I0812741

IMAGES
of America

THE SETAUKETS, OLD FIELD, AND POQUOTT

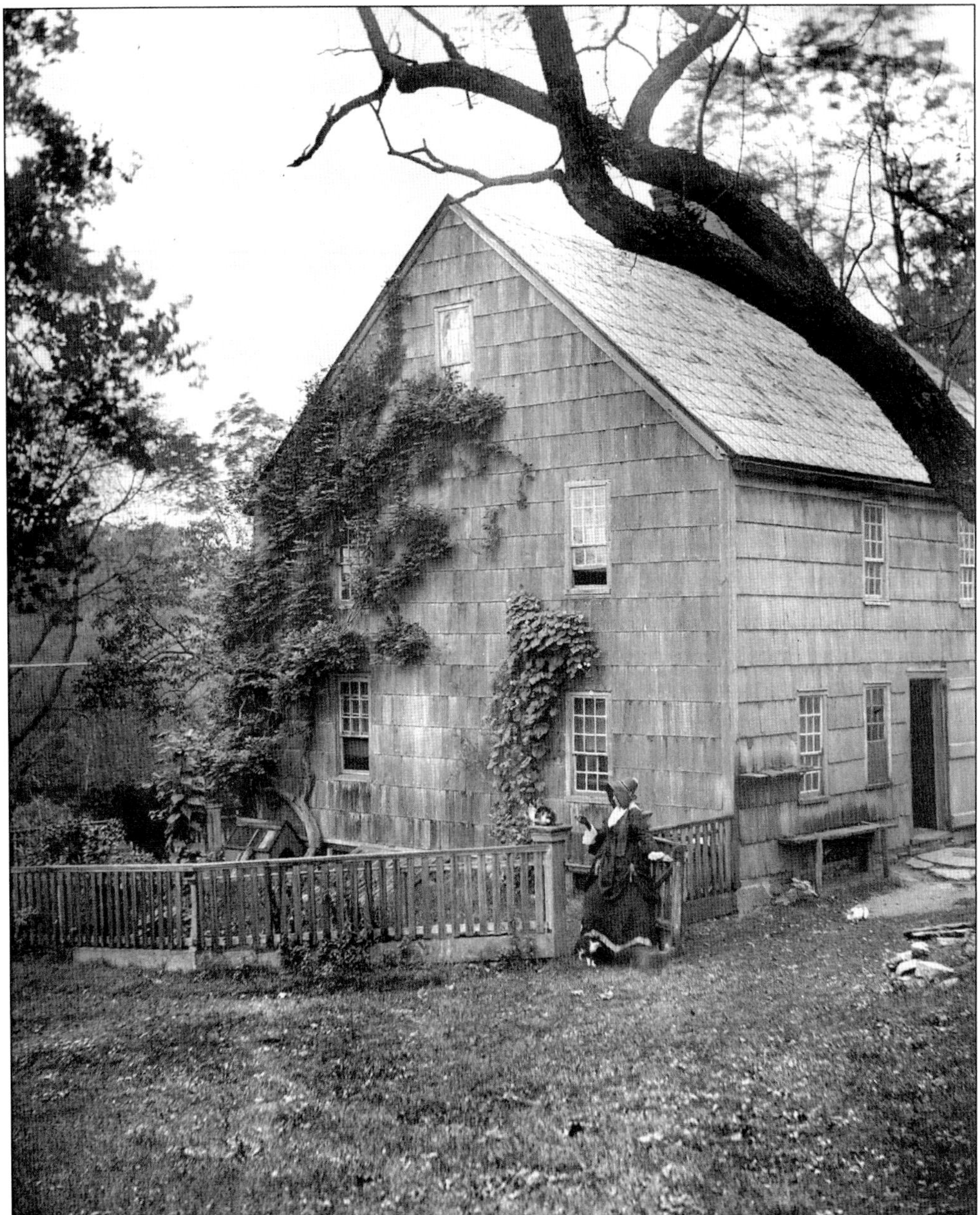

TIMOTHY SMITH HOUSE, SETAUKET, BUILT C. 1695. Julia Mills Smith, seen in this *c.* 1927 photograph, was locally known as "Miss Julia." She sold cakes and cookies from her back door on 55 Main Street. This house was the seat of Brookhaven town government from 1738 to 1788, when members of the Smith family served as the town clerks. The cemetery behind the house may contain the remains of the soldiers killed in the skirmish at the adjoining Jayne Tavern in 1778.

IMAGES
of America

THE SETAUKETS, OLD FIELD, AND POQUOTT

Three Village Historical Society

ARCADIA
PUBLISHING

ISBN 978-0-7385-3866-2

Published by Arcadia Publishing
Charleston, South Carolina

Printed in the United States of America

Library of Congress Catalog Card Number: 2005926066

For all general information contact Arcadia Publishing at:
Telephone 843-853-2070
Fax 843-853-0044
E-mail sales@arcadiapublishing.com
For customer service and orders:
Toll-Free 1-888-313-2665

Visit us on the Internet at www.arcadiapublishing.com

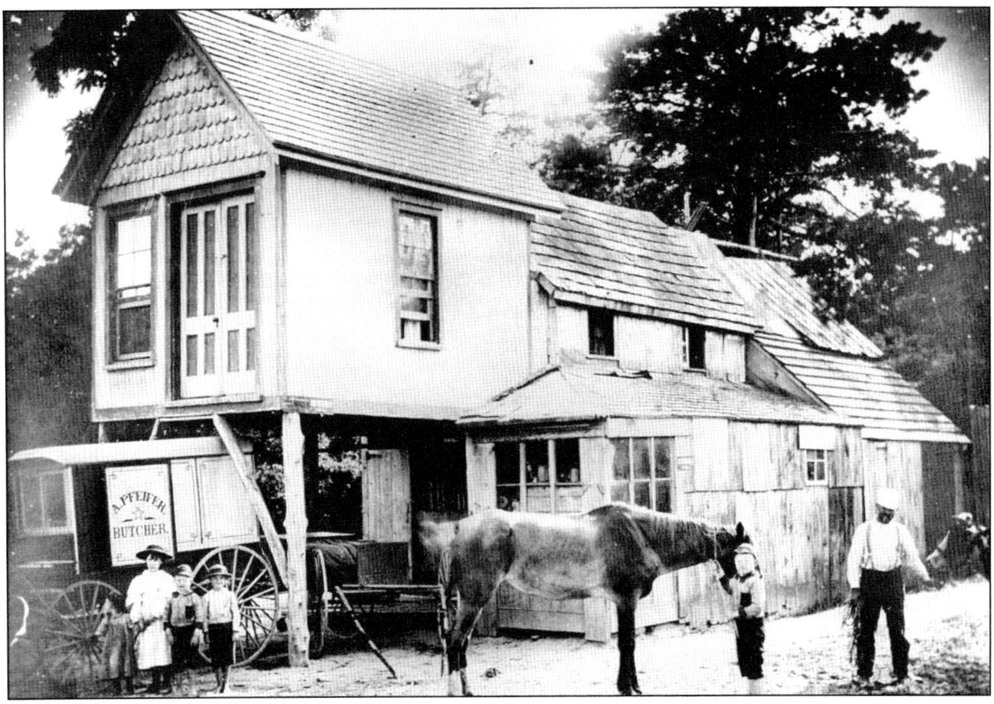

PFEIFFER'S CORNER, RIDGEWAY AVENUE AT NORTH COUNTRY ROAD, PHOTOGRAPH C. 1898. Adolph Pfeiffer operated a butcher shop on the ground floor and lived with his family on the second floor. The building in this view faces Ridgeway Avenue with the gable end facing North Country Road.

Contents

ACKNOWLEDGMENTS

This book is written in the memory of Joan Berry Weinstein. Joan was the moving force behind Images of America: *Stony Brook*, and she was the genesis of this volume. Joan was a longtime member of the society, a trustee, and a tireless volunteer. She was a passionate worker in our archives, who recovered the history of families, houses, and neighborhoods, and helped as well to restore the Colonial cemeteries. The scope of her contributions have become apparent only with her passing. Her wisdom, encouragement, and companionship will be missed by all who had the privilege to work with her.

Many individuals and organizations have contributed to the development of this book. We are indebted, first, to the staff and board of trustees of the Emma S. Clark Memorial Library, which generously houses the archives of the Three Village Historical Society and provides assistance to the increasing number of people using the collection for research. We thank in particular Edward V. Elenausky, library director, and Constance F. Sobel, adult services librarian. We owe a considerable debt to Sy Robbins, chairman of the society's historic districts committee, whose singular project of tracing local deed histories and wills and computerizing this information on a GIS mapping program has provided much historical basis for the text. Finally, and most important, we thank the many residents and their families who over the years have contributed personal photographs, diaries, memoirs, and legal documents, without which this book could never have been assembled. Many donors remain anonymous, but we can name a good number of people whose gifts and stories enriched this book: Fred Bryant, Julia Darling, Jean Darrow, the family of J. Ward Melville, Dr. R. Sherman Mills, Steven Poulos, John Strong, and Beverly Tyler. Unless otherwise specified, all photographs are the property of the Three Village Historical Society and are part of a collection of documents and photographs known as the Captain Edward R. Rhodes Memorial Collection of Local History.

Finally, we would like to thank the true authors of this book: Harold (Hap) Barnes, Gene (Sticky) Cockshutt, Carlton (Hub) and Nellie Edwards, Robert (Buddy) Gerard, Margaret Gwyrine, John Hewlett, Susan Jayne, Estelle Lockwood, Preston Pautch, and Kenneth (Lightning) Tuck. This book would not have been possible without their many contributions of pictures and documents, as well as their often uncanny ability to identify faces from the past, as well as long-gone residents and structures.

—Frank Turano, Karen Martin, Elizabeth (Betty) Voss, and Beatrice (Bee) Jayne

INTRODUCTION

Originally founded in 1655 as Ashford, then renamed Brookhaven and finally Setauket, this village was the first settlement in what is now the Town of Brookhaven. The original patentees "purchased" the land from a Native American group now called the Setalcott Indians. During the 16th and 17th centuries, this group, as well as all other native groups in North America, had had their numbers severely reduced by introduced diseases. The English settlers moved onto the land around the Setauket Millpond that the native people and their ancestors had been using for more than 3,000 years.

Setauket attracted the English because there was a good freshwater source and level, arable land near a well-protected harbor with relatively deep water. The salt meadows to the west of the settlement (and hence West Meadow) provided salt hay for the cattle in winter. Initially almost all the inhabitants were subsistence farmers, individually producing all of their needs. By the early 18th century, a road wandered along the north shore of Long Island, dotted with occasional ordinaries, taverns, and inns to accommodate travelers. Dr. Alexander Hamilton was one such traveler. In 1744, he described Setauket as "a small scattered village standing upon barren rocky land near the sea."

After the Battle of Long Island in August 1776, the British occupied the entire island and quartered their troops in villages along the north shore. Since Port Jefferson was not founded until 1796, Setauket was strategic because it controlled the surrounding harbor complex with its access to cordwood, the vital fuel for the army. In November 1780, the Colonial patriots attacked the Setauket Presbyterian Church, which had been fortified by the British. After capturing 54 prisoners, the Colonial force moved on to destroy the British hay supply in Coram. Although there was a significant British presence in Setauket, Washington's most successful spy ring developed here. It included Benjamin Tallmadge, Austin Roe, Abraham Woodhull, Robert Townsend, Caleb Brewster, and Anna Smith Strong.

During the War of 1812, Fort Nonsense, with a single 32-pound gun, was built on Tinker's Bluff to protect Port Jefferson Harbor, although it did not stop a British raid. In 1826, Mark Chase described Suffolk County as "towns and edifices mean and impoverished. Even its churches would be mistaken for unpainted barns, in ruins." By the early 19th century, shipbuilding had become a significant activity along Shore Road in East Setauket. Because of this concentration of activity, a second business district developed along Main Street.

William Sidney Mount, a Setauket native and portrait painter, painted many local scenes between the 1830s until his death in 1868. He always returned home to paint because he loved the quality of the light here.

In 1858, the Nunns and Clark Piano Company moved its operation to Setauket. Their factory was on Route 25A, opposite the Setauket United Methodist Church. In 1876, the Long Island Rubber Company purchased the factory, which became one of the largest employers in Suffolk County. An annex was built down Main Street (Route 25A), in the area occupied by the pond in East Setauket Pond Park. The factory operated under several names before it burned in 1904.

Many local men enlisted to serve in the Civil War, and there were several casualties. In the post–Civil War era, the Setauket area was discovered by upper-middle class and wealthy families as a summer haven from the perils of New York City. These people sought shorefront and view locations that were of little concern to the local farmers. The completion of the Long Island Railroad to Port Jefferson in 1873 facilitated their travels. The local population remained as farmers, shop-keepers, and part-time baymen.

In the period just before World War II, many buildings were moved from their original locations and adapted to new uses. These changes supported the sub-urbanization of Setauket and Stony Brook that began in the early 1960s, when many farm fields were turned into housing developments.

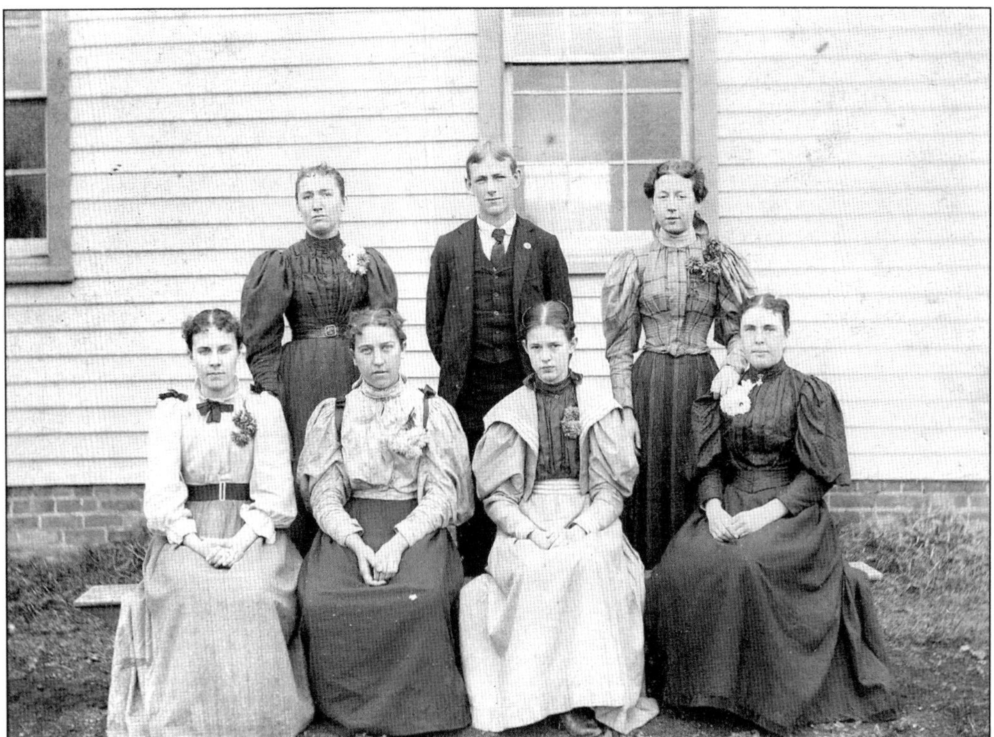

GRADUATING CLASS, C. 1900. The entire high school graduating class of the Coach Road School poses for a photograph.

One

East Setauket and Poquott

The shipyards along Shore Road were the focus of development in East Setauket. The narrow marsh with high, dry land behind it provided an ideal location for the yards and housing for the owners. Known as Dyers Neck, the picturesque nature of the location also made it attractive for boardinghouses and a hotel. Many local residents converted and/or expanded their homes into boardinghouses to accommodate summer visitors. When the fortunes of the rubber factory were at their height, an annex was built at the East Setauket Pond Park. With the concentration of rubber factory and shipyard workers, a business district developed to serve their needs as well as the needs of the summer people. Count de Teixeira's factory for manufacturing castings and metal plating also attracted workers to the area.

In the early 20th century, large portions of George's Neck came into the hands of Edward Larocque Tinker, a world traveler, businessman, financier, and photographer. His estate is a central portion of the village of Poquott, incorporated in 1930. At about the same time, an amusement park was developed at what is now the Poquott Village Beach on Port Jefferson Harbor. This attraction led to the development of the eastern side of Poquott as a summer community.

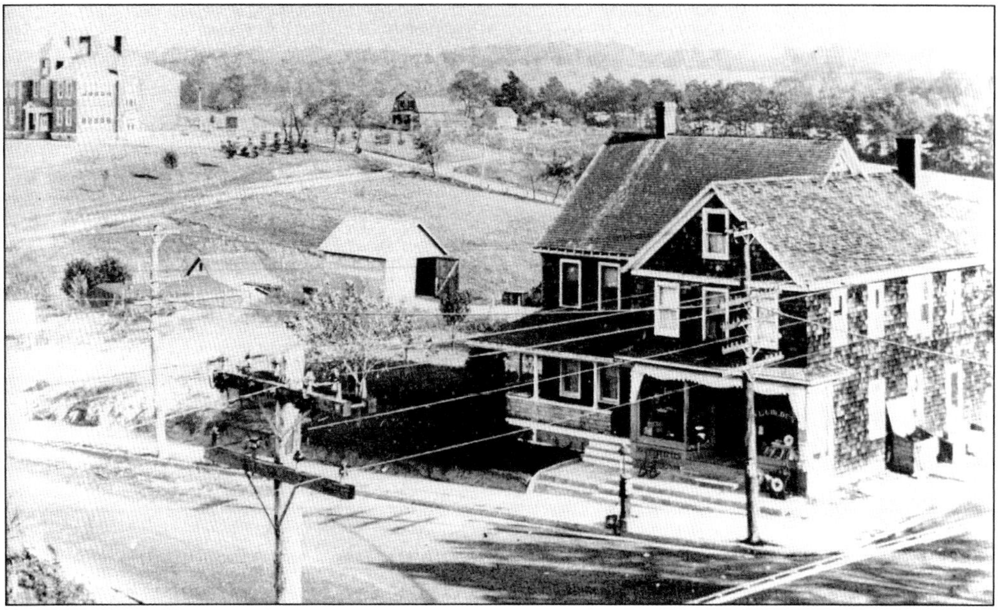

GOLDEN'S CORNER, ROUTE 25A (MAIN STREET) AT OLD TOWN ROAD, OCTOBER 1921. Golden's store and house is at the right. Herman (universally known as "Hymie") Golden operated a Laundromat on the ground floor, and there were gas pumps along Old Town Road. The Setauket Union Free Grade and High School No. 2 is on the hill at the left. This photograph was taken from the top of the Setauket United Methodist Church steeple by Ray Tyler.

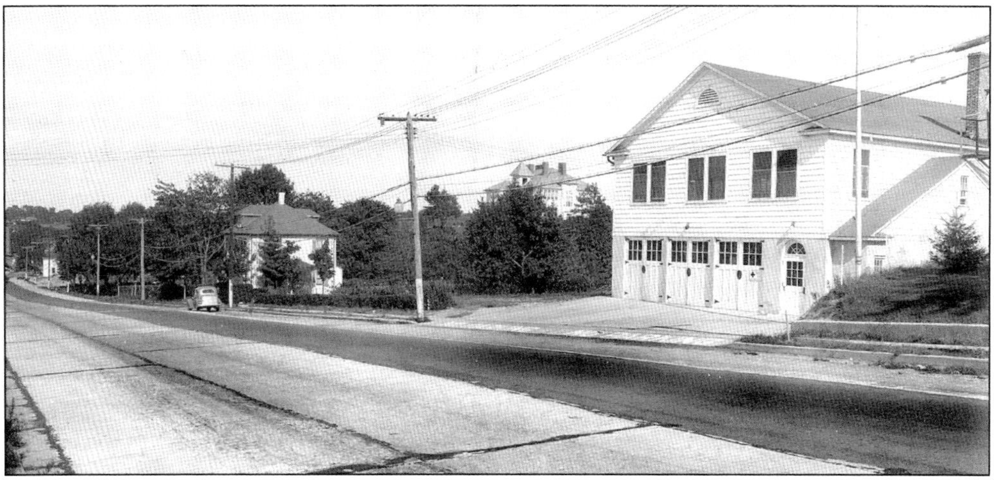

SETAUKET FIREHOUSE, MAIN STREET (ROUTE 25A), C. 1938. The second floor of the original three-bay firehouse, designed by Preston Lyon, was used in the 1930s and 1940s by the Setauket school as a gymnasium and auditorium. Teachers Annie Taffs and Ruth Derbyshire lived in the house at 194 Main Street. The Setauket Union Free School is on the hill in the background. The "sandpit" on the north side of the road was the site of numerous fire-department carnivals. This site is now occupied by a shopping center. In about 1880, John W. Rick, a farmer from Stony Brook, loaned two mules to a farmer in Mount Sinai. The farmer was reluctant to return them, but finally, after much pressure, John went and retrieved them. As he began to drive the mules toward Stony Brook, both died and were buried in the lot across from the firehouse. Legend has it that the mules were poisoned.

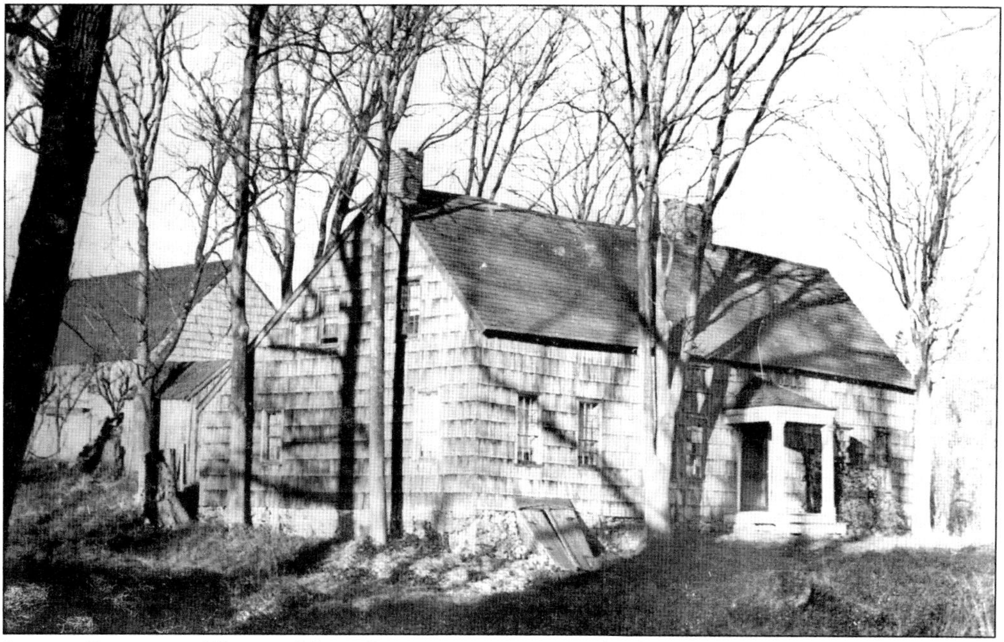

JOSEPH BREWSTER HOUSE, MAIN STREET, C. 1910. At the beginning of the 19th century, two separate houses were moved to this site, where they were combined and a saltbox extension was added. This house was depicted by local artist William Sidney Mount in his painting *Long Island Farmhouses* in 1854. The house was built in 1665.

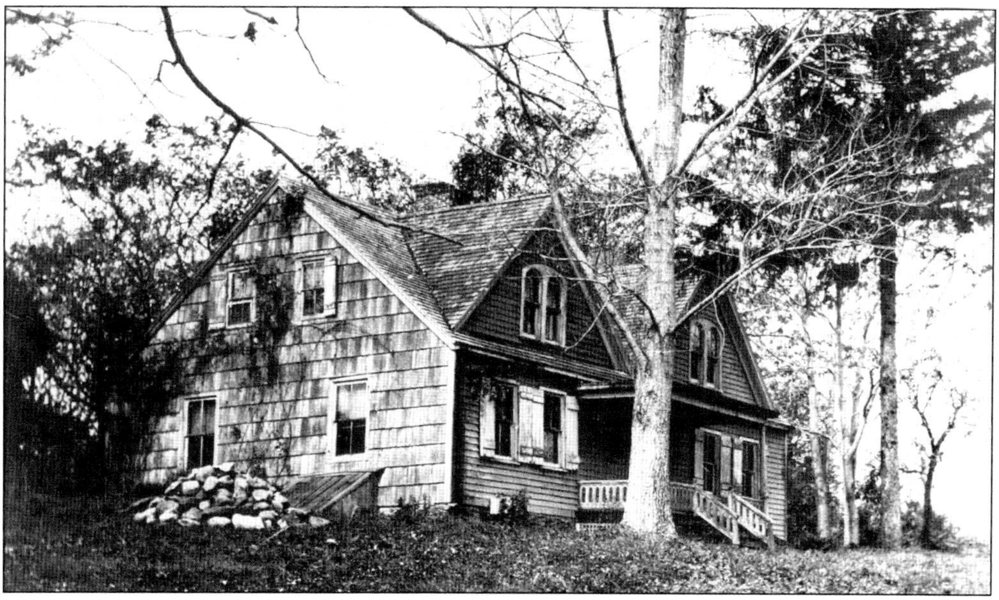

UNDERHILL HOUSE, 18 RUNS ROAD, BUILT C. 1750. This was the home of Robert Mount, musician and dancing teacher, the brother of William Sidney Mount. In 1833, Robert married Mary Thompson Brewster. His family lived in this second Brewster house, which can be seen in the background of William's painting *Long Island Farmhouses*. William Sidney Mount died in this home in 1868. The dormers were added in the late 19th century. The house was razed around 1942; the site is now occupied by a contemporary house. (Courtesy of Betty Voss.)

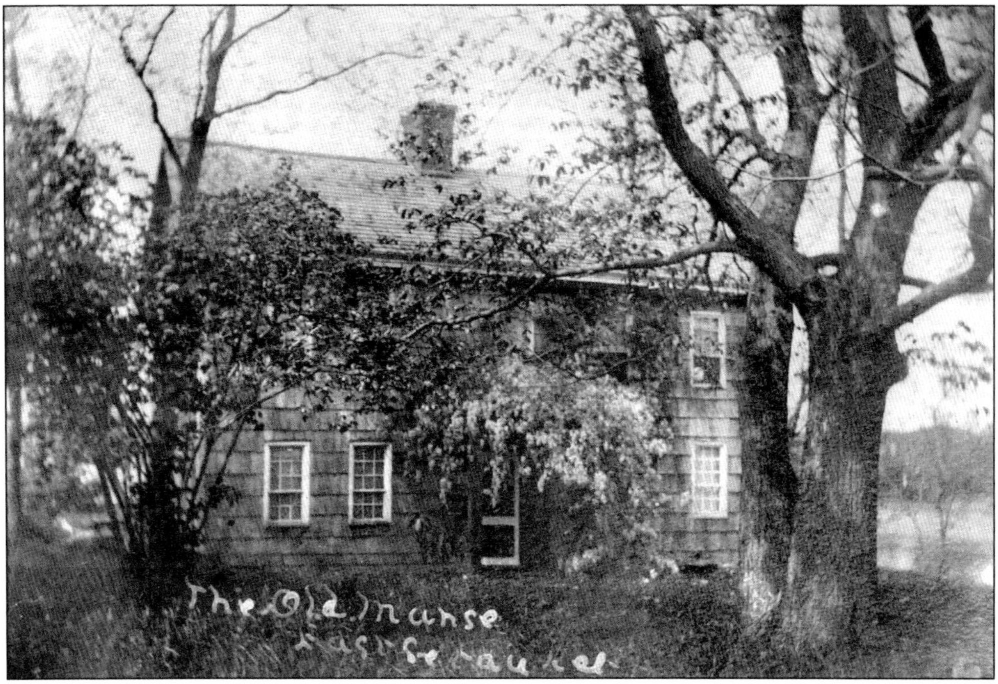

THE OLD MANSE, 30 RUNS ROAD, BUILT C. 1730. This was the parsonage for the Presbyterian church and the birthplace of Benjamin Tallmadge, who is of Setauket spy-ring fame. Tallmadge was the second son of Presbyterian minister Rev. Benjamin Tallmadge. The church divided the property around 1860 and built a new parsonage on the western half. This photograph was taken around 1910. (Courtesy of Betty Voss.)

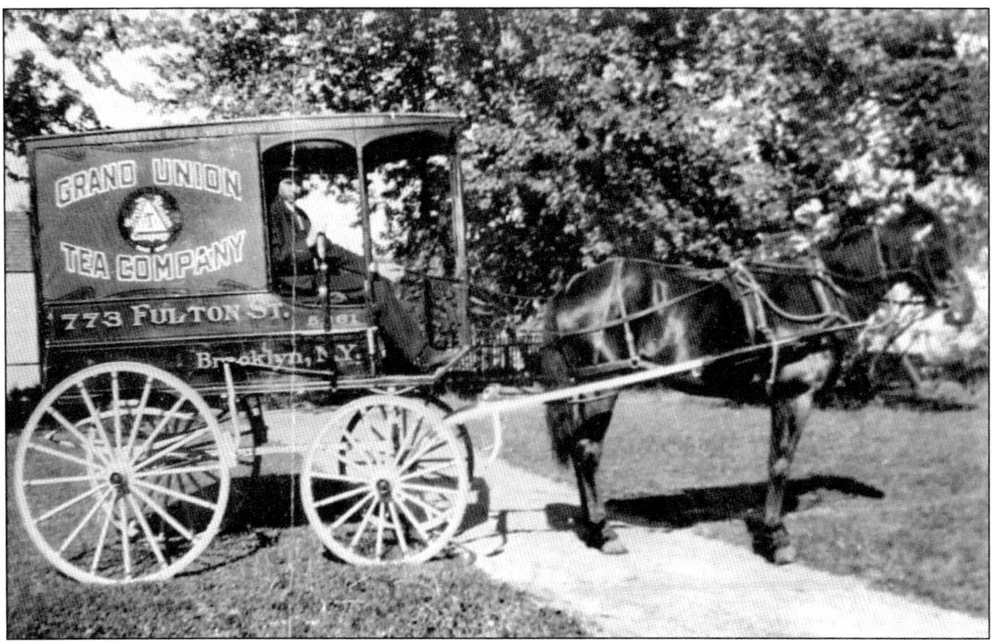

GRAND UNION TEA COMPANY SALES WAGON, C. 1920. Tom Lyon, seated in the wagon, was the company agent in the Setauket area.

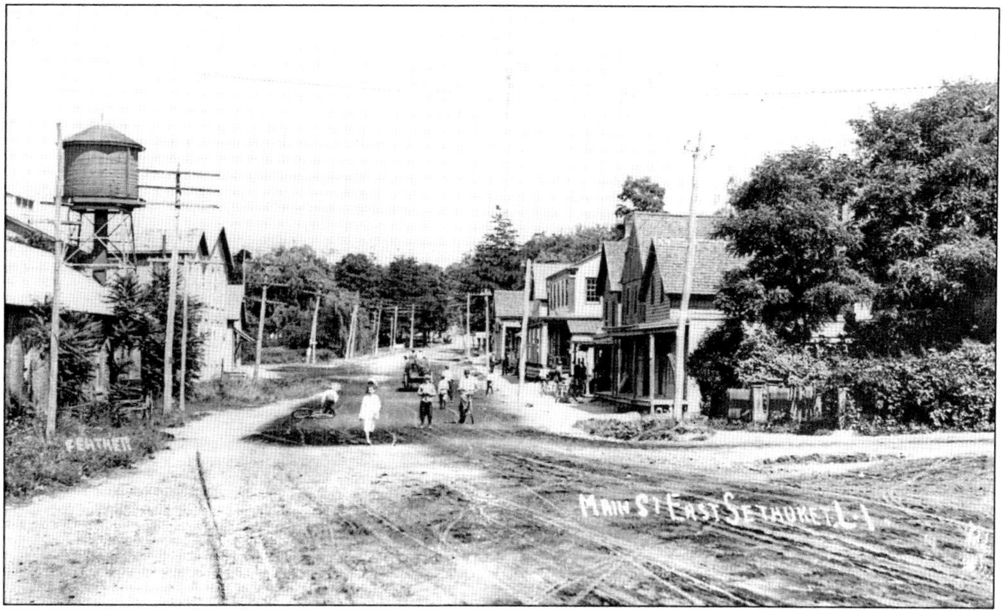

MAIN STREET (ROUTE 25A), LOOKING EAST FROM GNARLED HOLLOW ROAD. The lower rubber factory buildings are on the left. The East Setauket post office occupies the last building at the corner of Shore Road. Most of the East Setauket business district is along the south side of Main Street. Gnarled Hollow Road has had a series of names, including South Street (1873), Depot Avenue (1909), and Station Road (1917). (R. S. Feather photograph, *c.* 1915.)

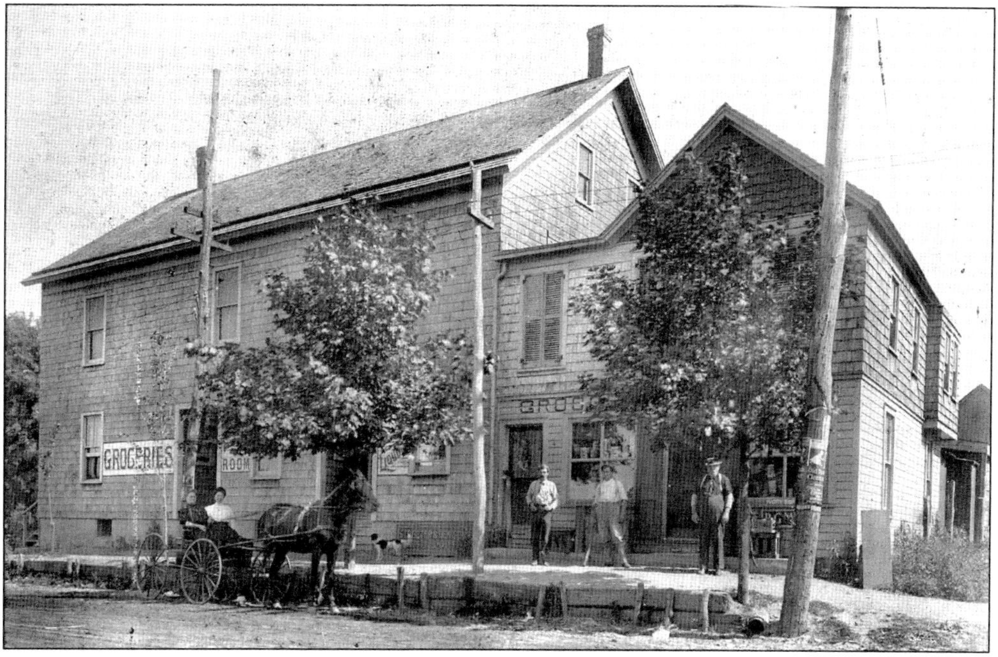

MCDOWELL'S STORE, C. 1910. This store was located on the southwest corner of Main Street (Route 25A) and Gnarled Hollow Road. From left to right are Mrs. Pat McDowell, Mary McDowell, Jim McDowell (Mary's husband), unidentified, and Pat McDowell. This building is presently known as Country Corners. (Courtesy of Betty Voss.)

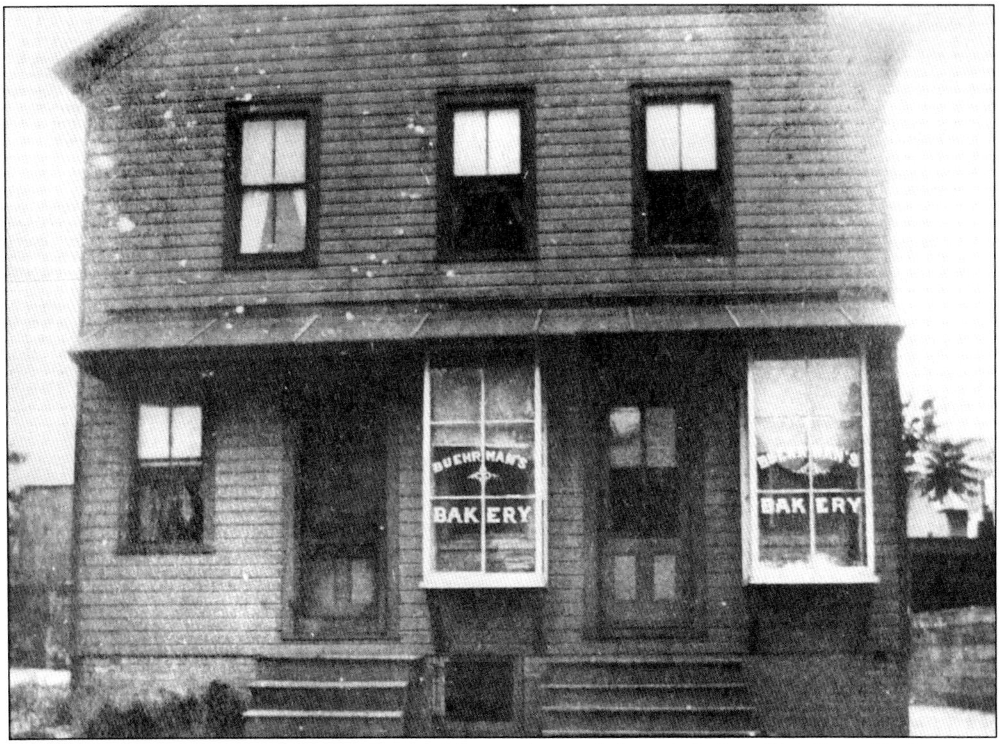

BUEHRMAN'S BAKERY, C. 1900. This building is located directly behind McDowell's Store on Gnarled Hollow Road. (Courtesy of Betty Voss.)

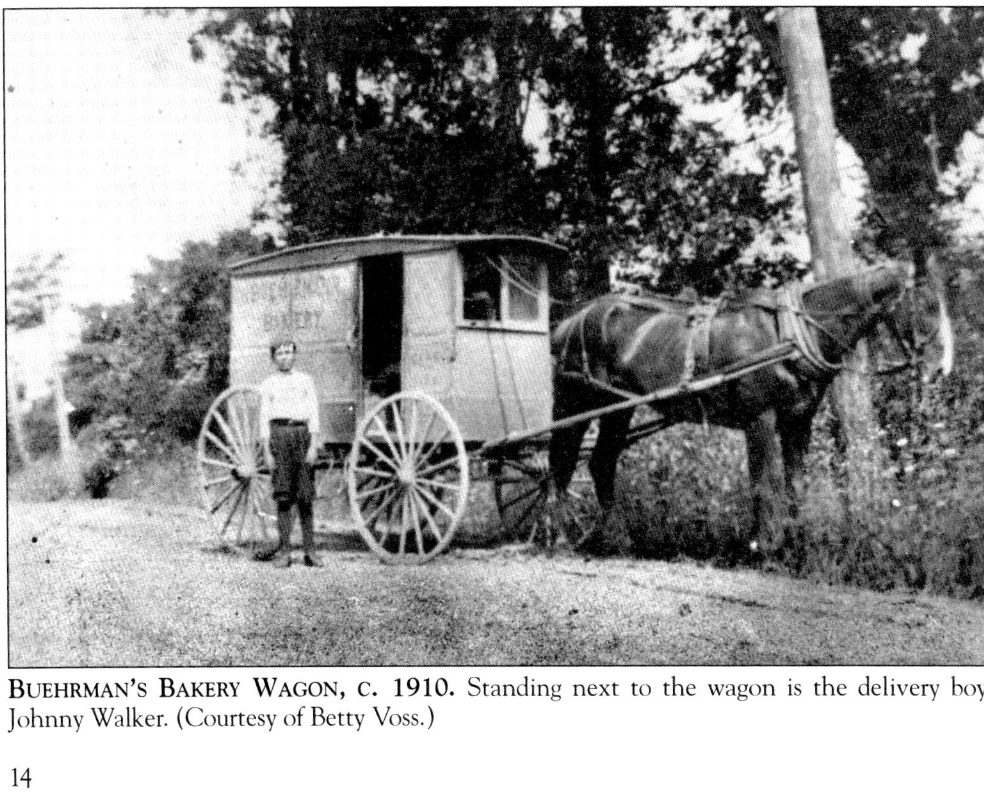

BUEHRMAN'S BAKERY WAGON, C. 1910. Standing next to the wagon is the delivery boy, Johnny Walker. (Courtesy of Betty Voss.)

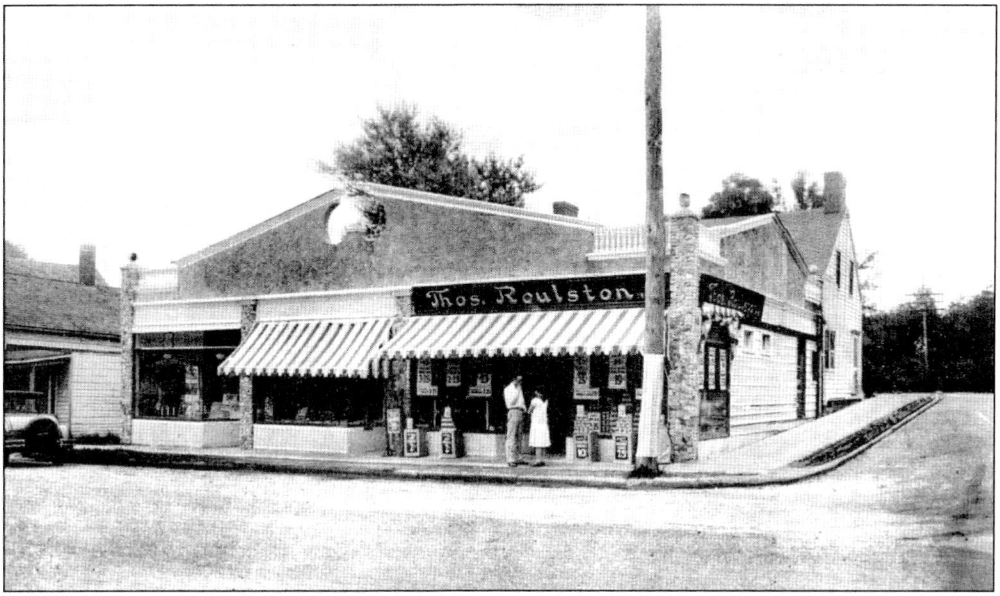

THOS. (THOMAS) ROULSTON'S STORE, C. 1920. Roulston's, shown here on the southeast corner of Main Street (Route 25A) and Gnarled Hollow Road, was a chain of co-op grocery stores that existed in small villages. Behind the store is the Old Ida Jones House (7 Gnarled Hollow Road), later owned by William Smith and Sara Ann Sells. Sara Ann, who was part American Indian, lived to be 100. She made her living as a mother's helper and later took in laundry. She was known in the community as "Aunt Sara" and "Sarry Ann." (Courtesy of Betty Voss.)

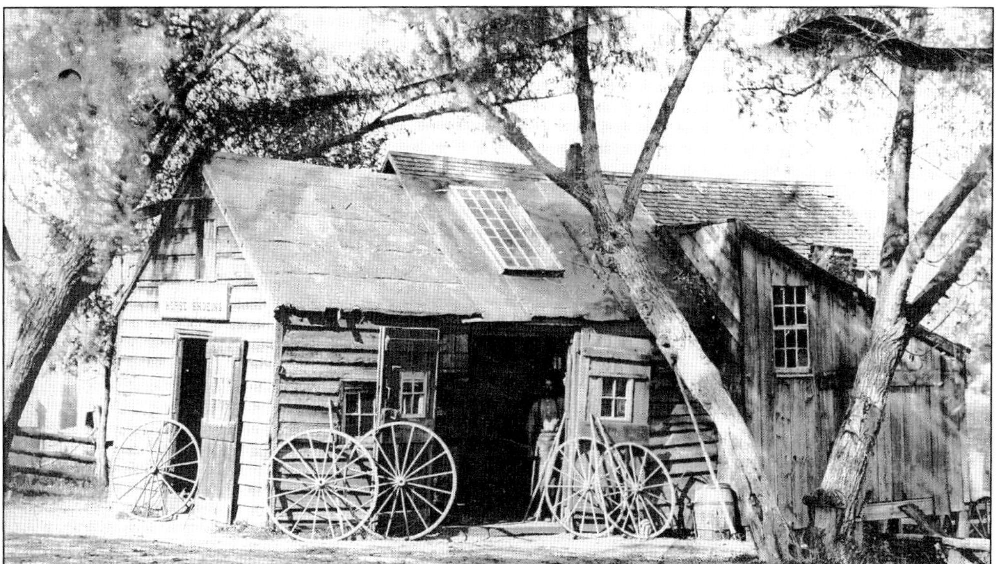

SAMUEL HARVEY WEST'S ORIGINAL BLACKSMITH SHOP, C. 1890. This blacksmith shop was established on 21 Gnarled Hollow Road in 1875. It advertised the following: "Blacksmithing and Horse shoeing a specialty. Carriage and Wagon work in all its branches. Work neatly and promptly executed. Agricultural implements." In 1881, West had a new shop built on the site and eventually added a two-story building next door, where carriages were repaired. Samuel West died in 1938. (Courtesy of Betty Voss.)

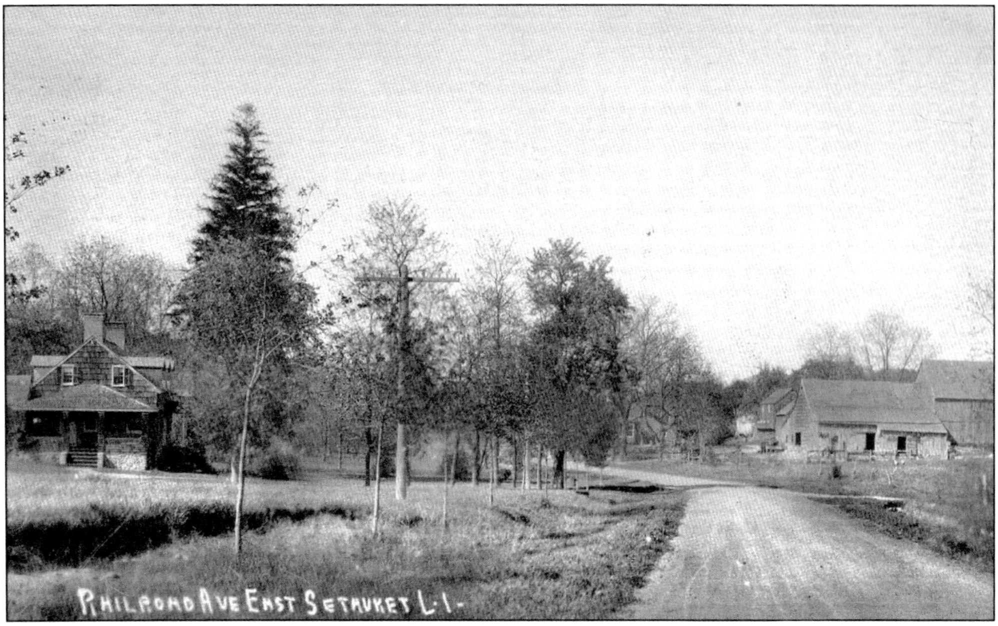

GNARLED HOLLOW ROAD (AKA RAILROAD AVENUE), C. 1910. Looking north from the junction of Old Town Road, the Satterly farm can be seen on the right. On the left at 56 Gnarled Hollow Road is the Floyd Smith house, built around 1820. The barn may date back to 1750, when another home occupied the property. In 1917, J. W. Angel operated a chicken farm at this site, which is now Benner's Farm. (Courtesy of Beverly and Barbara Tyler.)

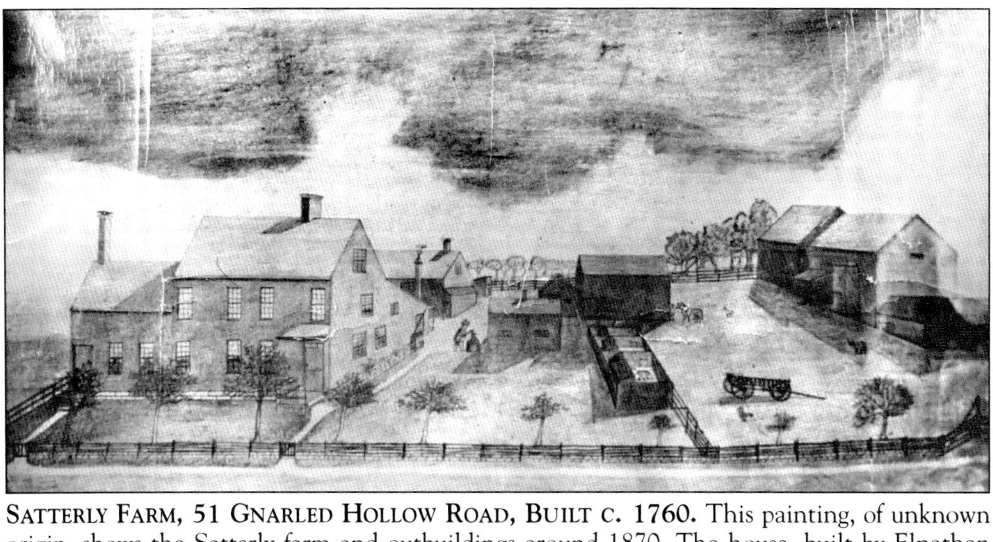

SATTERLY FARM, 51 GNARLED HOLLOW ROAD, BUILT C. 1760. This painting, of unknown origin, shows the Satterly farm and outbuildings around 1870. The house, built by Elnathan Satterly, is constructed of both oak and chestnut beams. Satterly was a very successful farmer, as well as the ancestor of a longtime prominent local family. The property remained in the Satterly family until 1937.

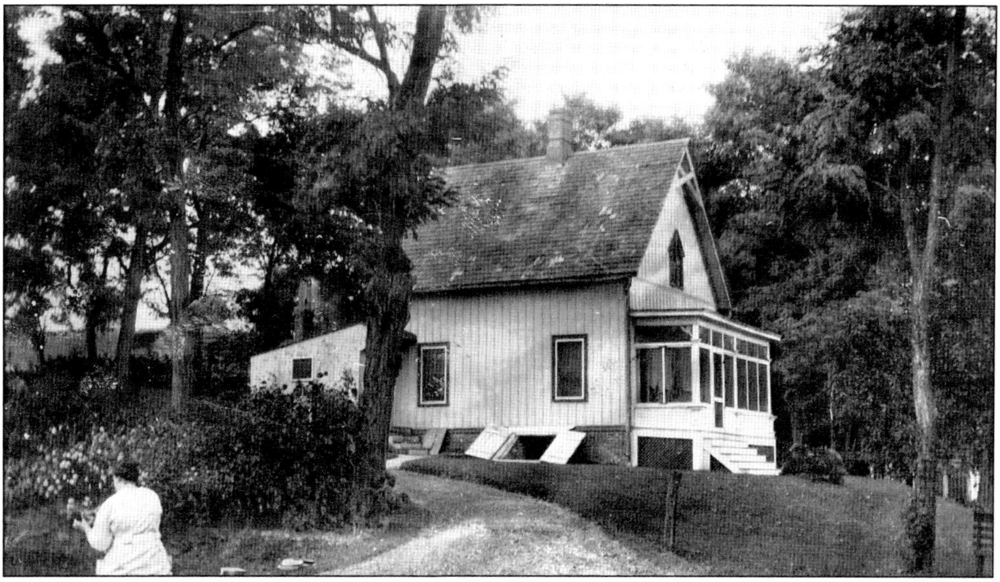

Tyler House, 185 Old Town Road, Built c. 1920. This house was originally built on the property of Walter Hudson and his wife, Florence Tyler Hudson, at 46 Gnarled Hollow Road. This photograph shows the house in about 1925, after it was moved to its present location. Walter Hudson was the area's last surviving local Civil War veteran. (Courtesy of Betty Voss.)

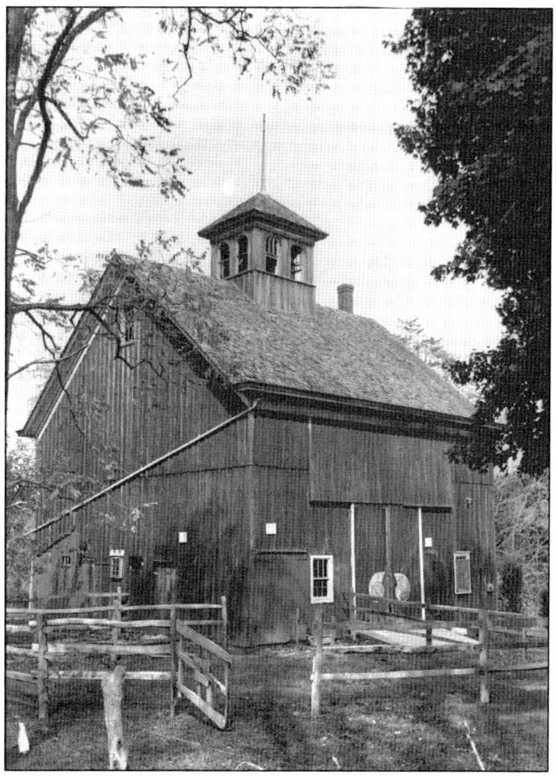

Hawkins Barn, Built c. 1850. Bryant Coleman Hawkins was a piano manufacturer and worked for Nunns. He and his wife, Rebecca Brewster, built the house and barn on 162 Old Town Road. Thornton Hawkins owned the property from 1948 to 1968. Hawkins farmed and raised sheep, cows, pigs, chickens, and hunting dogs. His horse Buttercup was locally famous and lived to be 35 years old. From 1969 to 1976, the house was the national headquarters for the Environmental Defense Fund, and the barn was the home of the Environmental Centers of Setauket-Smithtown. Pictured here around 1985 is the barn, which was torn down in the late 1990s. (Courtesy of Beverly and Barbara Tyler.)

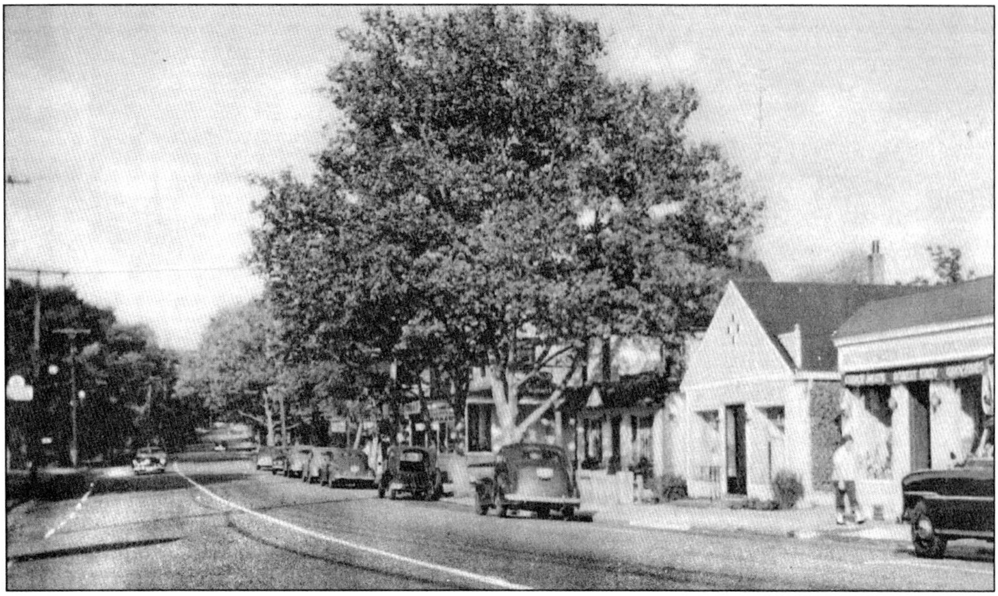

Main Street (Route 25A) Looking East, c. 1950. The Shore Road intersection is at the center left. The stores, from right to left, are Eikov's Liquor Store, Meister's Drug Store, Sheppard's Bar and Grill, and Steven Bossey's Grocery.

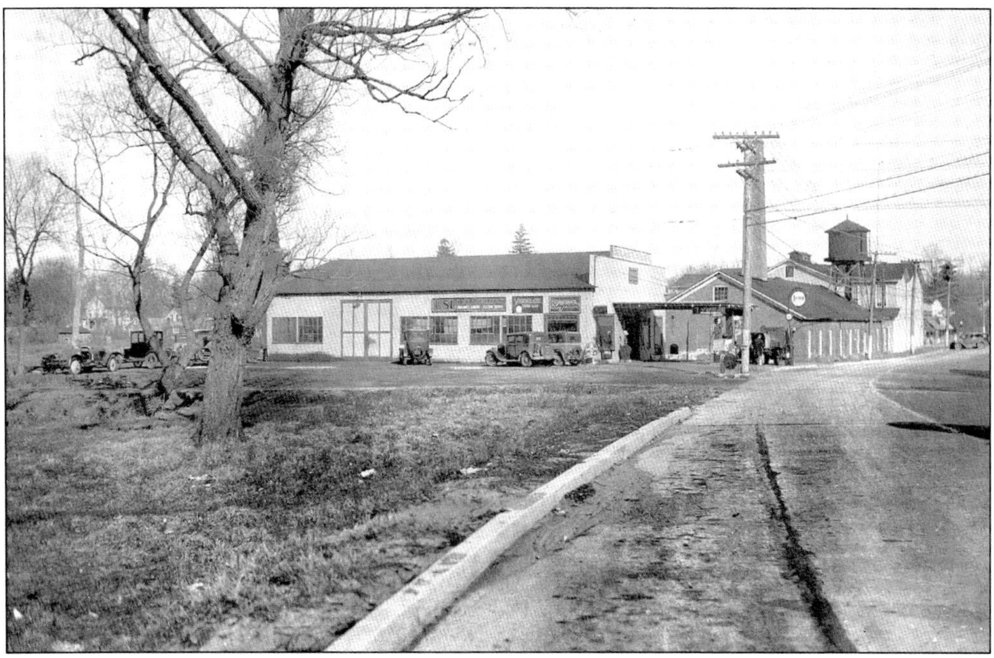

Ruhland's Garage, Main Street Looking East, c. 1926. From left to right are Ruhland's Garage, the Rubber Factory, the A&P, and Lyon Brothers Hardware. The traffic light at Gnarled Hollow Road was a blinker. The lower rubber factory remained empty for most of the 1920s, and according to Sam Golden, it served bootleggers as a spot "for making hooch." By the time of this photograph, the old East Setauket post office had been moved behind the corner store facing Shore Road.

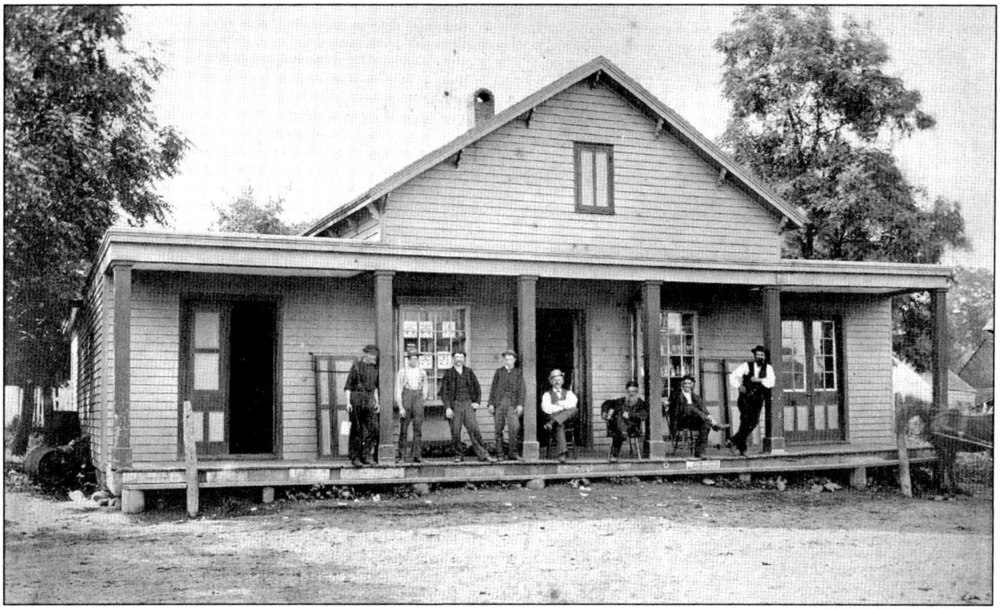

Walter Jones Sr., General Store, c. 1895. This store, on 300 Main Street (Route 25A), was on the site of the original Tinker National Bank. From left to right are an unidentified gentleman, Ed Newton, John Barrett, Benjamin Risley, Walter Jones Sr., Walter Smith, Harry Tyler, and Ansel Jayne. In later years, ladies of dubious reputation were alleged to have frequented the back rooms of this building. (Courtesy of Betty Voss.)

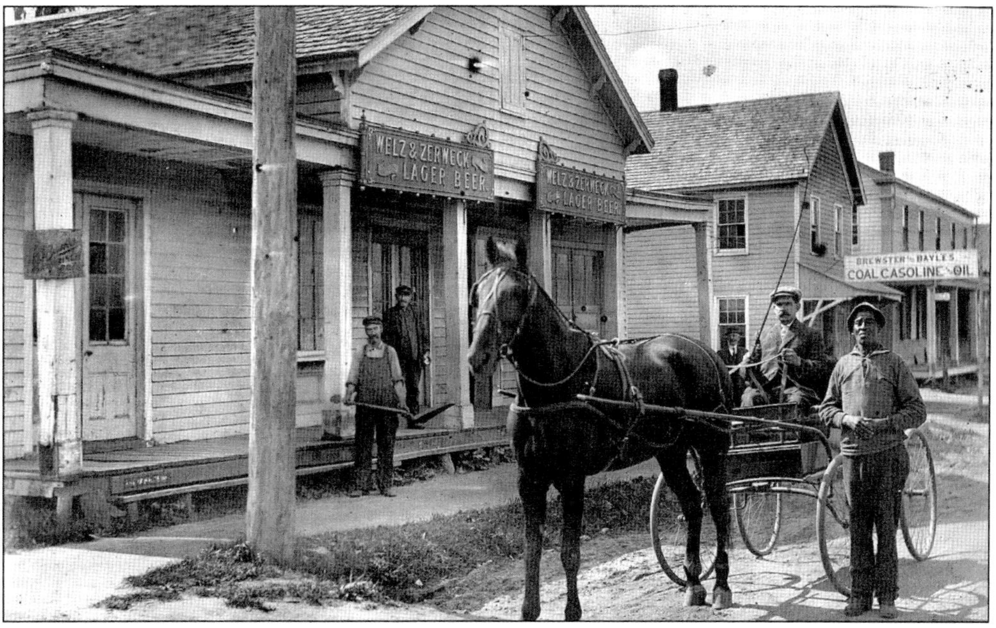

Walter Jones Store and Bar, Featuring Welz and Zerweck Lager Beer, c. 1915. From left to right are William Howell, Henry Christie, Charles Smith, Walter D. Jones (driving Sporting Bill), and Andrew Woodhull. Woodhull reportedly was rescued as a baby from an ice flow in Long Island Sound by Walter D. Jones. He remained with the Jones family for the rest of his life.

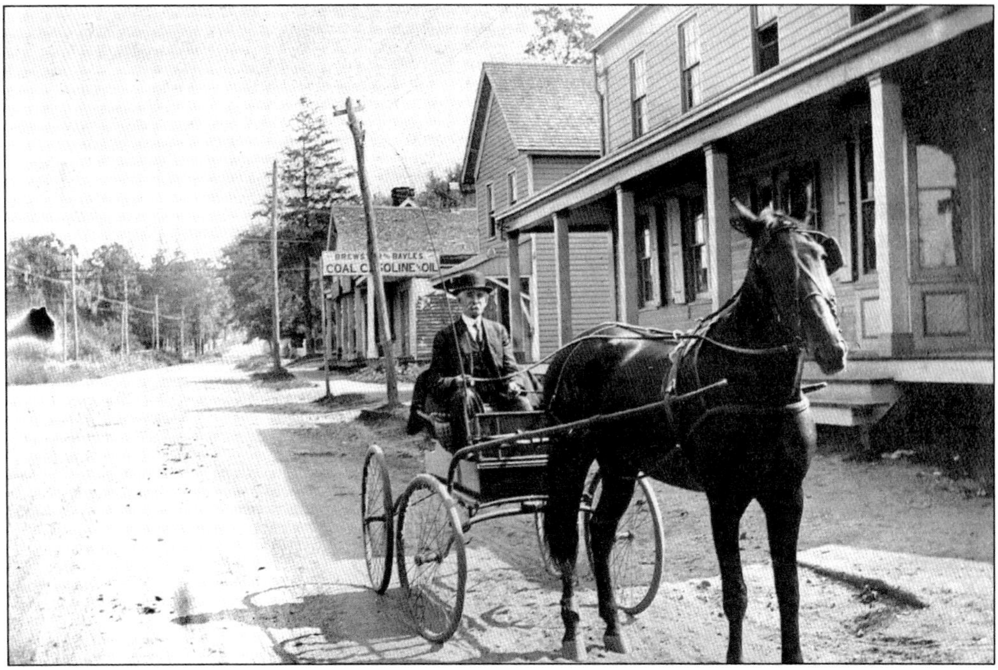

CHARLIE E. SMITH, DRIVING SPORTING BILL ON MAIN STREET, C. 1915. The sign in the background is for Brewster and Bayles, Coal, Gasoline and Oil. All his life, C. E., as he was known, was a lover of good trotting horses and delighted in driving them. His last horse, Sporting Bill, was a spirited one. On April 22, 1923, at the age of 82, Smith was fatally injured when he was dragged under the teeth of a hay rake attached to Sporting Bill. (Courtesy of Betty Voss.)

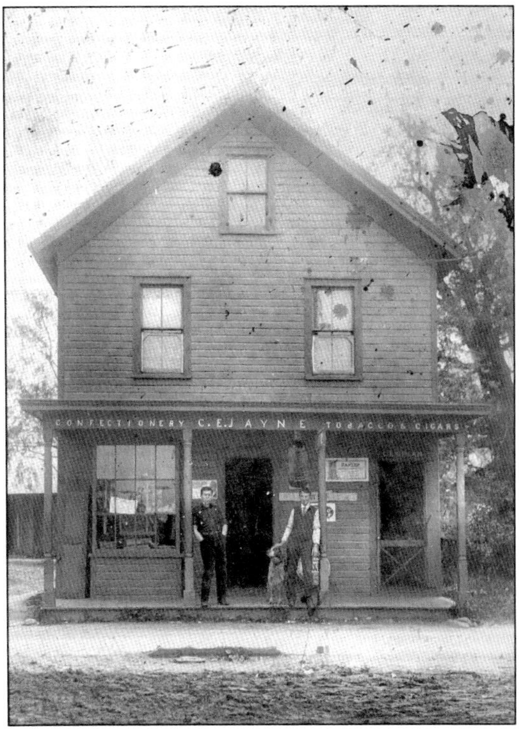

CHARLIE JAYNE'S CONFECTIONERY, TOBACCO AND CIGARS, C. 1910. Barney Jayne (right) stands with his dog Rover. When Barney Jayne took over the store at 290 Main Street, the menu was expanded to include a continuous poker game in the back room. (Courtesy of Betty Voss.)

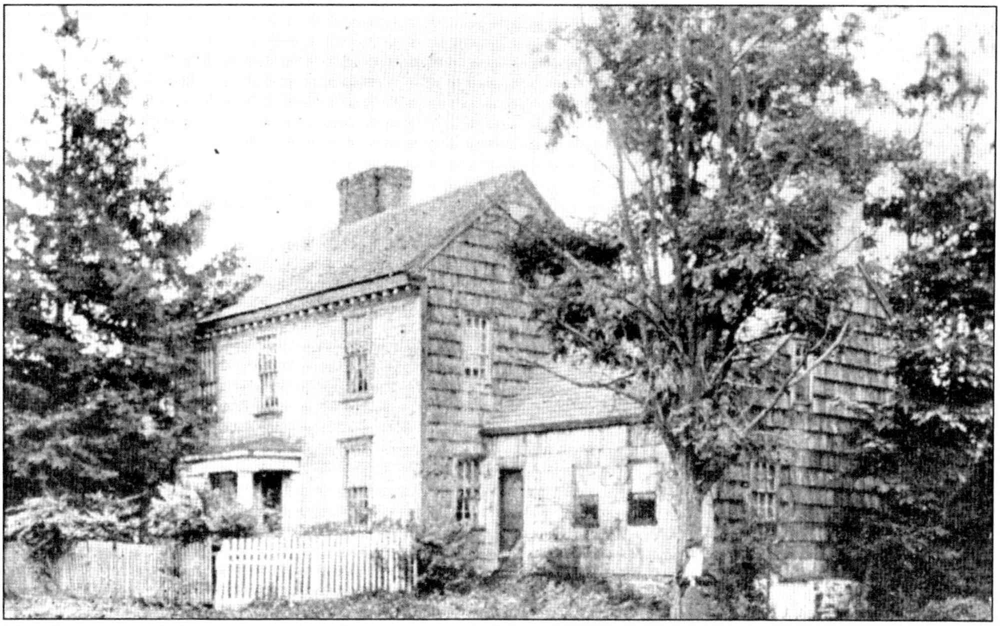

THE MANSION HOUSE, OR OLD SHINGLESIDES, BUILT 1754. This c. 1890 photograph shows Old Shinglesides, built by Jeffrey Smith, great-grandson of Richard (Bull) Smith. Purchased in 1760 by Ebenezer Jones, the house on 316 Main Street stayed in that family for several generations. In 1921, it was opened as a teahouse. To make way for the construction of the new post office, J. Ward Melville moved the home to 33 Gnarled Hollow Road at Mills Lane in 1962.

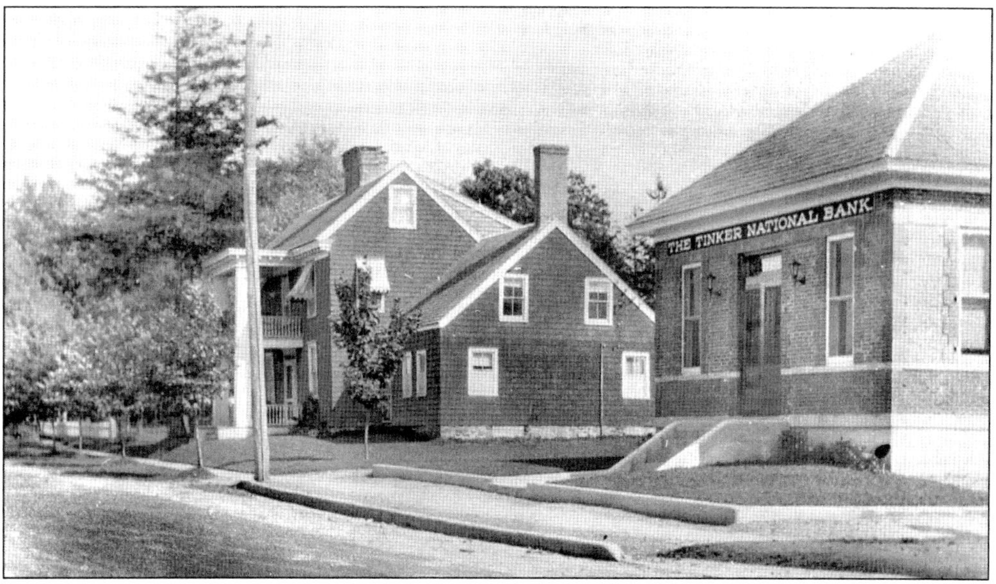

THE MANSION HOUSE (OR OLD SHINGLESIDES) AND TINKER NATIONAL BANK, 300 MAIN STREET. Tinker National Bank, founded by local businessman Edward L. Tinker, opened its doors on Saturday, August 28, 1920. On opening day, it took in $135,000 in deposits and opened 125 accounts. The original building, designed by George E. Hand, was remodeled in 1953. It merged with Marine Midland in 1969 and is now HSBC Bank. The photograph dates to about 1940.

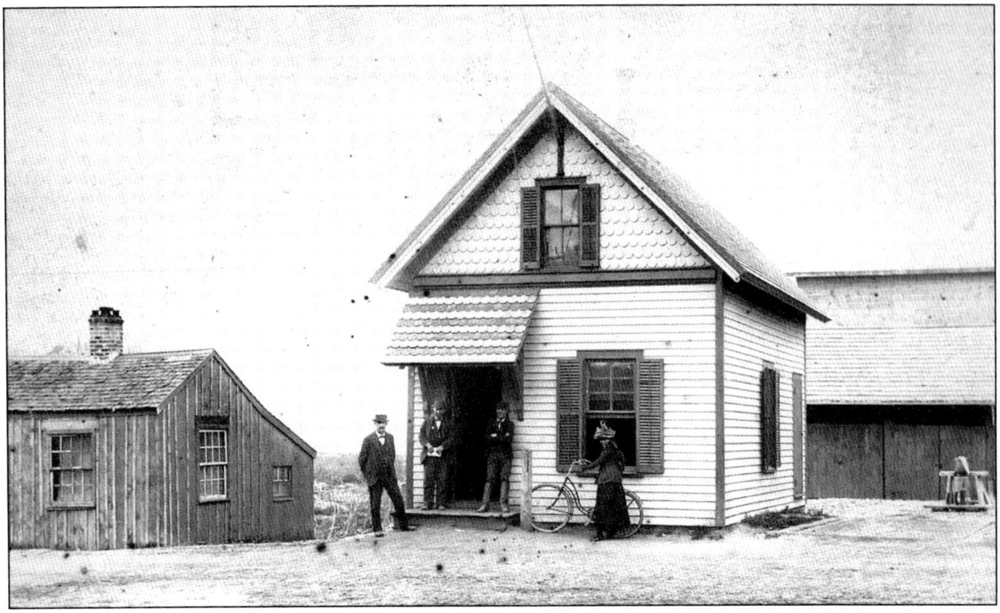

OLD EAST SETAUKET POST OFFICE, MAIN STREET AND CORNER OF SHORE ROAD, C. 1890. This photograph was taken before the construction of the lower rubber factory in 1894. Mrs. Walter Hudson is standing by the bicycle. Henry M. Rakow's blacksmith shop is at the right behind the post office. The post office was moved around the corner to Shore Road in the 1920s and is now the back of Fox's Hardware. The building at the left is unidentified. (Courtesy of Betty Voss.)

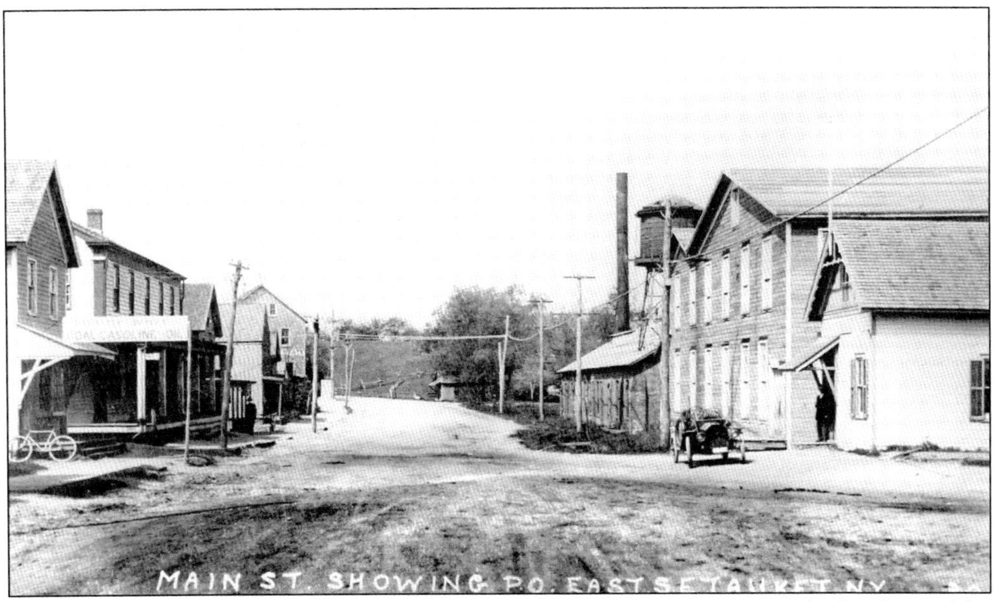

LOOKING WEST ON MAIN STREET, C. 1910. In this image, a 1910 Essex is parked in front of the post office, and the lower rubber factory is next door. The rubber factory was prone to destructive fires. The building shown here is a reconstruction after the October 25, 1898, fire. This fire also consumed the post office, an empty store, B. F. Jayne's Coal Yard, and James Warren's residence. This fire was preceded by a fire in 1895.

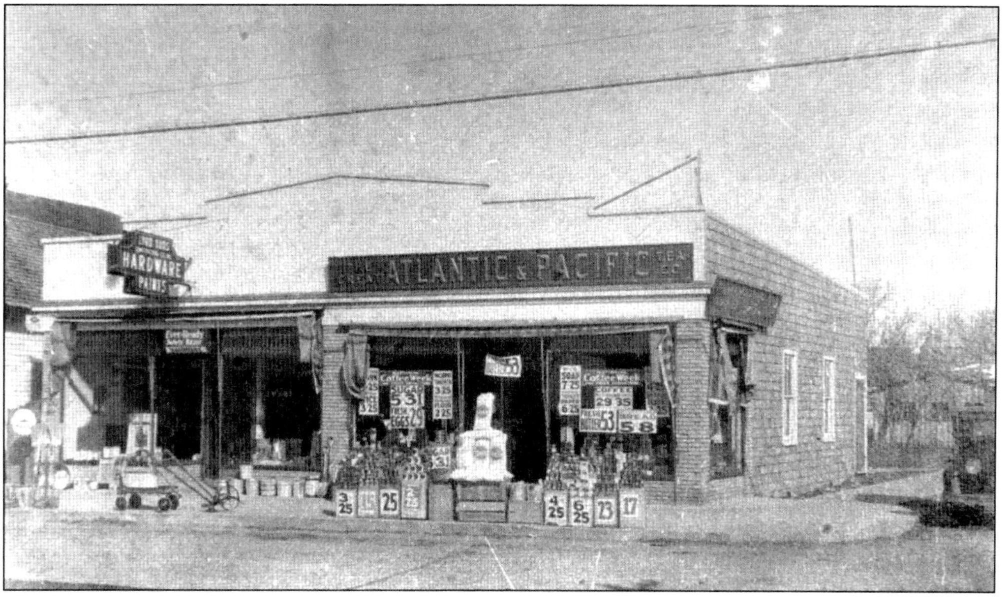

THE GREAT ATLANTIC AND PACIFIC TEA COMPANY, C. 1920. Some of the items on sale at this store, located on Main Street at the northwest corner of Shore Road, include fresh butter, 53¢/pound; five pounds of sugar, 31¢; fresh eggs, 29¢/dozen; three pounds of rice, 75¢; two pounds of flour, 25¢; six rolls of toilet paper 25¢; 8 O'clock coffee, 29¢/pound; Red Circle coffee, 35¢/pound; and P and G (Proctor and Gamble) soap, seven for 25¢. Lyon Brothers Hardware shares the building. Today this is Fox's Hardware. (Courtesy of Beverly and Barbara Tyler.)

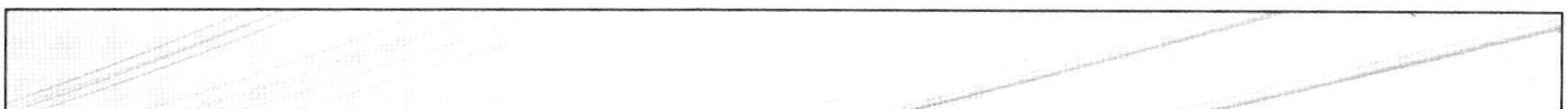

MAIN STREET AT THE CORNER OF SHORE ROAD, C. 1930. Mather's Drug Shop now occupies the corner building along with Lyon Brothers Contracting Company, which sells hardware and paints. The old East Setauket post office has been moved around the corner, directly behind the drug store, facing Shore Road. The new Great Atlantic and Pacific Tea Company building was constructed on the former site of the post office; today this is Se-Port Deli.

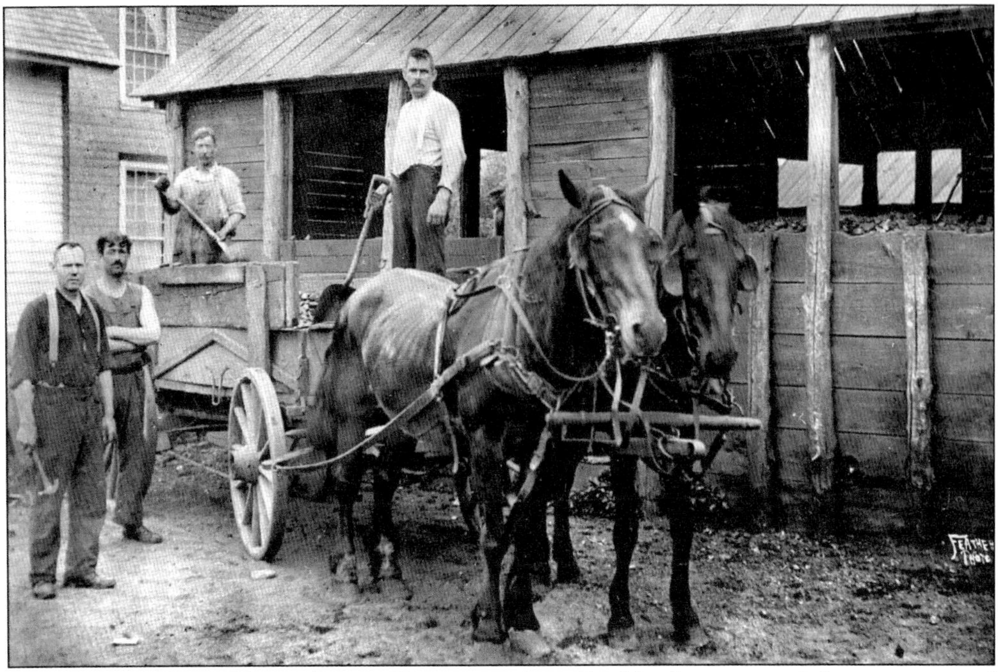

HENRY JONES COAL YARD, SHORE ROAD, C. 1911. Scudder Jayne owned this property and buildings and leased the coal yard to Jones, his cousin. The yard was on Shore Road, behind the present-day Fox's Hardware Store. The lower rubber factory is in the background. Pictured, from left to right, are Henry Rakow, Art Gerard, Chet Hawkins, and Walter Jones.

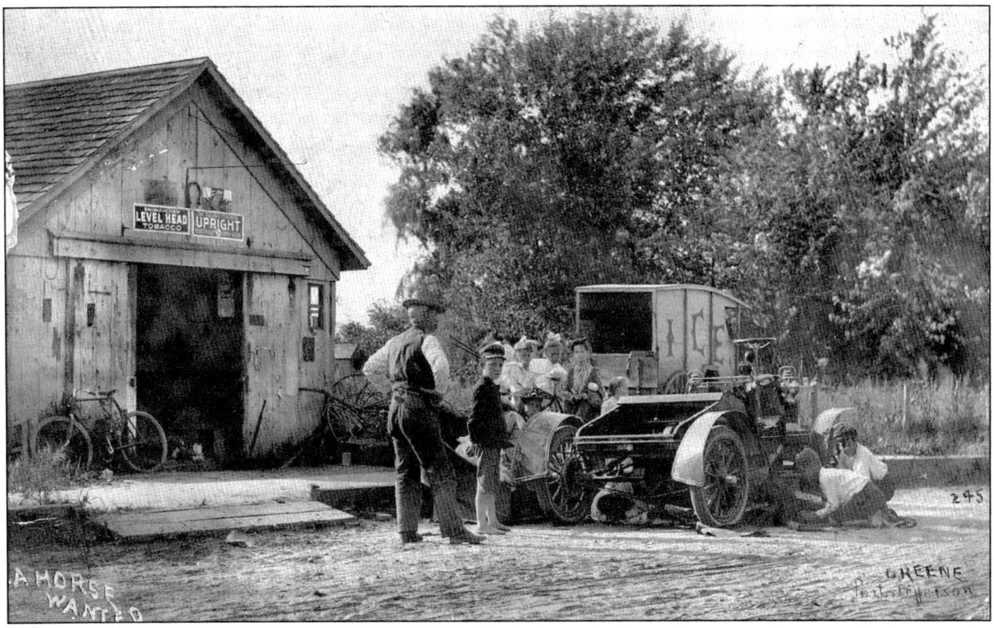

HENRY RAKOW'S BLACKSMITH SHOP, C. 1900. This Arthur Greene photograph shows the blacksmith shop, at approximately 26 Shore Road, that later became the first home of the Setauket fire department. A mechanic is under a 1903 Winton attempting repairs. (Courtesy of Beverly and Barbara Tyler.)

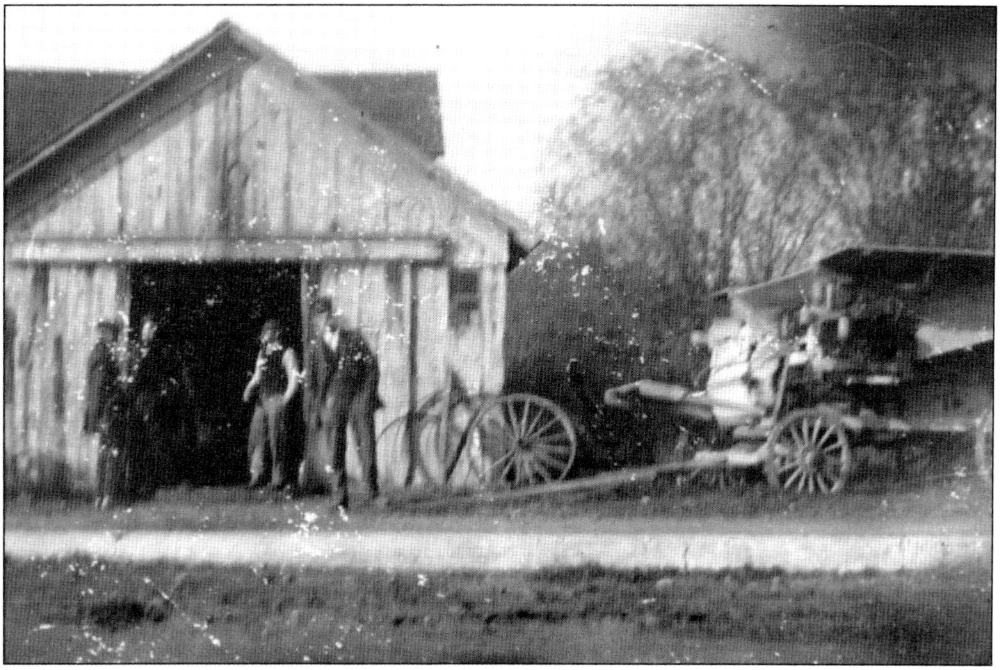

RAKOW'S BLACKSMITH SHOP, C. 1905. Pictured are, from left to right, two unidentified customers, Henry M. Rakow (blacksmith), and George Fordham. The shop was located at about 26 Shore Road. (Courtesy of Betty Voss.)

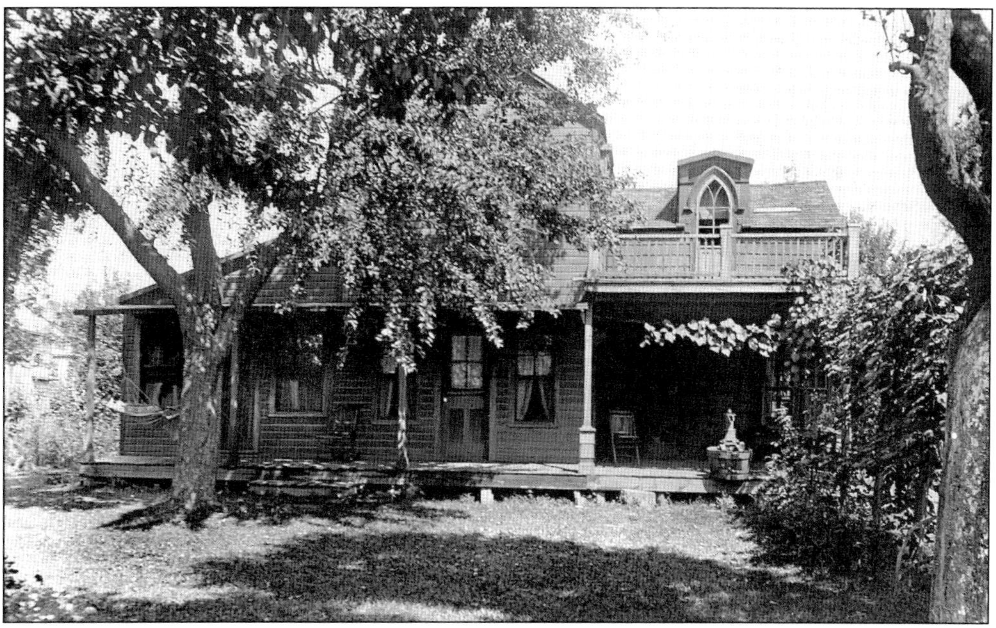

DEVERELL HOUSE, 41 SHORE ROAD, BUILT C. 1890. In this house, the Gothic window/door in the small dormer opened onto the roof. The window reportedly came from the St. James Catholic Church on Main Street, Setauket, when the church was remodeled in 1907. (Courtesy of Betty Voss.)

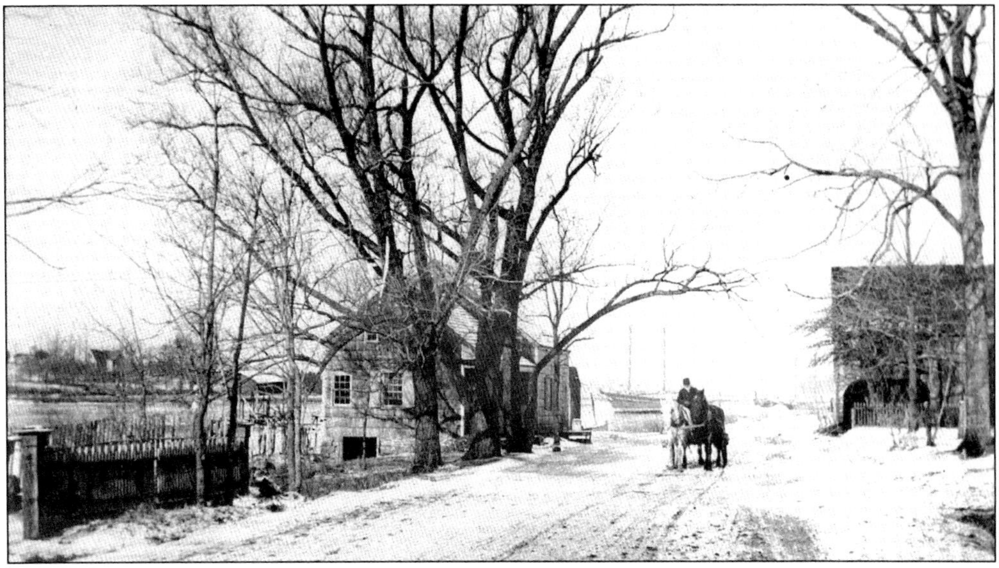

PHILIP LONGBOTHUM HOUSE, 46 SHORE ROAD, BUILT C. 1825. In the early 20th century, when this photograph was taken, this was the home of Richard (Dick) Risley. Tom Rowland, who had a shipyard around the corner on Shore Road, is shown driving the wagon. Risley's son Jim worked for Rowland as a ship caulker. This 19th century house was demolished and replaced with a barge, which was converted to a houseboat around 1928. At the left across the water, the Vingut House that was behind the Presbyterian church is visible. There is a two-masted schooner anchored in the harbor. (Courtesy of Betty Voss.)

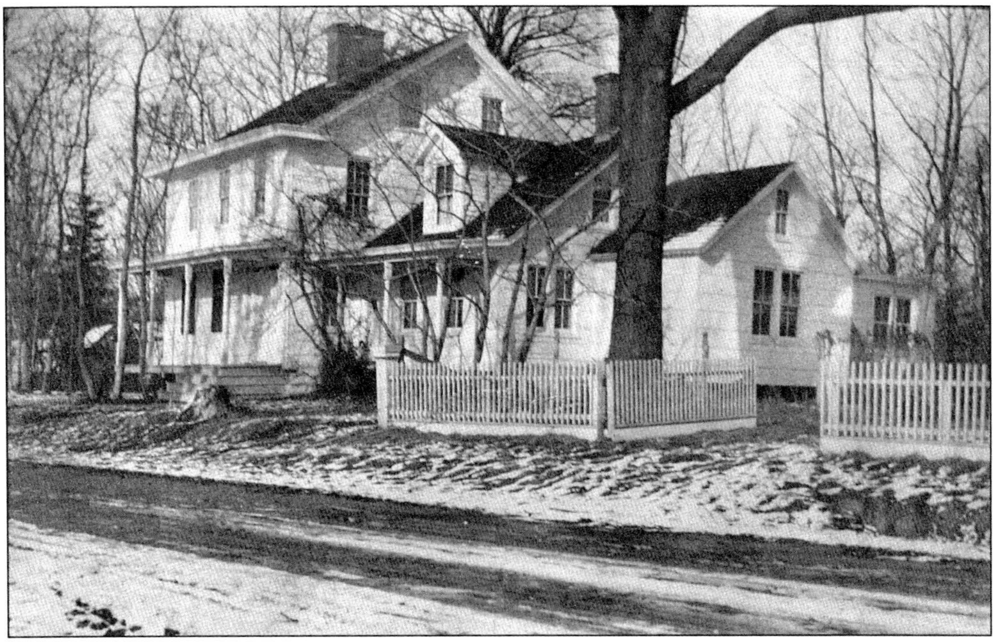

CAPT. BREWSTER HAWKINS HOUSE, 49 SHORE ROAD, BUILT C. 1825. This c. 1920 photograph shows the house that was constructed on a foundation of an earlier building. Captain Hawkins was married twice and had 13 children with his first wife and 3 with his second. Hawkins operated a ship's chandlery opposite his home. (Courtesy of Betty Voss.)

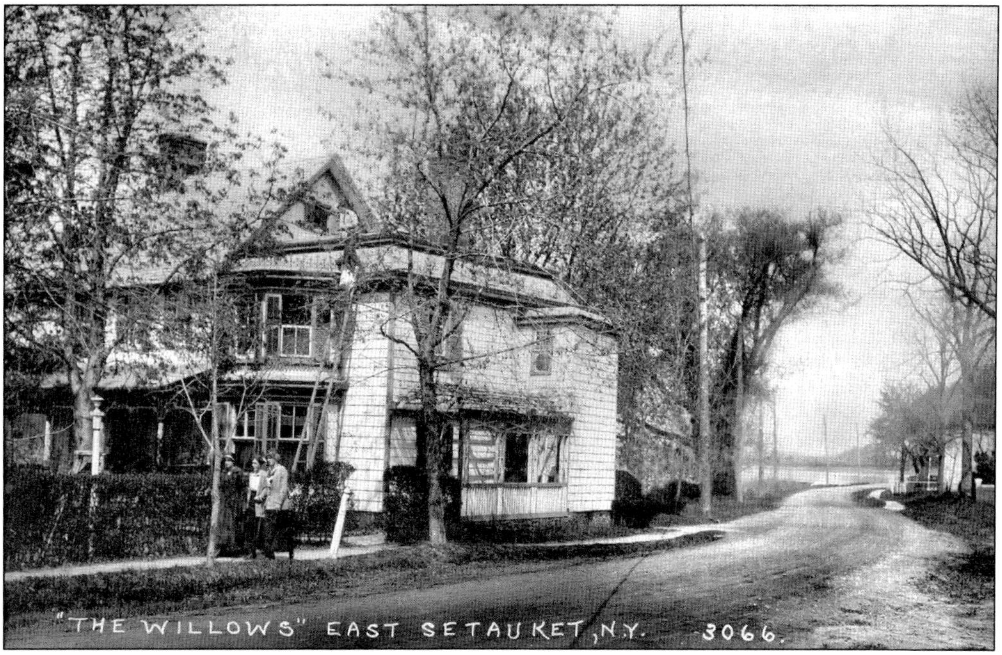

DAVID CLEAVES HOUSE, THE WILLOWS, BUILT C. 1800. David Cleaves operated a boatyard adjacent to this house on 44 Shore Road from 1820 to 1835. The late-19th-century extension near the road was added when the home operated as a summer boardinghouse. (Courtesy of Susan White Picroth.)

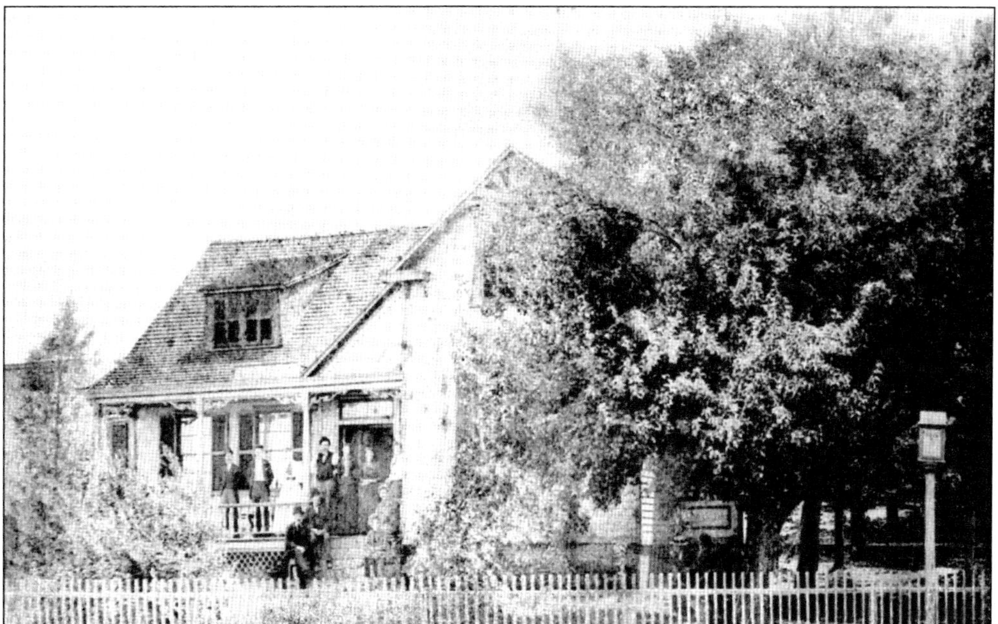

HENRY TYLER HOUSE, 61 SHORE ROAD. Built in the late 18th century, this is the oldest house on Shore Road. In 1909, it was known as the Atlantic Hotel and was operated by Mary McDowell as a boardinghouse. This photograph, taken around 1910, shows a wing that was subsequently removed. (Courtesy of Betty Voss.)

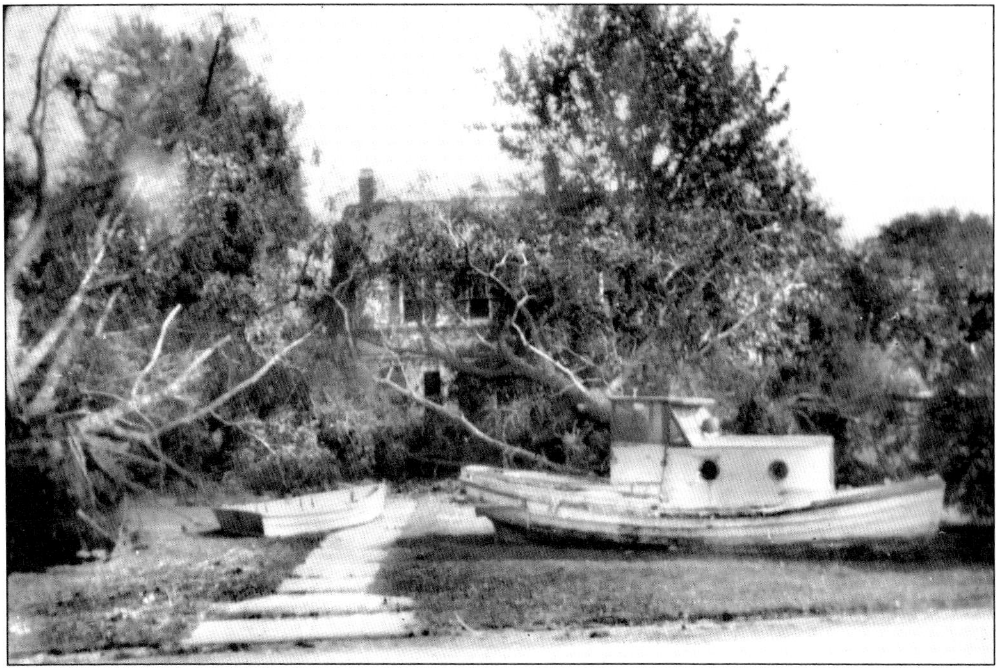

JOSHUA BUNCE HOUSE, 69 SHORE ROAD, BUILT C. 1858. This photograph shows the aftermath of the 1938 hurricane. Bunce was a ship carpenter who worked in the yards along Shore Road. The house was extensively remodeled in the 1920s.

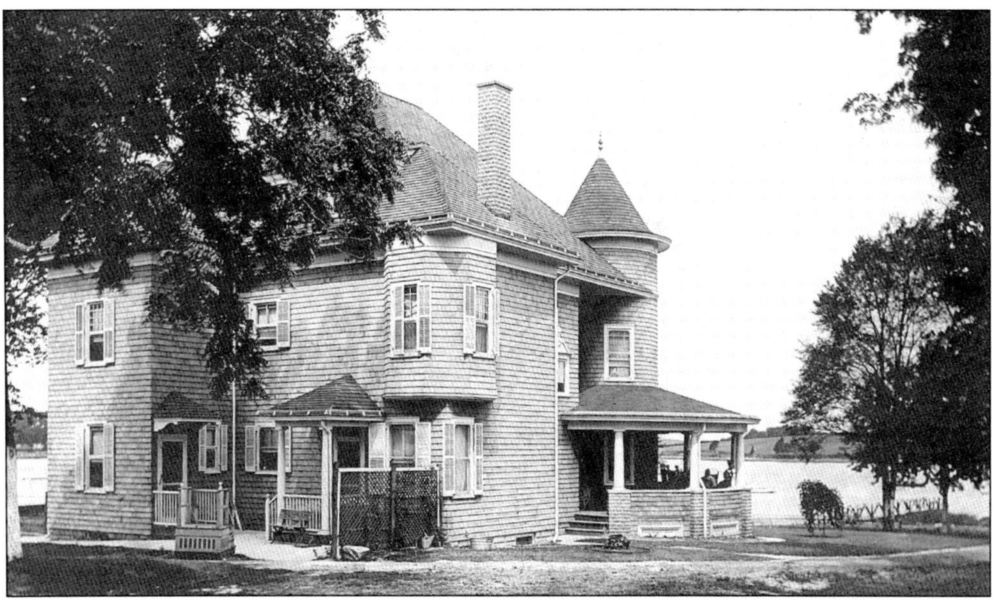

MARK MURPHY HOUSE, SHORE FARM, BUILT C. 1910. This house, at the corner of Bayview Avenue at 73 Shore Road, was built for vaudeville stars Mr. and Mrs. Mark Murphy. It was renamed Westwind in 1929, when Benjamin West purchased the property. West owned a farm on the south side of North Country Road, from the present Ridgeway Avenue to the Stop and Shop.

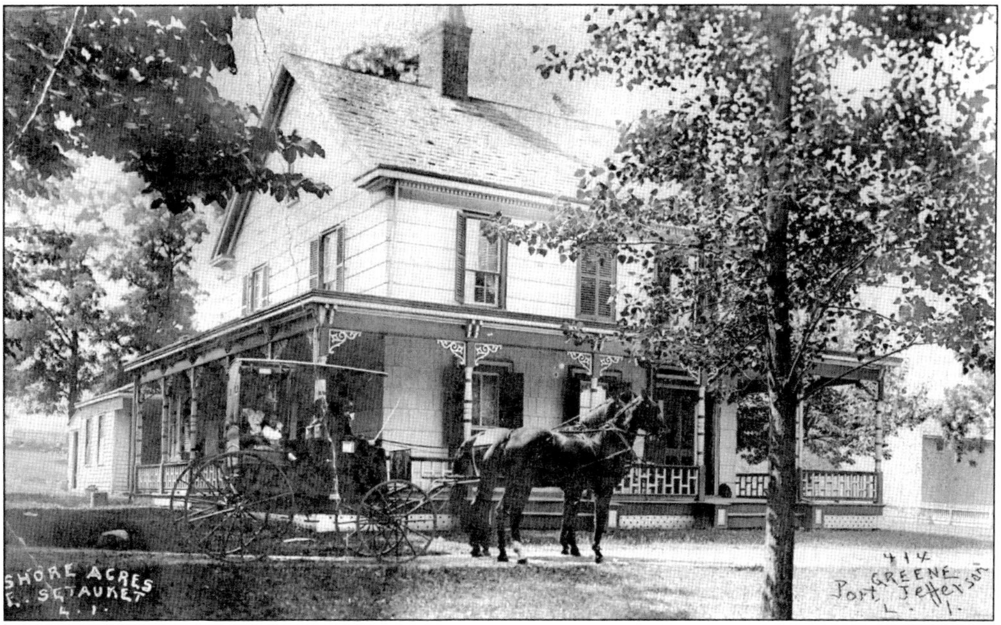

SHORE ACRES, WILLIAM DECATUR OAKES HOME, BUILT c. 1823. In this *c.* 1900 Arthur Greene photograph, William Decatur Oakes is driving the carriage and his wife, Julia Augusta (Jayne), and daughter Lillian are in the backseat. The carriage is being pulled by Ella and George. The house was located on 83 Shore Road. (Courtesy of Julia Oakes Darling.)

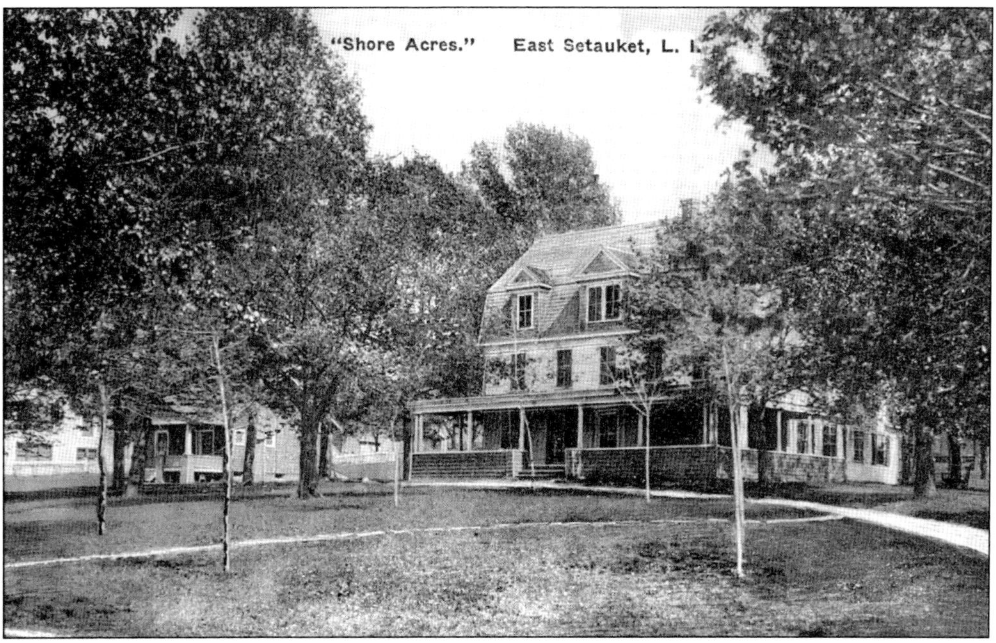

SHORE ACRES AS A BOARDINGHOUSE, 83 SHORE ROAD, c. 1910. This summer boardinghouse at 83 Shore Road is an expansion of the Oakes home (shown in the top photograph). It was operated by William and Julia Oakes. Their daughter Julia Augusta Darling taught fourth grade at the Setauket Union Free School. The boardinghouse was torn down in 1962.

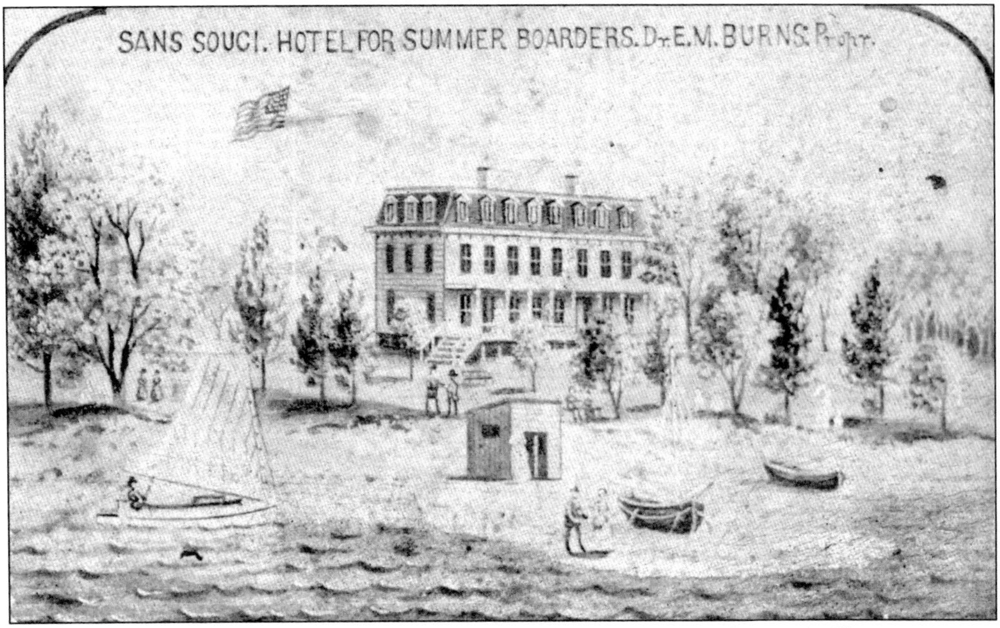

"SANS SOUCI. HOTEL FOR SUMMER BOARDERS. DR. E. M. BURNS, PROPR." This is a portion of a c. 1875 collage of Setauket. The collage is signed, "For Sale by Edw. Lange, Art., Suff. Co. N.Y." This is the only known representation of the hotel, which was located on the water at Van Brunt Manor Road and Tinker Lane.

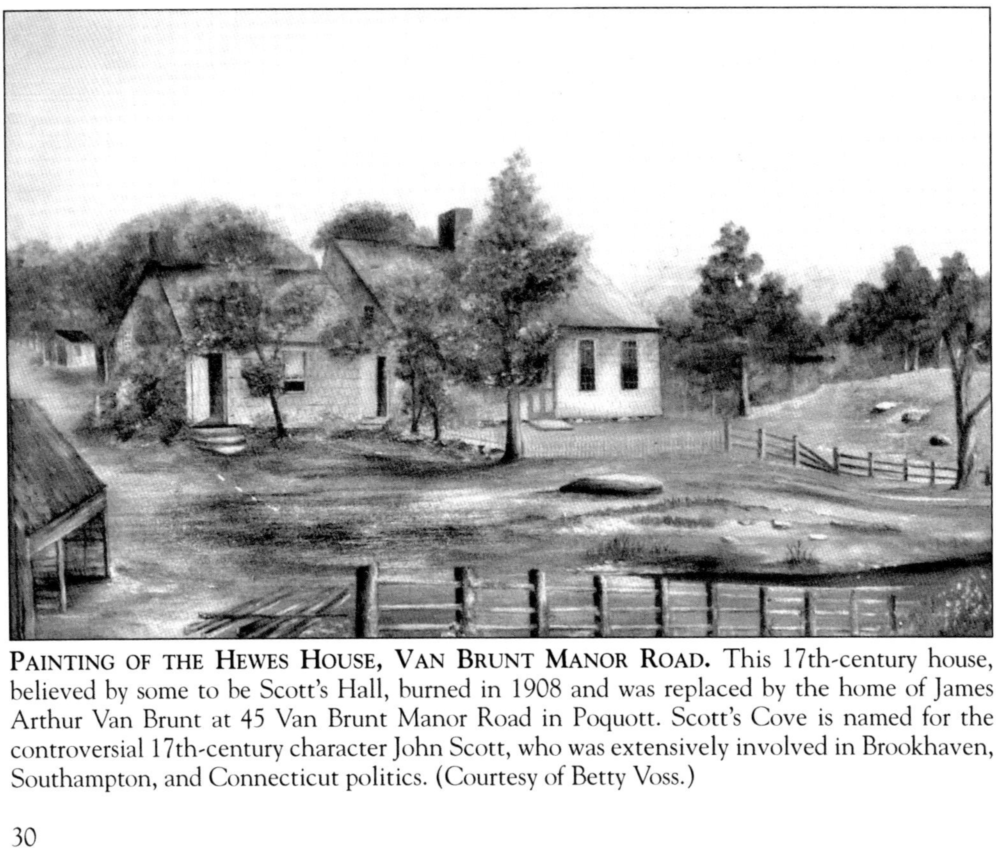

PAINTING OF THE HEWES HOUSE, VAN BRUNT MANOR ROAD. This 17th-century house, believed by some to be Scott's Hall, burned in 1908 and was replaced by the home of James Arthur Van Brunt at 45 Van Brunt Manor Road in Poquott. Scott's Cove is named for the controversial 17th-century character John Scott, who was extensively involved in Brookhaven, Southampton, and Connecticut politics. (Courtesy of Betty Voss.)

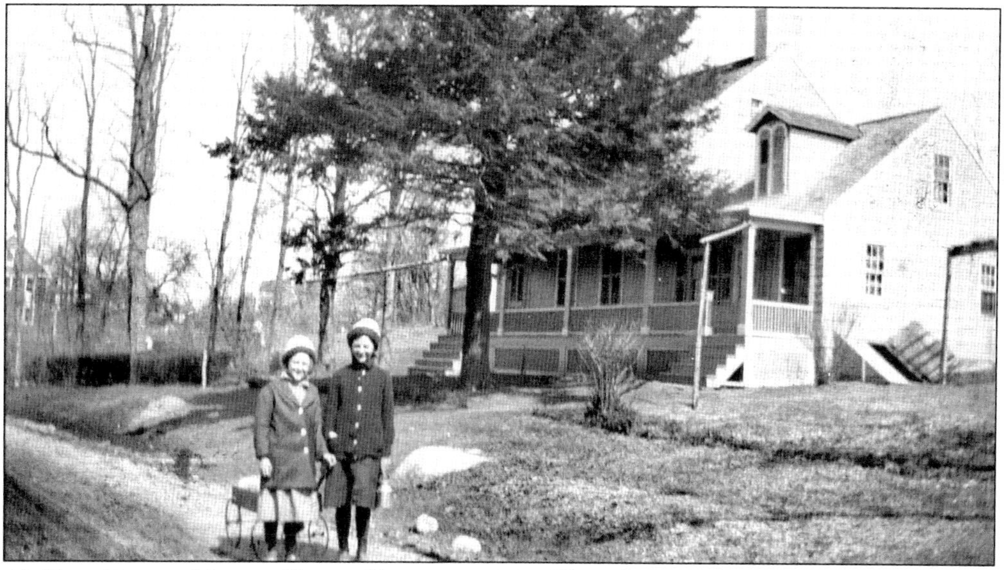

41 VAN BRUNT MANOR ROAD, BUILT C. 1880. This photograph was taken around 1915. (Courtesy of John Lane.)

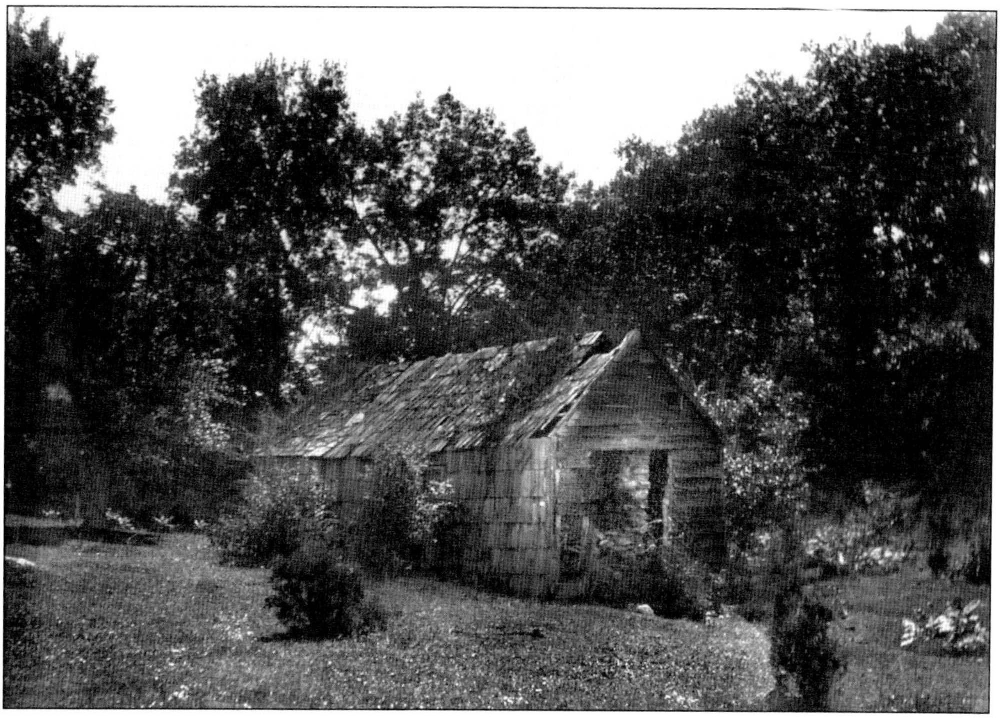

VAN BRUNT SLAVE QUARTERS, DYERS NECK, POQUOTT, C. 1935. The remains of the stone chimney are at the near end of the building.

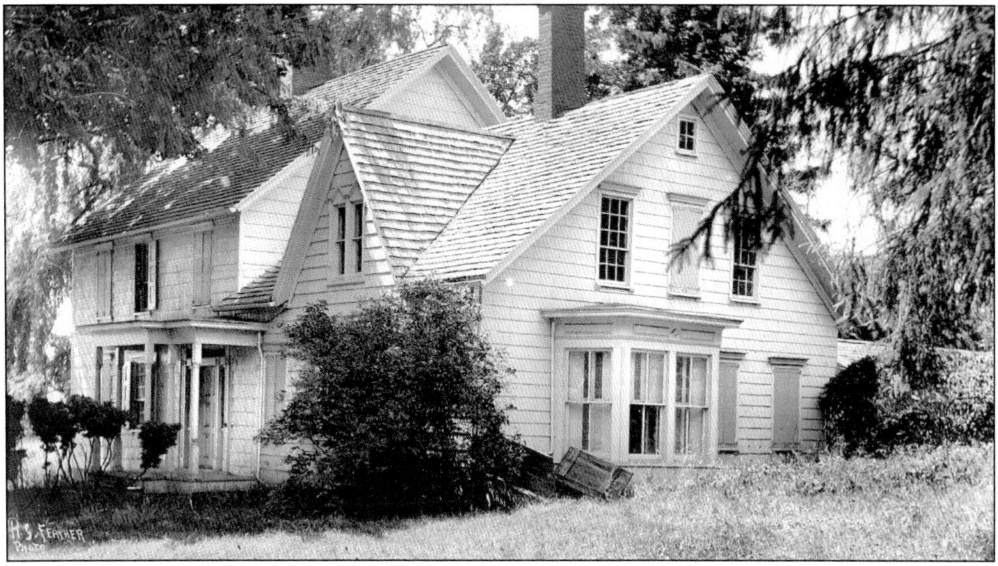

ROE TAVERN, MAIN STREET AT BAYVIEW AVENUE, BUILT C. 1703. Constructed as a private home, Austin Roe converted this building into a tavern just before the American Revolution. This was a focal point for the operation of the Setauket spy ring. Pres. George Washington stayed here during his 1790 tour of Long Island. In 1936, when New York State widened Route 25A, Wallace Irwin, homeowner and novelist, moved the tavern to Millie Lane off Old Post Road on Briar Hill. The DeHart Moving Company of Port Jefferson did the moving. (R. S. Feather photograph, *c.* 1900.)

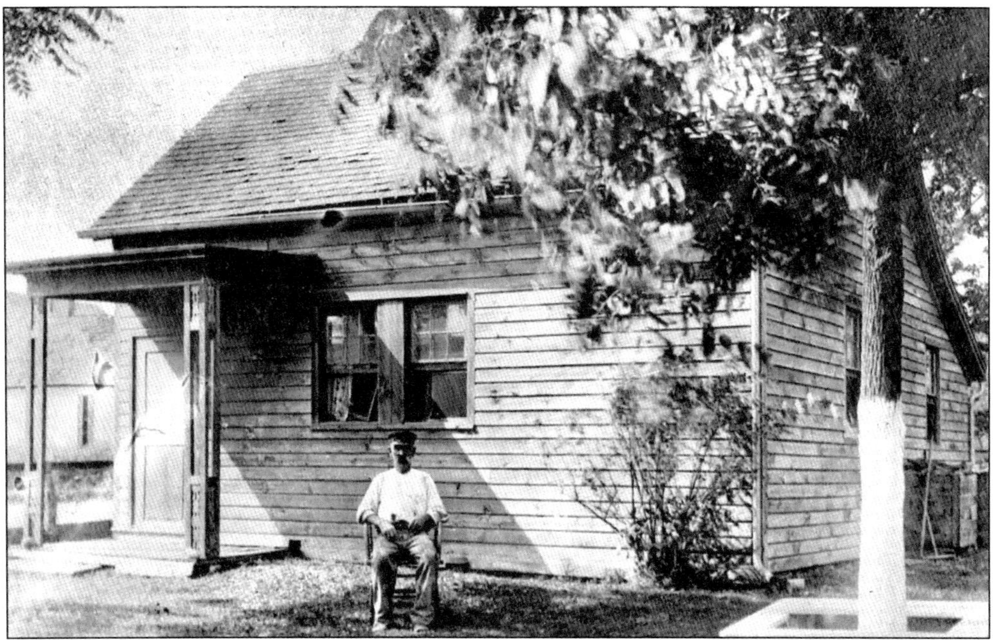

CAPT. ALBERT J. NELSON, 1908. Nelson was skipper of the schooner *Louise*, which was abandoned in Scott's Cove. This house, originally next to the Roe Tavern on Route 25A, was moved with the tavern to Old Post Road. It was rebuilt and preserved through the efforts of the Three Village Historical Society.

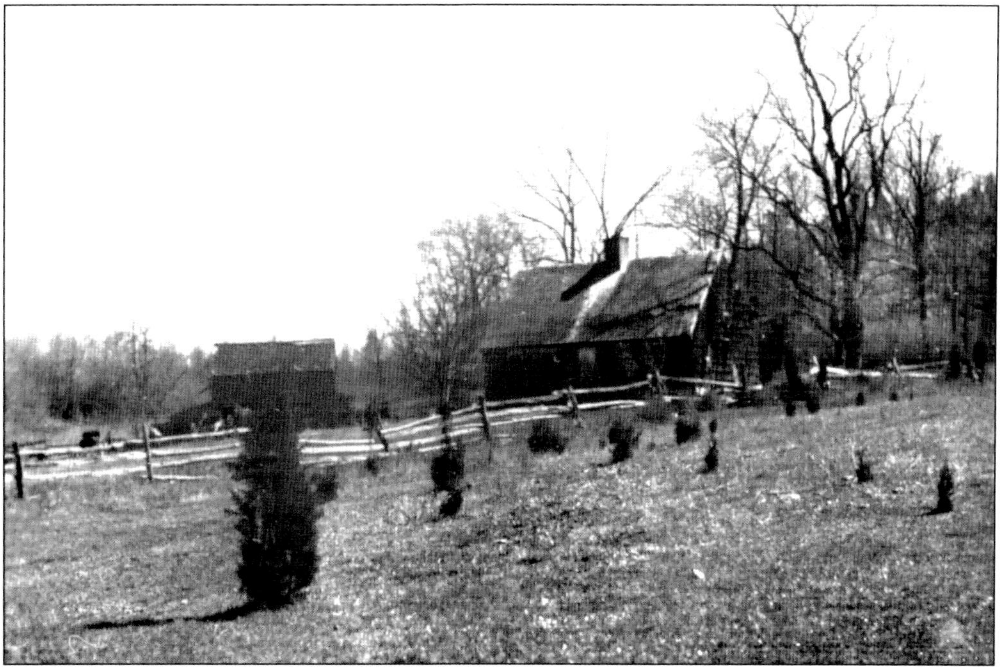

James Hulse House, 40 Old Post Road, Built c. 1750. In 1832, James Hulse owned this 70-plus-acre farm. The house was restored by the Society for the Preservation of Long Island Antiquities in the 1960s.

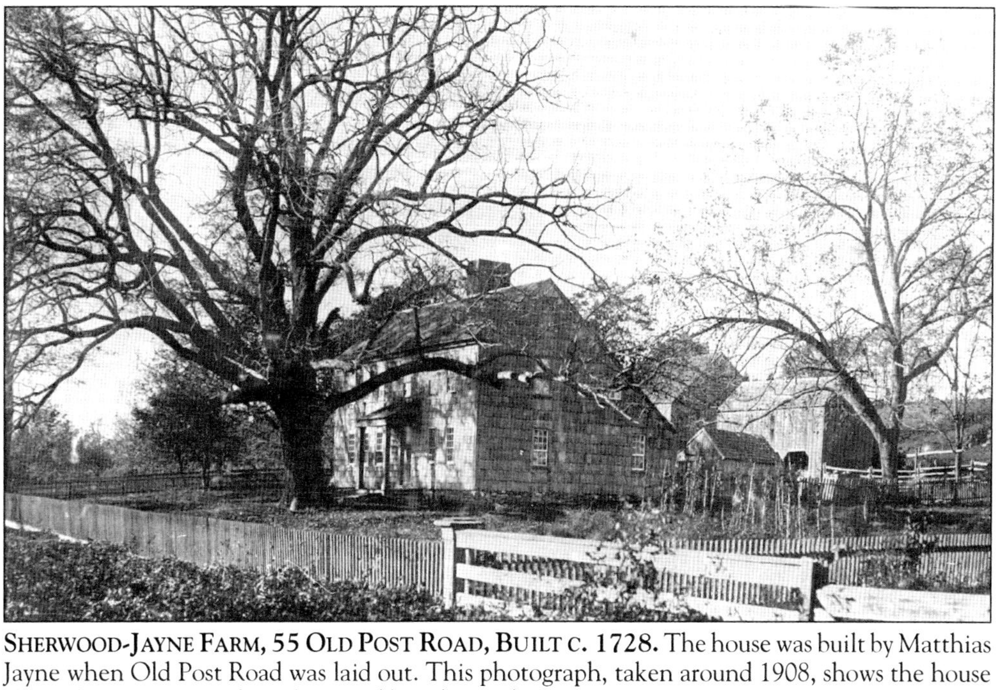

Sherwood-Jayne Farm, 55 Old Post Road, Built c. 1728. The house was built by Matthias Jayne when Old Post Road was laid out. This photograph, taken around 1908, shows the house about the time Howard C. Sherwood bought it. Sherwood was the founder of the Society for the Preservation of Long Island Antiquities, which now owns this property. (Courtesy of Beverly and Barbara Tyler.)

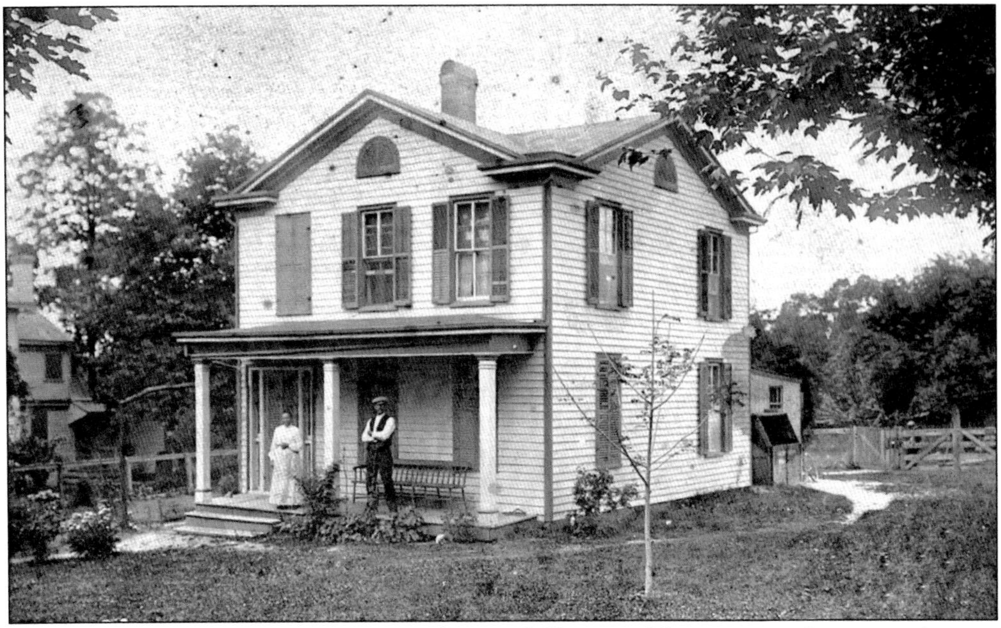

HAMMON HOUSE, BUILT C. 1840. Matthias and Christina Hammon are shown standing on the porch of their 393 Main Street home, which was purchased in 1899. According to the 1900 census, Matthias, a farm laborer, and his wife came to the United States from Germany in 1886. (Courtesy of Betty Voss.)

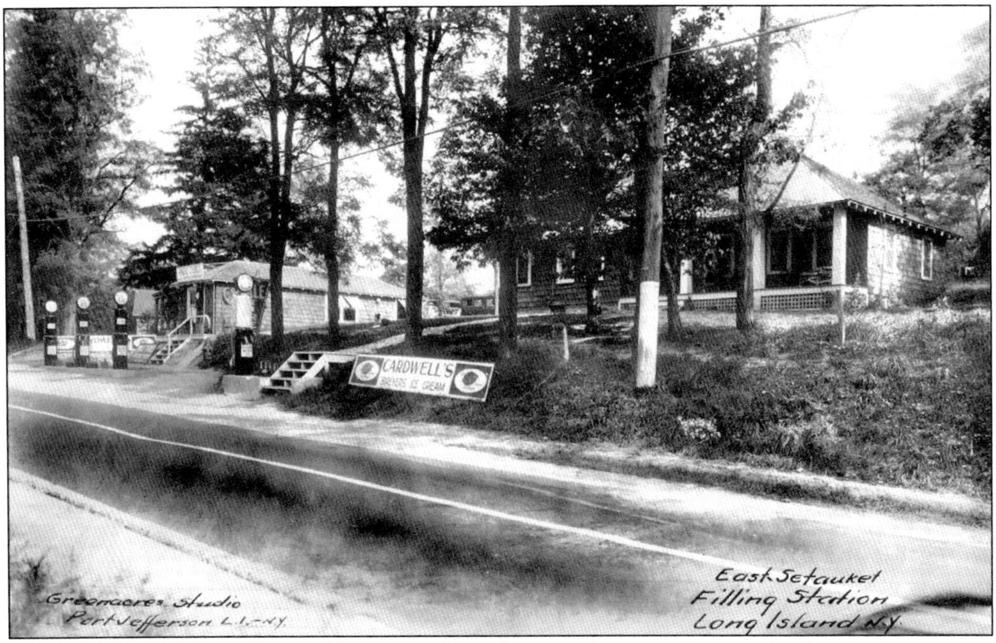

CARDWELL'S CORNER, MAIN STREET AT VAN BRUNT MANOR ROAD. Cardwell's Corner was also known as "Suicide Bend" because it was so difficult to navigate at a high rate of speed when coming from Port Jefferson. This *c.* 1930 Arthur Greene postcard photograph shows Cardwell's Filling Station, which sold gasoline, kerosene, and ice cream. The Setauket baseball field was directly across Main Street (Route 25A). (Courtesy of Susan White Pieroth.)

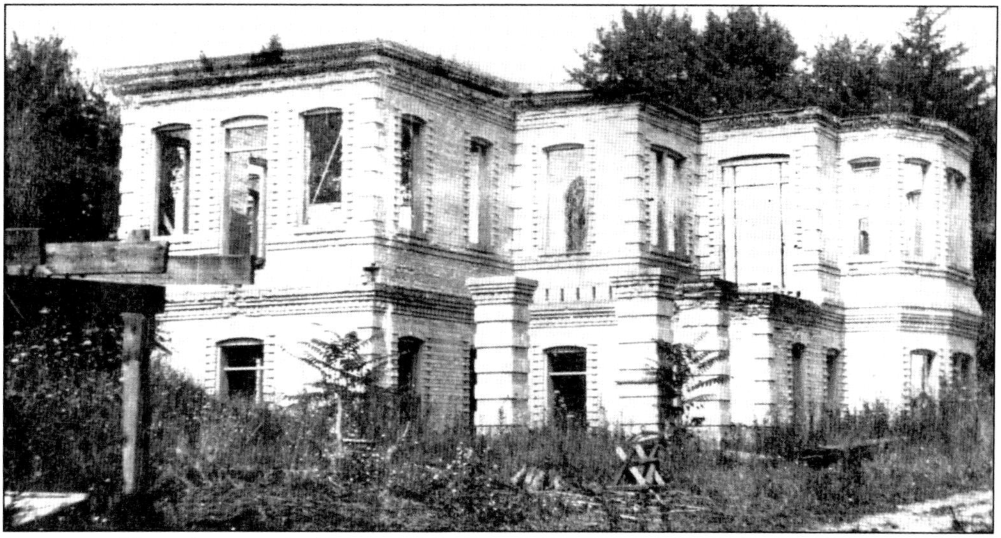

DIAMOND HILL CASTLE, 22 BAYVIEW AVENUE, BUILT C. 1915. "The Castle," shown here around 1927, was to be the home of Brazilian count Eugenio Goncalves de Teixeira and his wife, Leona (Hand). It was never completed and was demolished in 1940. The de Teixeira family had owned the Piricaua Mines in the Amazon Valley since Colonial times. About 1914, this mine produced a five-pound, 24-carat gold nugget with a 4-carat diamond embedded in it, thus the castle name of Diamond Hill. Although he actually lived at 9 Carlton Avenue, de Teixeira listed his address as "Diamond Hill Castle, Villa Teixeira, L.I., N.Y." He wanted to tunnel to the bay to facilitate unloading "freight" but stopped because he could not excavate under other people's property. (Courtesy of Dr. Sherman Mills and Lois Schaub.)

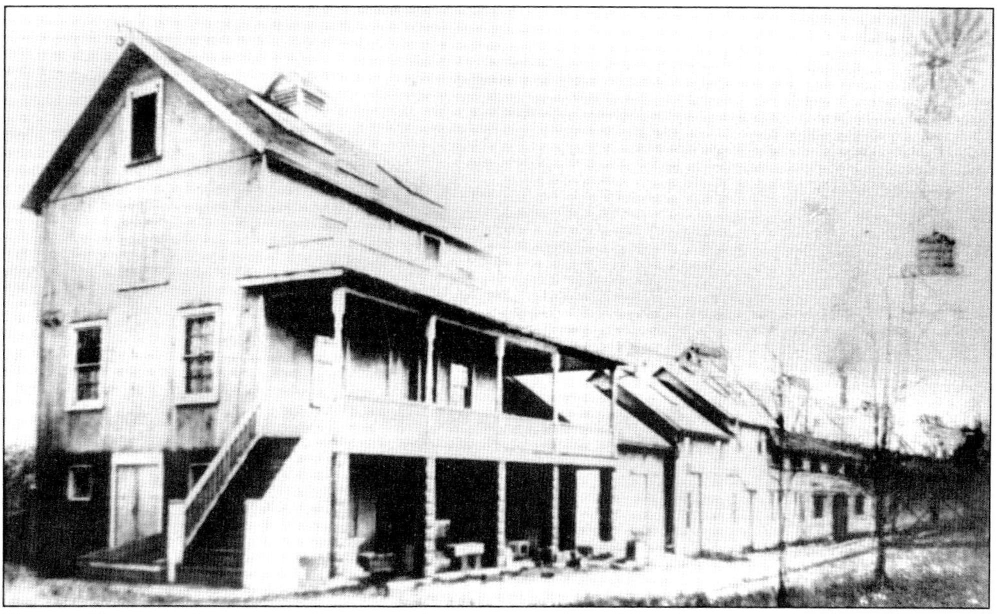

THE DE TEIXEIRA FACTORY, CARLTON AVENUE, C. 1927. This factory produced metal castings and carried out nickel, copper, bronze, aluminum, gold, and silver plating. The factory also produced Teixeirite, a ceramic used for decorative castings with a hardness similar to brick. (Courtesy of Dr. Sherman Mills and Lois Schaub.)

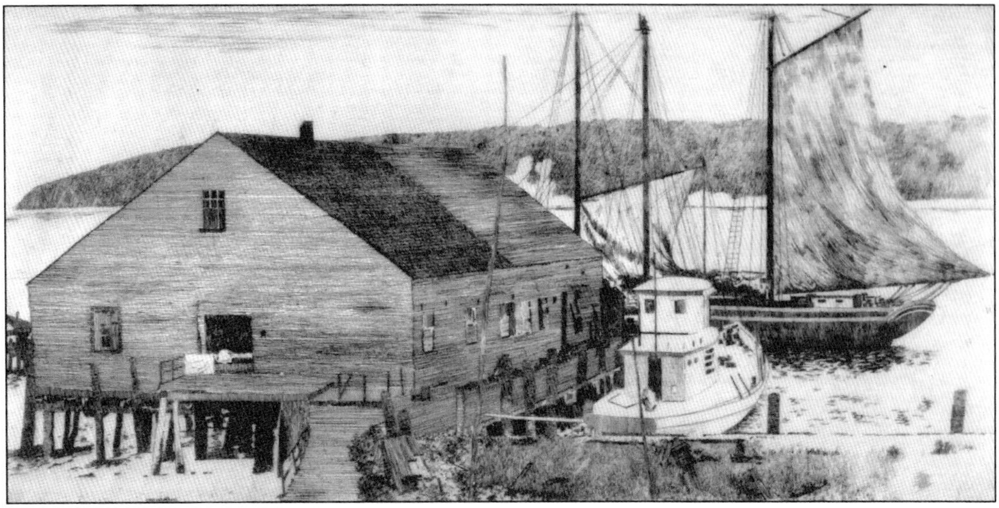

OYSTER HOUSE AT CALIFORNIA GROVE, POQUOTT. This September 2, 1923, drawing by Ray Tyler was copied from one of his photographs. The oyster house was at the end of Washington Avenue, at the Poquott Village Beach, and operated as the Suwasset Oyster Company, owned by Henry Schmeelk. When the oyster house was dismantled in 1934, a portion of it was moved and became part of the house at 91 Sheep Pasture Road. (Courtesy of James McNamara.)

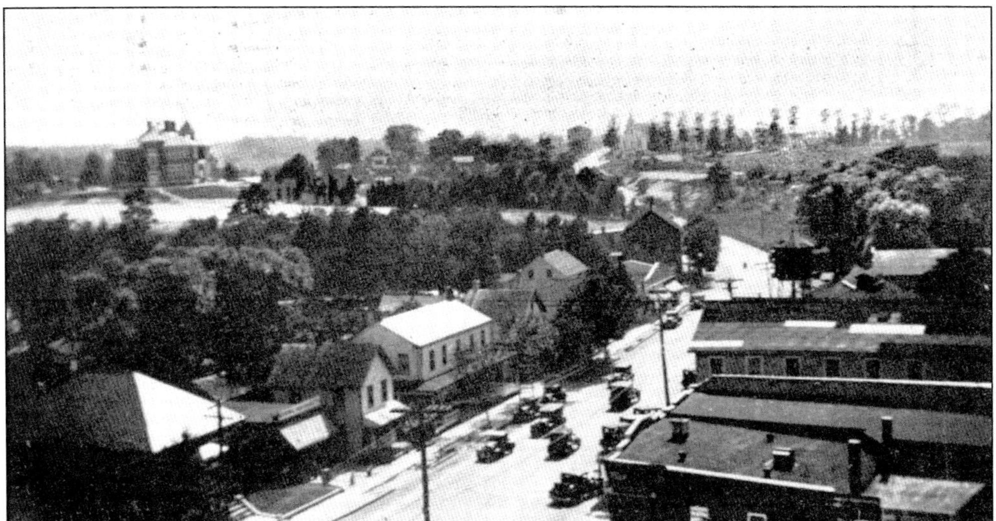

MAIN STREET, LOOKING WEST, C. 1930. This photograph was taken by Ray Tyler from the top of the flagpole in the East Setauket Memorial Park, on Shore Road's north side. From east (bottom) to west (top) are Meister's Drug Store, Lyon Brothers Hardware, the Great Atlantic and Pacific Tea Company (later Roulston's Market), the two rubber factories (one wood, one brick with a wood-barrel water tower), Ruhland's Garage, Brewster House (behind trees), the sandpit, two residences, a real estate office, and the Setauket United Methodist Church. On the south side, from east to west, are Tinker National Bank, Edith Kloh's Liquor Store, Roulston's Grocery Store, Karl Huter's Fine Foods, Barney Jayne's Tavern (290 Main Street, later Sheppard's Tavern and Bolduc's Saloon), the post office, Roulston's Grocery Store (corner of Gnarled Hollow Road), and Jack Michaels Country Corner. The upper rubber factory is in the distant center opposite the Methodist church. On the hill at the upper left is the Setauket Union Free School.

Two

Setauket and Strong's Neck

The Setauket stream that was ultimately dammed to form the millpond was the central feature that attracted, first, Native Americans and, later, white settlers in 1655. It provided freshwater for both man and beast and eventually powered a series of gristmills. The original business district developed near the mills, on Main Street. The post office was the subject of the usual political ebb and flow. Over the years, it seems to have been located in at least six different buildings in four locations within the business district. The Setauket Village Green is one of only a few surviving village greens on Long Island. It provided the central meeting place for many forms of community activities.

When the piano factory and then the rubber factory opened, some of the business and social activity shifted up Main Street to the vicinity of the Setauket United Methodist Church. Several of these businesses survived into the 1950s and 1960s to serve the expanding population of the village, and a few of their structures were adapted to new uses and/or moved.

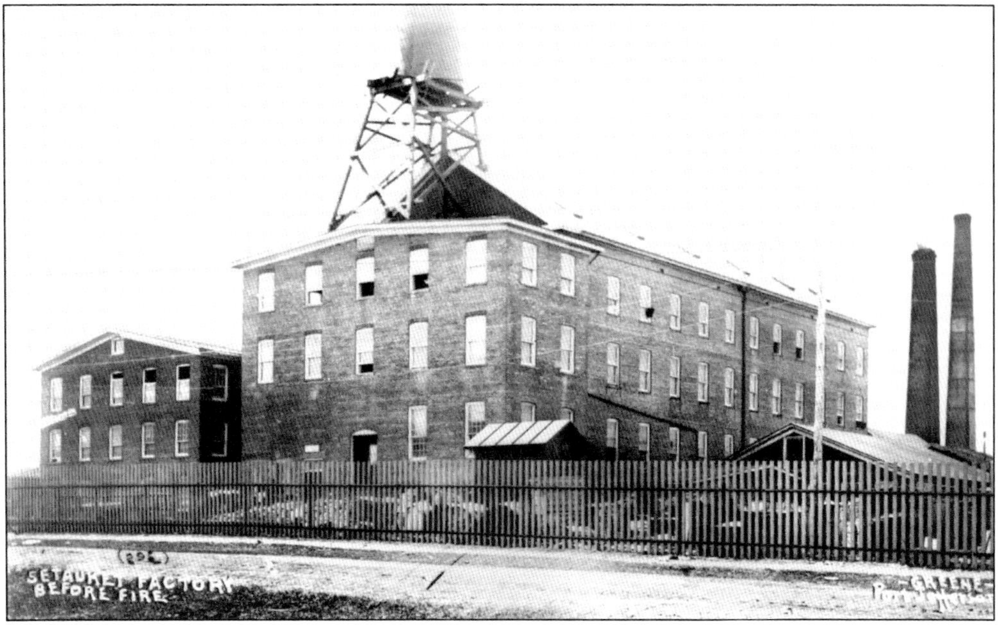

SETAUKET RUBBER FACTORY, C. 1900. Known as the "upper" rubber factory, this building was located across from the current North Fork Bank at approximately 46 Route 25A. This area was locally known as "Chicken Hill." The factory was founded as the Nunns and Clark Piano Factory before the Civil War, and then it was occupied by the rubber company. The company that operated the rubber factory changed its name many times, but the principals tended to remain the same. This is an Arthur Greene photograph.

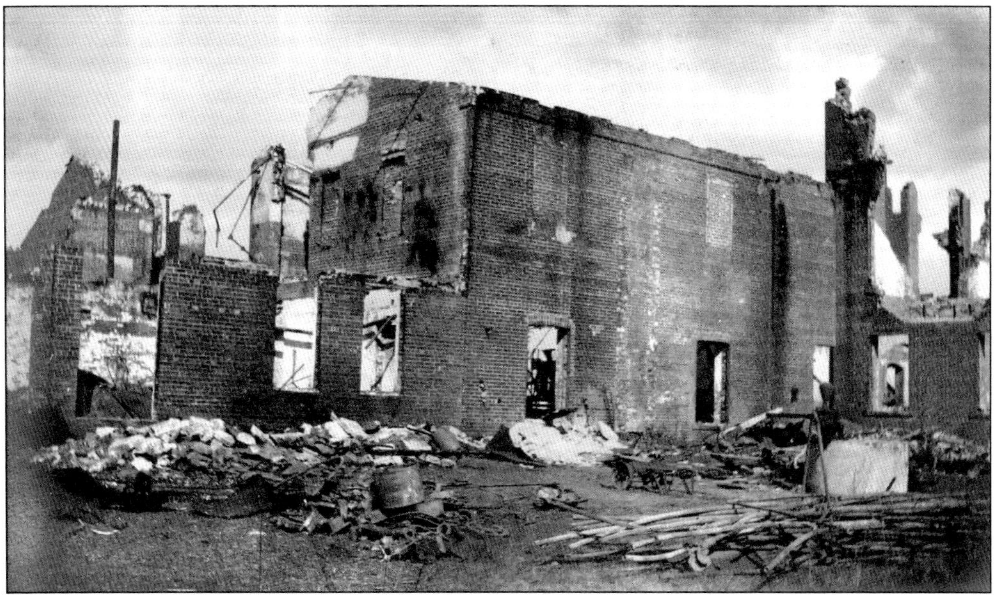

RUBBER FACTORY FIRE, OCTOBER 1904. This fire consumed almost all of the upper rubber factory, along with numerous frame houses surrounding it. The only portion of the building to survive was a small section closest to the road. This section was salvaged, and later the Jericho Laboratories operated a small drug and cosmetics factory at this location.

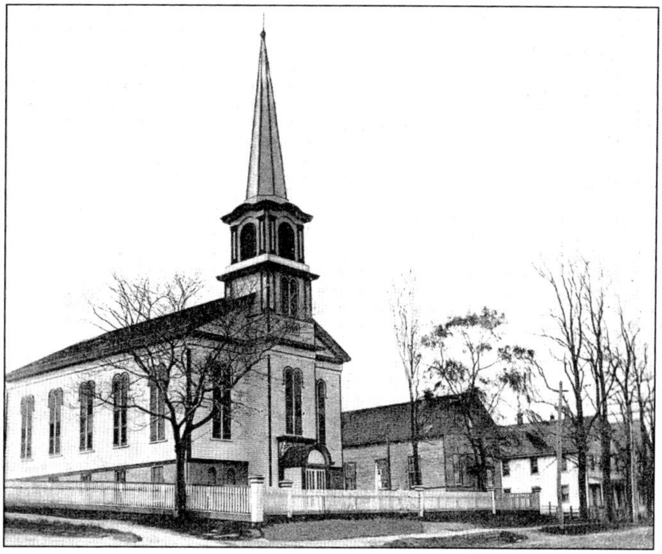

SETAUKET UNITED METHODIST CHURCH, 160 MAIN STREET, BUILT 1870. In this photograph from around 1909, Good Templars, or Mechanics, Hall is to the right. It was built as a Masonic temple and later used as a meeting hall for community groups, including the Boy Scouts. It also served as the school auditorium and was attached to the church building in about 1960. The twin-gabled buildings, to the right, are a residence and Pinnes' Meat Market, which later became Bob Eikov's Meat Market.

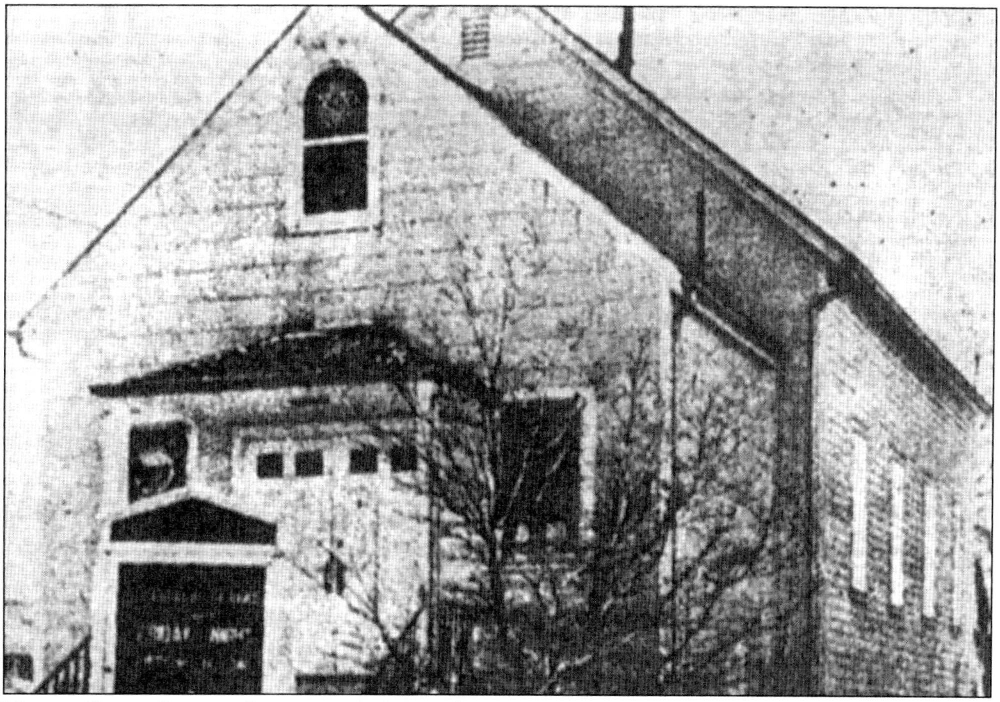

NORTH SHORE JEWISH CENTER, 152 MAIN STREET, BUILT 1890. This shul, the first synagogue in Suffolk County, was built by William Deckman on land donated by Herman Pinnes. Congregation Agudas Achim was incorporated November 28, 1893. The building, shown around 1950, was constructed to serve a growing European immigrant population, which found employment at the local rubber factory since the late 1870s. After the 1904 rubber factory fire, many of these families left the area to find employment, and the synagogue closed in 1914. It reopened during World War I to serve Jewish sailors stationed in Port Jefferson and Yaphank. Rededicated in 1948, as the North Shore Jewish Center, it served its congregation until 1971 when a new synagogue on Old Town Road was opened. (Courtesy of the North Shore Jewish Center.)

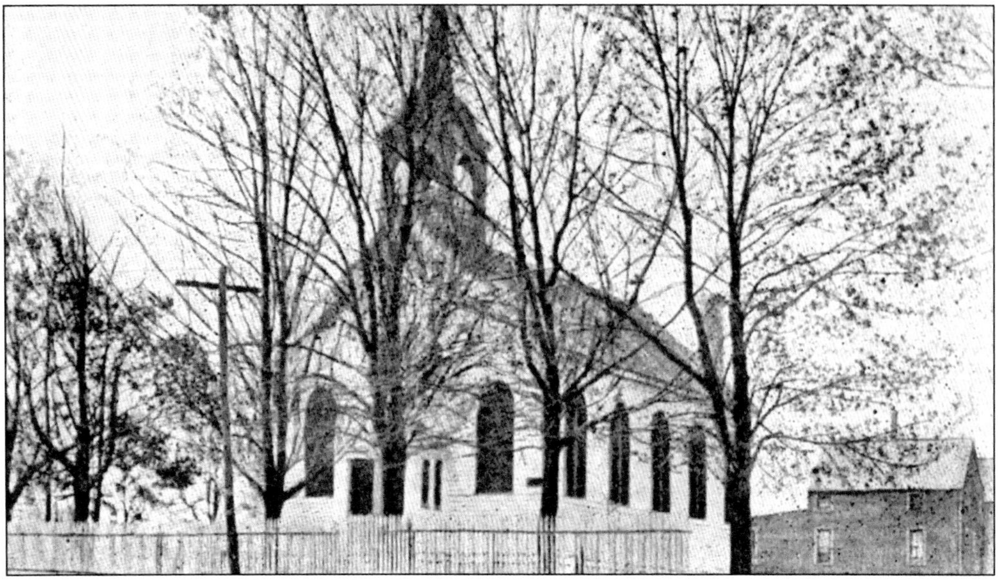

ST. JAMES CATHOLIC CHURCH, BUILT 1888. The church at 139 Main Street was remodeled by George Vingut for the wedding of his daughter Elizabeth to Count Charles D'Este in 1907. The count was a French cavalry officer in World War I. This building served the congregation of Setauket until 1968 when the new church at Ridgeway Avenue was built. This became the home of the St. Germain of Alaska Eastern Orthodox congregation in 1974 and, most recently, the Jerusalem Patriarchate Monastery of the Holy Cross. Two rubber-factory workers' houses are visible at the right. The photograph dates from before 1907. (Courtesy of Susan White Pieroth.)

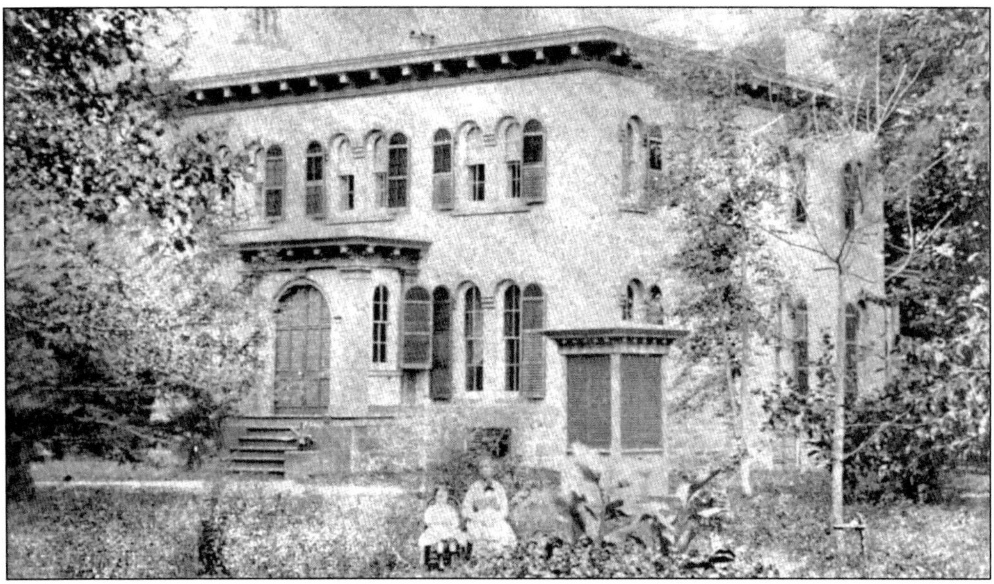

NUNNS-RIDGWAY HOUSE, BUILT C. 1845. Robert Nunns of the Nunns and Clark Piano Factory built this home at approximately 128 Main Street. By 1874, the house was owned by Phebe Ridgway. Seated on the lawn next to the well house in this photograph, taken around 1875, are likely to be Catherine Meade, the governess, and either Phebe or Caroline Ridgway. The house, which stood between the present Setauket School and the Emma S. Clark Memorial Library, was torn down around 1954.

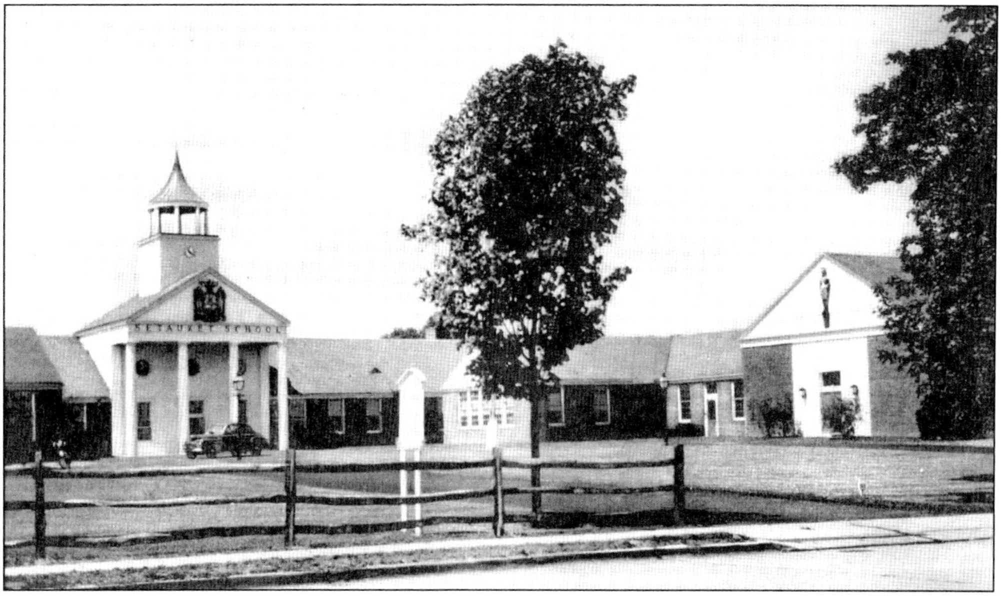

SETAUKET SCHOOL, BUILT 1951. Shown here soon after construction, the Setauket School at 134 Main Street was designed to serve students through ninth grade, replacing the Setauket Union Free School on the hill above Main Street (Route 25A). The polychrome statues on the front of the building were constructed by Frank Newsham.

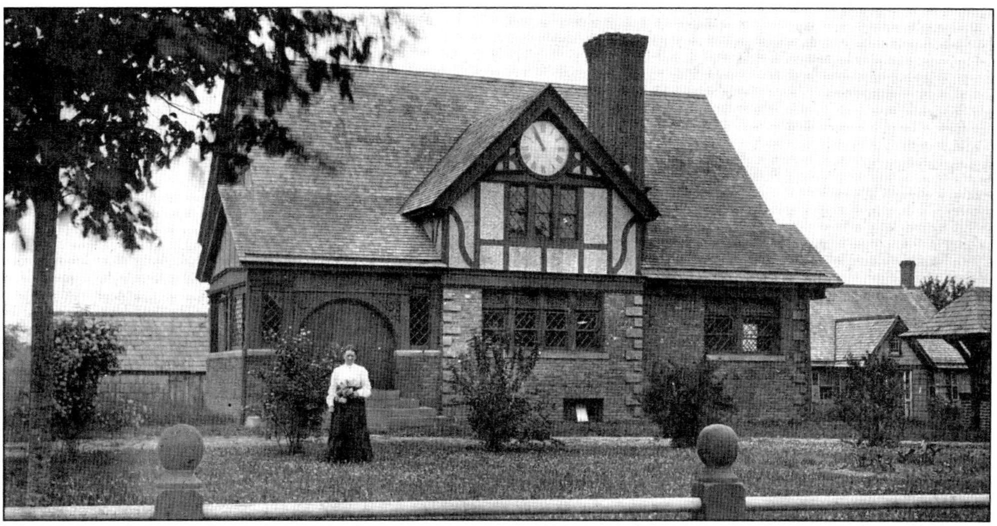

EMMA S. CLARK MEMORIAL LIBRARY, BUILT 1892. Anna Morand, the first librarian, stands in front of the library at 120 Main Street in this photograph taken around 1900. The library was opened on October 3, 1892, Emma Clark's birthday. Thomas Hodgkins, Emma's uncle and owner of Brambletye Farm, financed the construction of the library. Directly behind the library is a barn that was occupied by a local recluse. To the right rear of the library is the house and barn that originally belonged to Ebenezer Bayles, the town undertaker. The house was moved and set on a new foundation, and the widow of Dr. Ferdinand Bates lived there. Later it was a home for the librarian. Other tenants rented the house until it was destroyed by fire in 1945. This library is Suffolk County's oldest continuous service library that has remained at its original location. (Courtesy of Beverly and Barbara Tyler.)

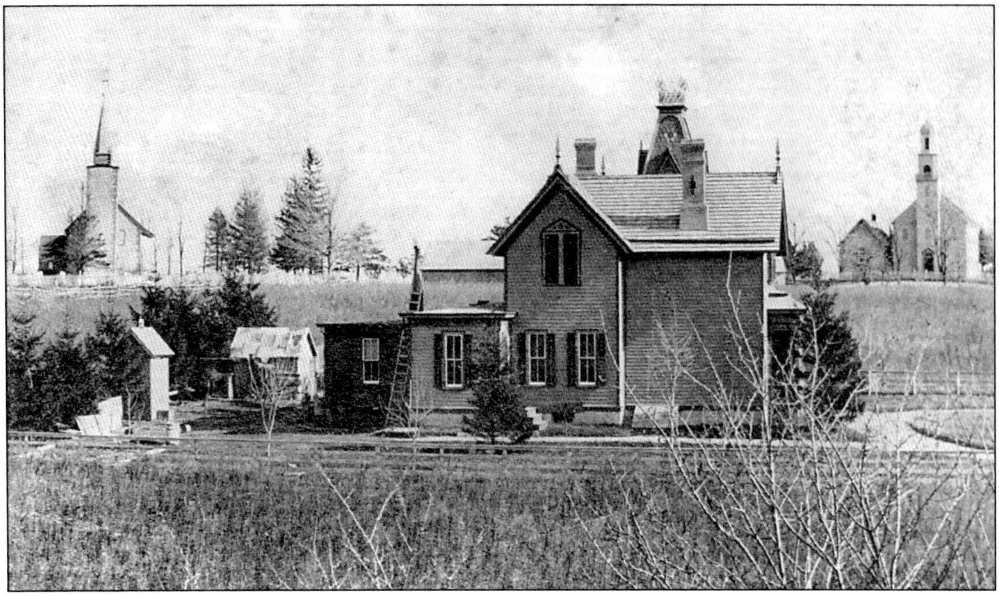

Allen-Bryant House, 109 Main Street, Built c. 1885. This *c.* 1890 photograph shows the Caroline Church in the left background. The Presbyterian church is at the right. Note that the entrances to both churches are at their west ends so that their congregations are facing east. English tradition dictated that the congregation was to face the east, and at burial, the feet of the deceased were to be oriented to the east. This permitted the faithful to face Christ at the second coming. (Courtesy of Beverly and Barbara Tyler.)

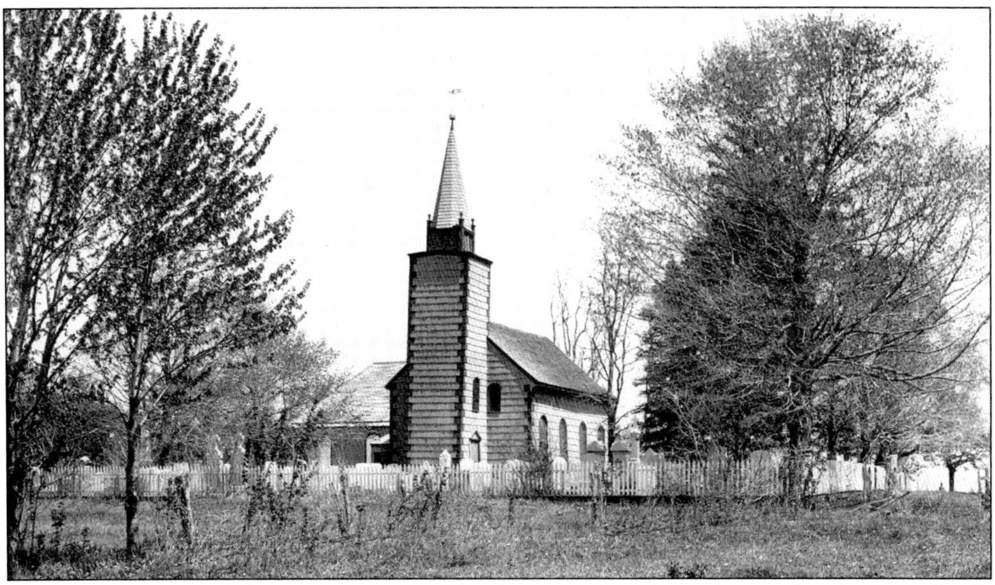

Caroline Church of Brookhaven, Setauket Green, Built 1729. This is Long Island's oldest Episcopal church. Queen Wilhelmina Karolina, wife of King George II, sent an altar cloth and silver communion service that is still used on special occasions. Caroline Church served as a British hospital during the patriot attack in 1777 and was not desecrated because it was the Anglican church, the official church of England. St. John's Church in Oakdale was founded as a mission church from Caroline. (Arthur Greene photograph, *c.* 1900.)

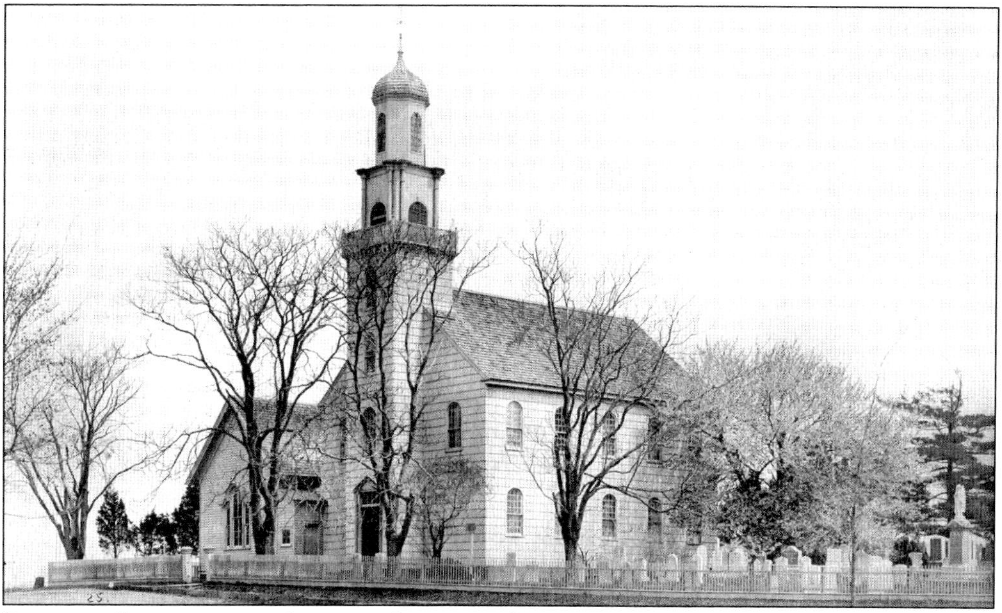

SETAUKET PRESBYTERIAN CHURCH, SETAUKET GREEN, BUILT 1812. This is the third building to occupy the site of the Setauket Presbyterian Church, but the congregation, founded about 1660, is the oldest in Brookhaven. The cemetery dates from the earliest days of the colony. In 1777, when the British seized the church as a garrison, they used tombstones and monuments to reinforce the fortifications, and the building became a stable. Zachariah Greene was a participant in the assault of August 1777. After the Revolution, he became the pastor of the church and dedicated the present building. This is an Arthur Greene photograph, taken around 1906. (Courtesy of Susan White Pieroth.)

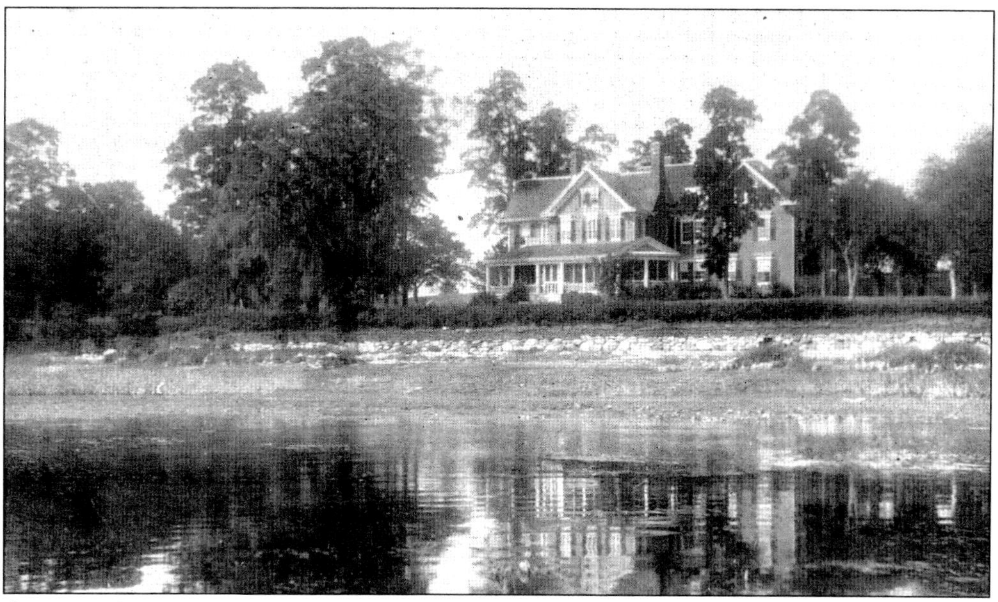

GEORGE VINGUT ESTATE, BUILT C. 1895. Pictured here in about 1962, this house burned down on November 29, 1966. Jacob Ruhland Sr. and George Mitchell Sr. were caretakers of the estate, which was located behind the Presbyterian church and faced Setauket Harbor.

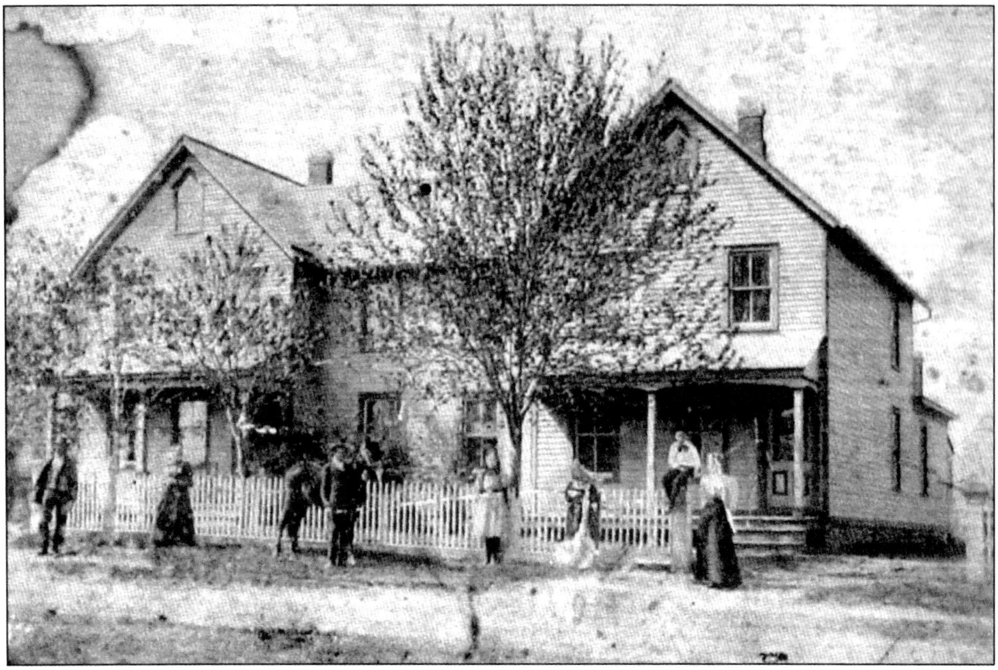

WILLIAM DECKMAN HOUSE, BUILT C. 1886. This photograph, taken around 1910, shows the only house in Setauket that was built as a two-family home. The homes had the addresses of 20 and 22 Caroline Avenue. (Courtesy of Robert and Wilma Gerard.)

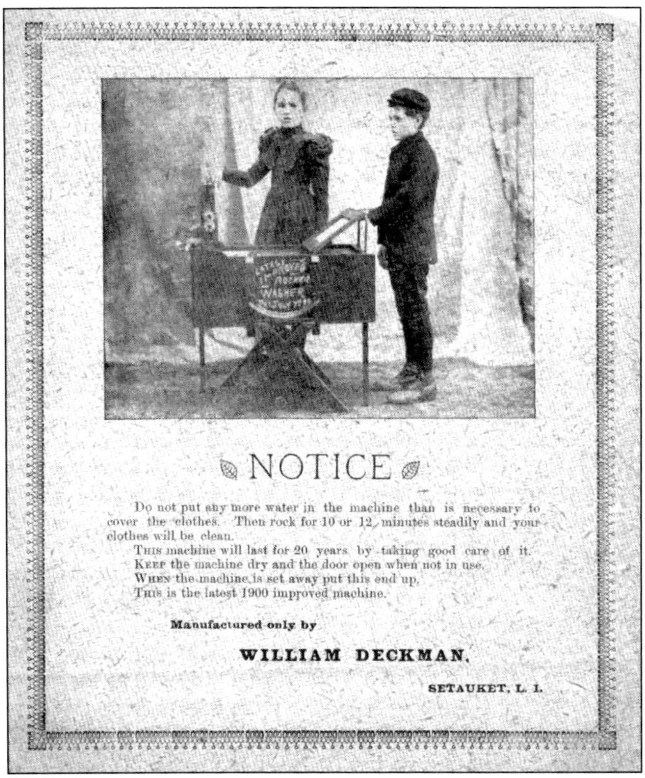

ADVERTISEMENT, WILLIAM DECKMAN'S WASHING MACHINE, C. 1905. This advertisement reads as follows: "Notice. Do not put any more water in the machine than is necessary to cover the clothes. Then rock for 10 to 12 minutes steadily and your clothes will be clean. This machine will last for 20 years by taking good care of it. Keep the machine dry and the door open when not in use. When the machine is set away put this end up. This is the latest 1900 improved machine. Manufactured only by William Deckman, Setauket, L.I." (Courtesy of Robert and Wilma Gerard.)

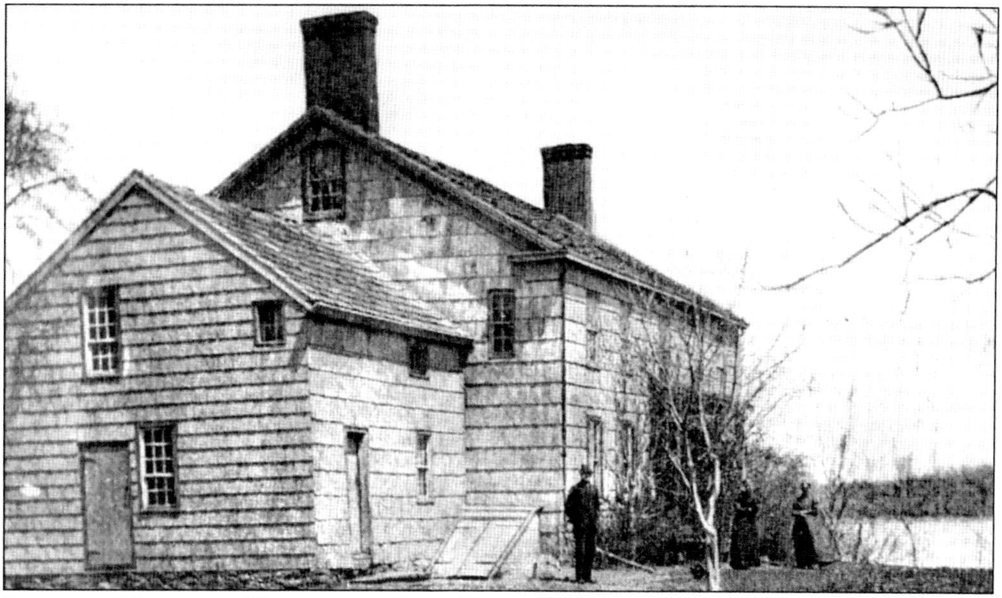

RICHARD WOODHULL HOMESTEAD, DYKE ROAD AT BOB'S LANE, BUILT 1690. This *c.* 1895 photograph shows the Richard Woodhull Homestead at the corner of Dyke Road and Bob's Lane. The small addition to the left is believed to have been the earliest portion of the house. The New York State historic marker at the site reads the following: "Site of home of Abraham Woodhull, Chief of Long Island Spies. Built by Richard Woodhull 1690 burned in 1931." (Courtesy of Beverly and Barbara Tyler.)

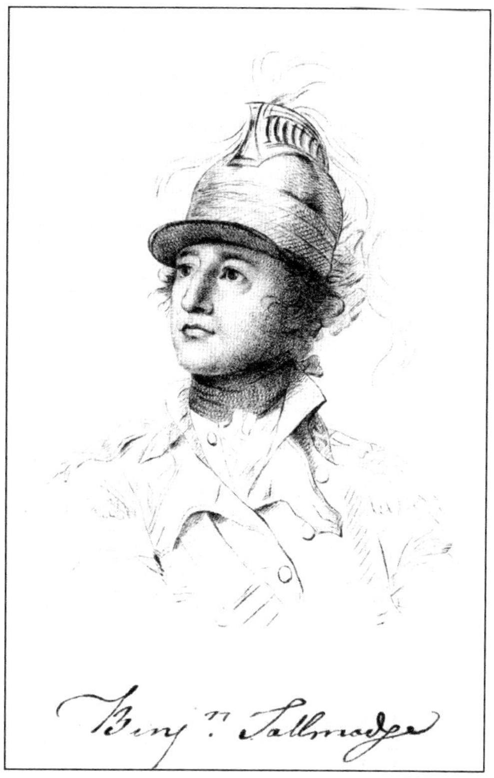

MAJ. BENJAMIN TALLMADGE (1754–1835). This image is from a lost drawing by John Trumbull. Setauket residents Abraham Woodhull, Caleb Brewster, and "Petticoat" Anna Smith Strong, along with Robert Townsend of Oyster Bay, were the nucleus of the Setauket spy ring. In 1790, George Washington came to Setauket to thank these people personally for their contributions to the war. This ring, however, remained largely unknown until 1939, when Morton Pennypacker of East Hampton uncovered the identities and function of its members. (Courtesy of Estelle Lockwood.)

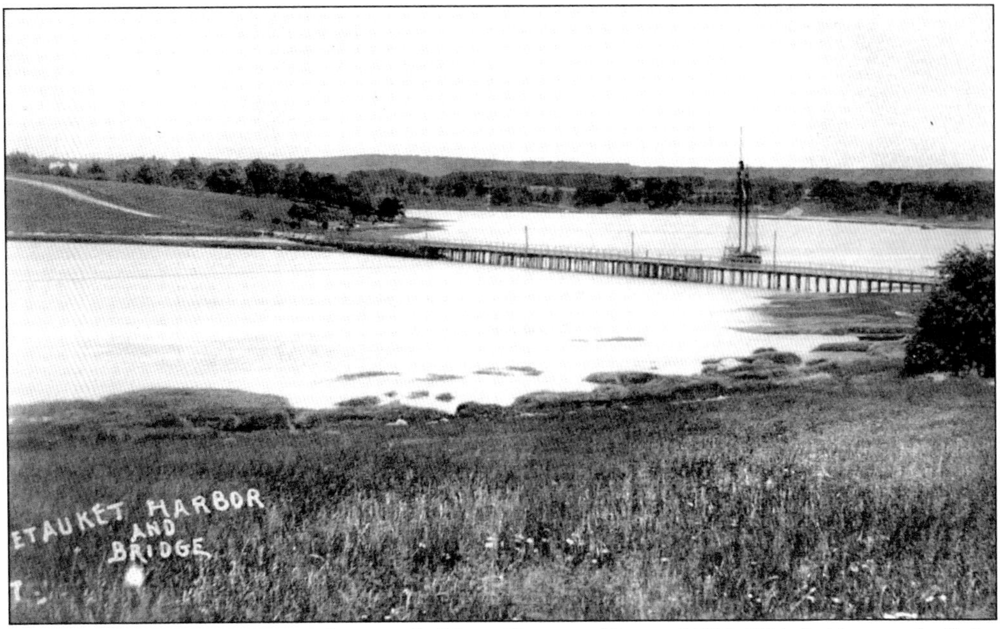

SETAUKET HARBOR AND THE STRONG'S NECK BRIDGE, BUILT 1879. This bridge was built by the Strong family. The bridge was severely damaged in the 1938 hurricane and was pulled down after the 1944 hurricane. Schooners, such as the *Two Sisters* or *Steven Tabor*, shown here around 1895, often tied up to the bridge to unload coal. Note the open landscape on Strong's Neck that is consistent with the William Sidney Mount painting *Eel Spearing in Setauket*. (Courtesy of Betty Voss.)

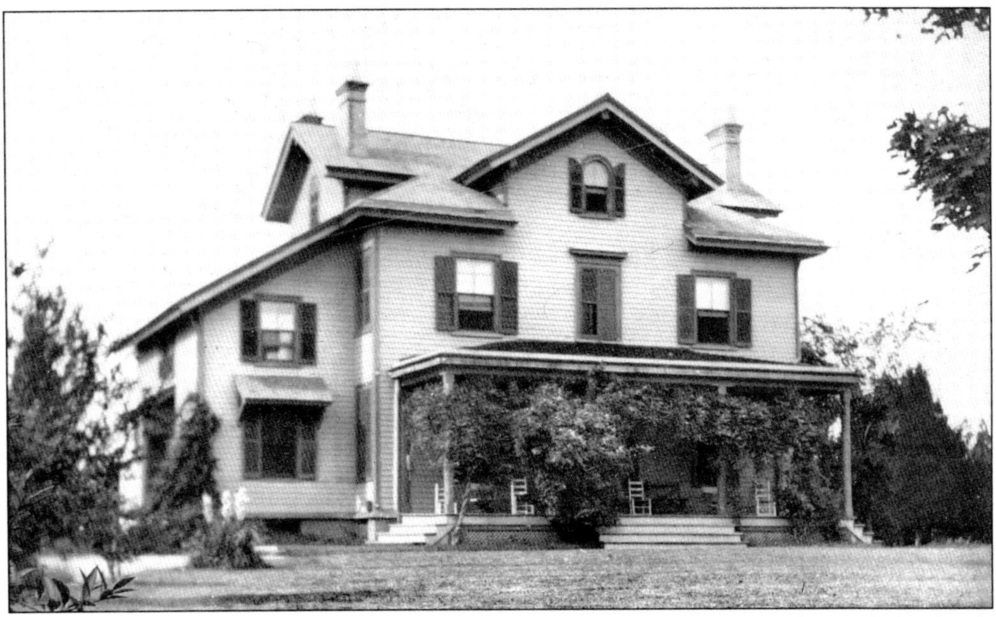

KATE WHEELER STRONG'S MANOR HOUSE, BUILT 1879. Frederic Diaper designed this family home and barn, shown here around 1905, for Selah B. Strong. Known as "the Cedars," it was also home to his daughter "Miss Kate," a local historian whose *True Tales* recounted stories of the past. She lived to be 98 years old. The house was located at 7 Strong's Lane on Strong's Neck.

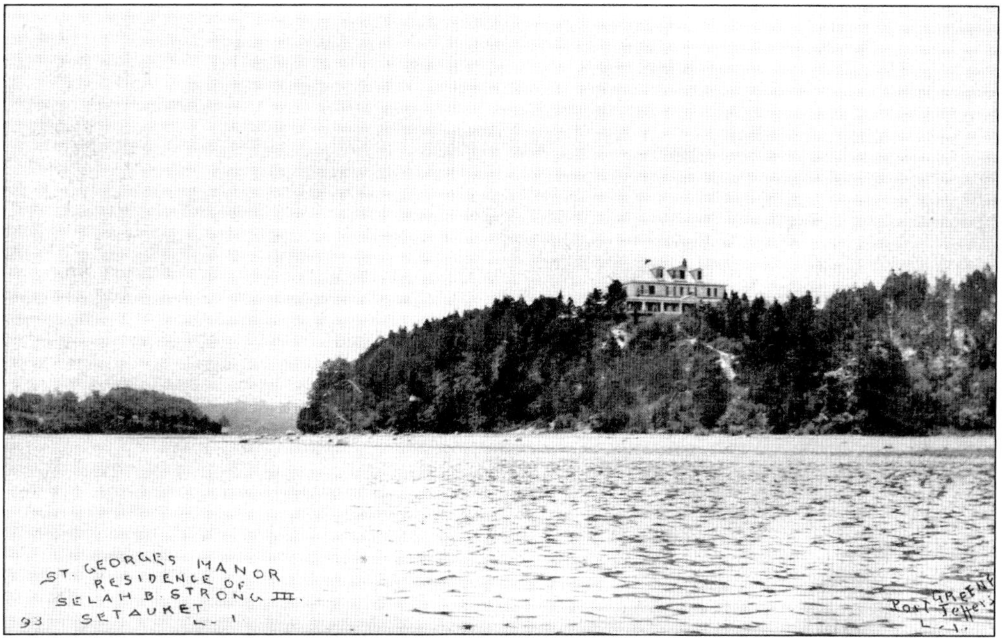

HOME OF SELAH B. STRONG III, AKA ST. GEORGE'S MANOR, STRONG'S NECK, BUILT C. 1900. This was the residence of New York State Supreme Court justice Selah B. Strong III. This photograph was taken from Whitehall Beach, looking south into Setauket Harbor. Tinker's Point, Poquott, is at the left. This is an Arthur Greene postcard that was mailed in 1909. (Courtesy of Susan White Pieroth.)

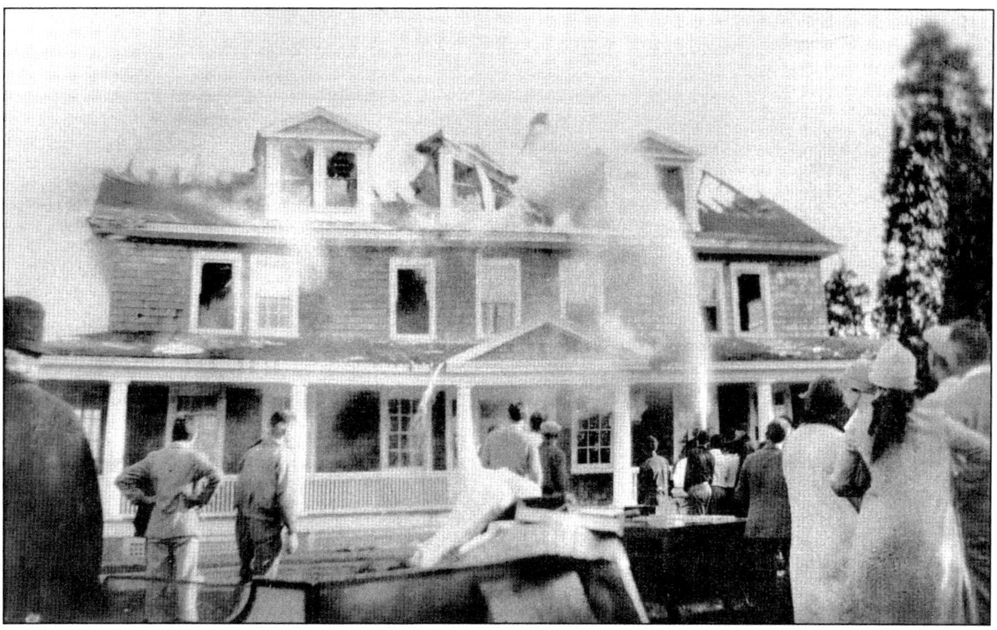

THE FIRE OF OCTOBER 11, 1928. Selah B. Strong III's residence was totally destroyed by this fire, but some family portraits, furniture, china, and glass were salvaged. At the time of the fire, the house was rented to Sinclair Lewis. It is alleged that a female occupant fell asleep smoking in bed. (Courtesy of Margo Arceri.)

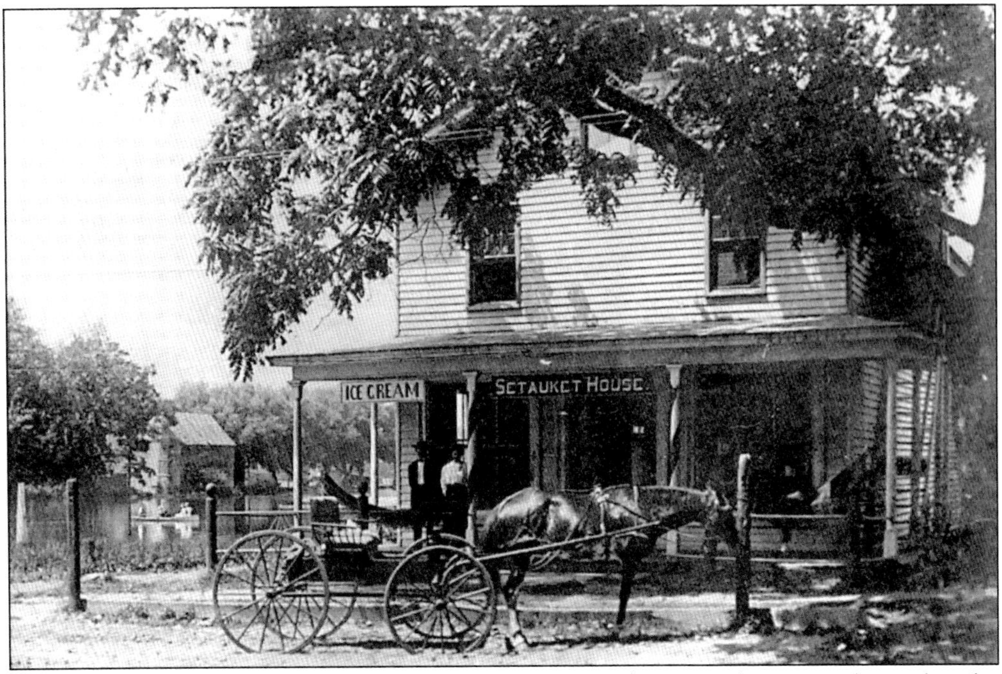

THE SETAUKET HOUSE, MAIN STREET, BUILT C. 1870. This general store was located at the approximate site of the present-day Setauket post office. It was the post office during the two Grover Cleveland administrations, 1885–1889 and 1893–1897, when Martha Isabel Bates, a Democrat, was postmistress. Note that the millpond at the left shows open water at this time. (Courtesy of Beverly and Barbara Tyler.)

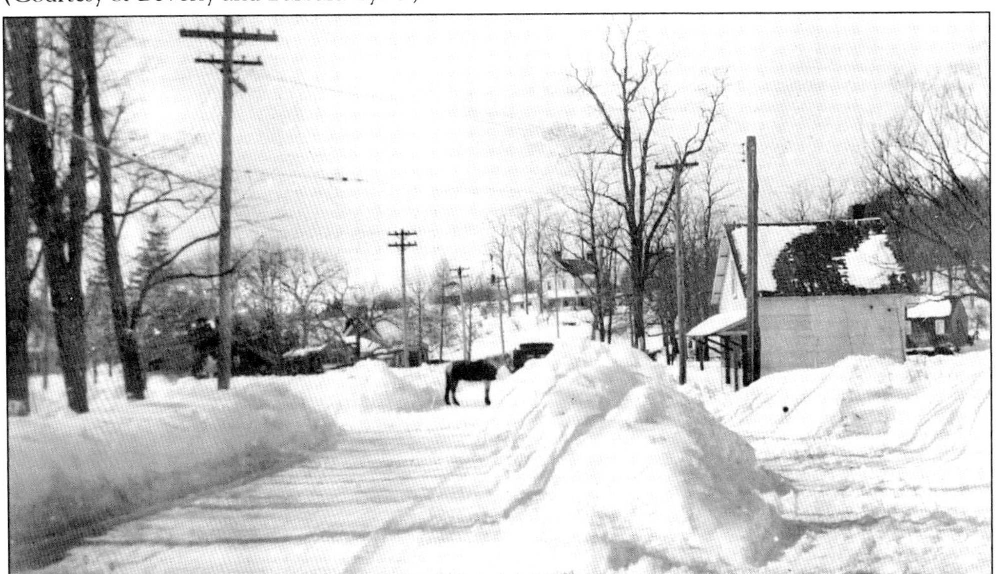

MAIN STREET, FEBRUARY 27, 1934. The storm pictured here lasted for three days and thoroughly isolated most communities on Long Island. The horse is tied up in front of the Setauket post office, sometimes known as "the Shack." Between 1900 and 1930, this building served Setauket as a post office, ice cream store, or butcher shop. It was demolished in 1930 to make way for the Setauket post office, now located at 78 Main Street.

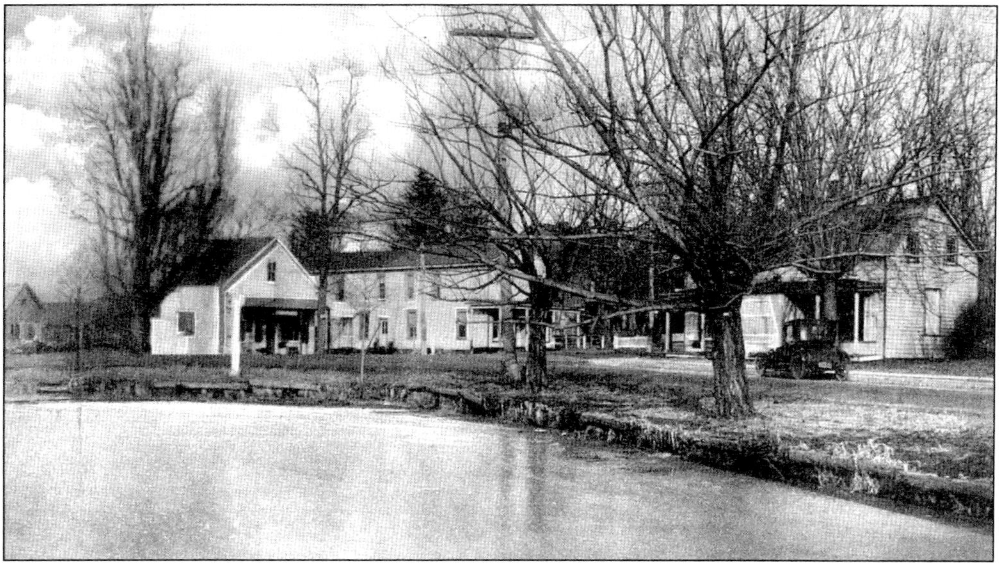

SETAUKET MILLPOND, C. 1915. The Setauket post office (the Shack), at left, was originally in the present driveway to the Frank Melville Memorial Park. The two-and-a-half-story building to its right was a Tyler general store (also known as the Setauket House) and is the present location of the Setauket post office (built in 1941). To its right is the Dr. Ferdinand Bates House (c. 1825) at 105 Main Street. At the far right of this photograph, facing the millpond, is the Tyler Brothers' Store that sat in front of 97 Main Street. In about 1942, the road grade was raised by about 12 feet from the Neighborhood House to the post office to alleviate flooding.

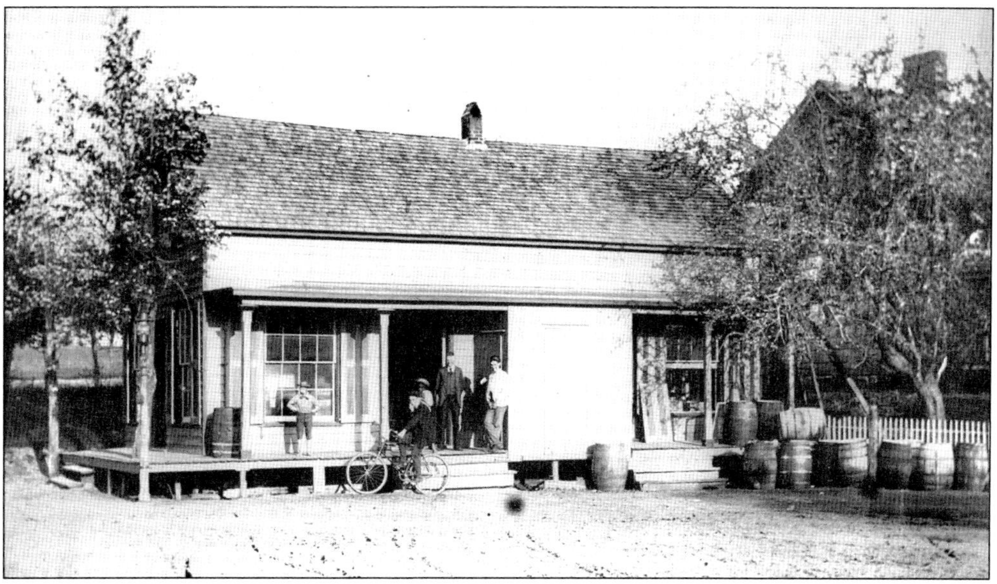

TYLER BROTHERS' GENERAL STORE, C. 1885. This store, located at 97 Main Street, was operated by Capt. Charles B. Tyler. At various times, it served the local community as a post office and general store. In 1930, it was moved to 150 Main Street and served as the American Legion hall until 1975. It has been heavily modified. To the right is the gable end of the Tyler home, also known as the Amos Smith house, built around 1740. Today this home is only a reminder of this bustling location. (Courtesy of Betty Voss.)

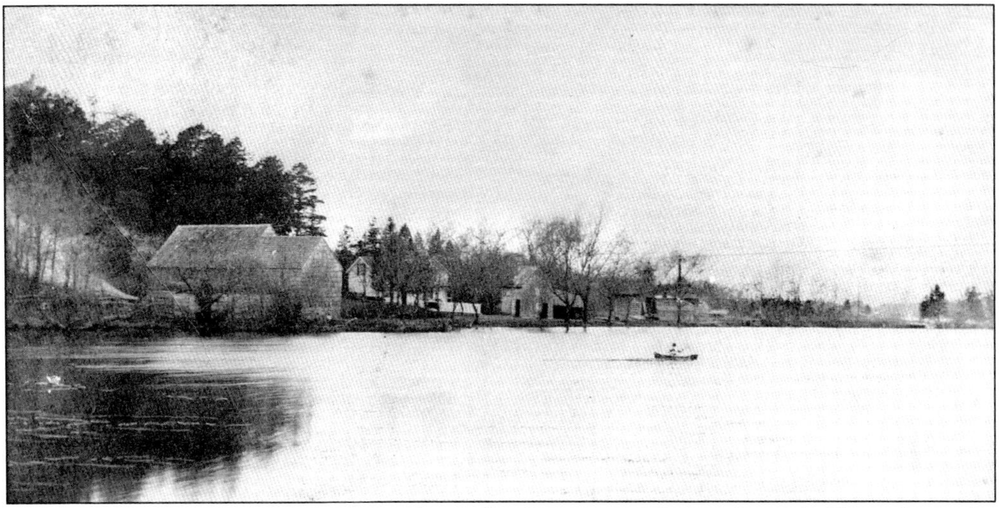

SETAUKET MILLPOND, C. 1910. At about the location of the rowboat, halfway down the present pond, an old dyke extended from the east shore with an opening for a mill at the west side. When silt accumulated behind the dyke, the mill was moved to the location in this picture. In 1930, there was open water between the old dyke and the new mill dam. By this time, the area in the foreground (south of the old dyke) silted up, hay was gathered on the land, and muskrats were trapped in the stream. The dyke remains under about three feet of water today. The present pond was dredged in 1936. Edward (Laddie) Acker Jr. built a rubble and earthen dam as a replacement for the dyke and base for the present simulated mill. The buildings, from left to right, are Satterly Barn, miller Everett Hawkins's house, Everett Hawkins's barn, and the Setauket Gristmill. (Courtesy of Beverly and Barbara Tyler.)

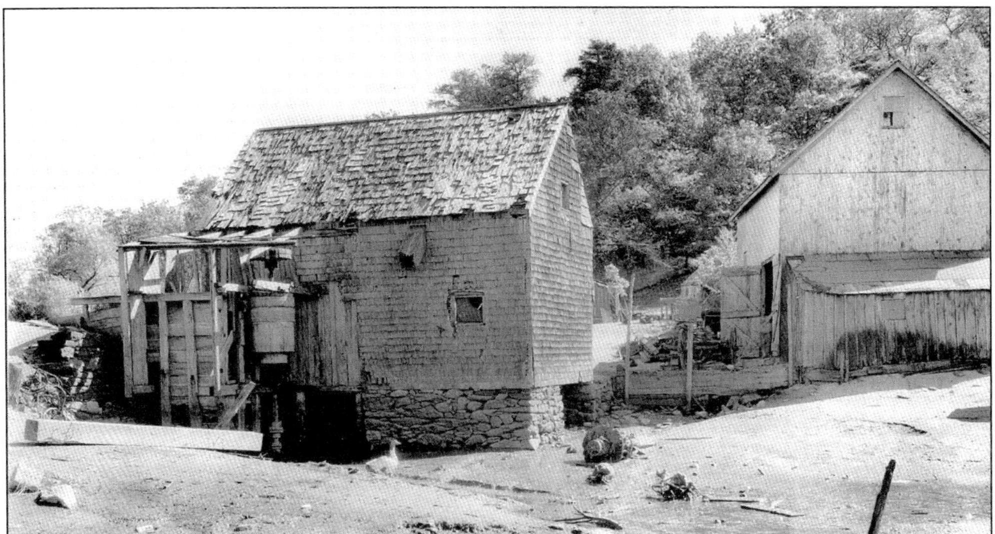

THE CORE OF THE SETAUKET MILL, C. 1935. The mill in this photograph had been converted from an overshot wheel operation to a tub or turbine. The turbine is the cylinder visible on the side of the mill. Note the chute near the roofline where the chaff from the wheat was blown into the harbor. A discarded mill shaft lies on the mudflat. Millers were well known for constructing "functional" additions that did not conform to any standard architectural principles. The mill operated until it was taken down for the construction of the Frank Melville Memorial Park in 1936.

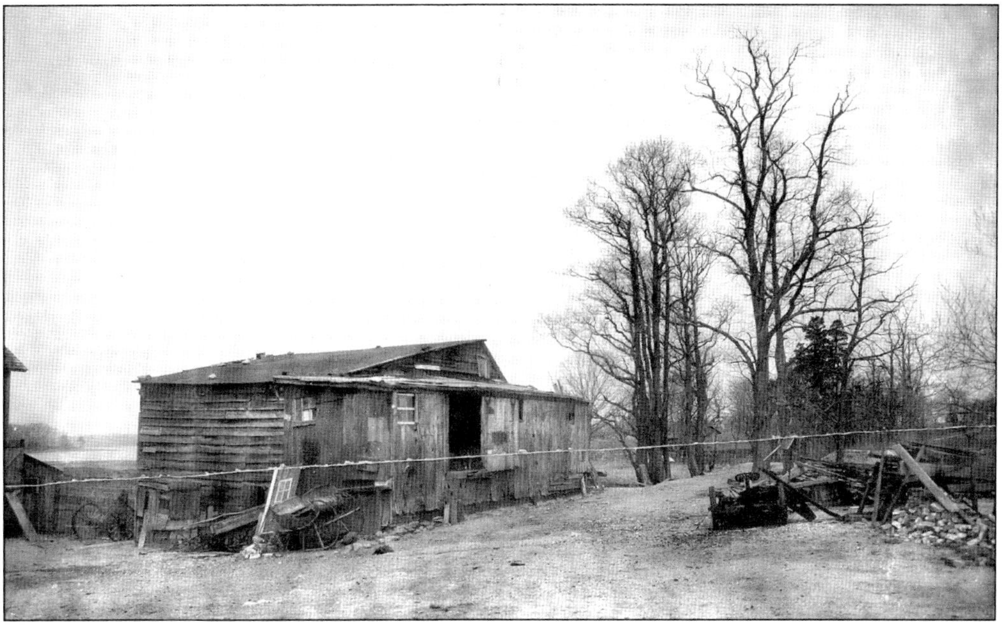

Old Shed at the Setauket Mill, c. 1930. Looking east, this is the Setauket Mill as it operated until the early 1930s. The large door in the south shed extension facilitated the loading and unloading of wagons. The shed extension on the west side extended the roofline of the mill with a long, gentle pitch. The turbine that powered the mill is on the far side of the building.

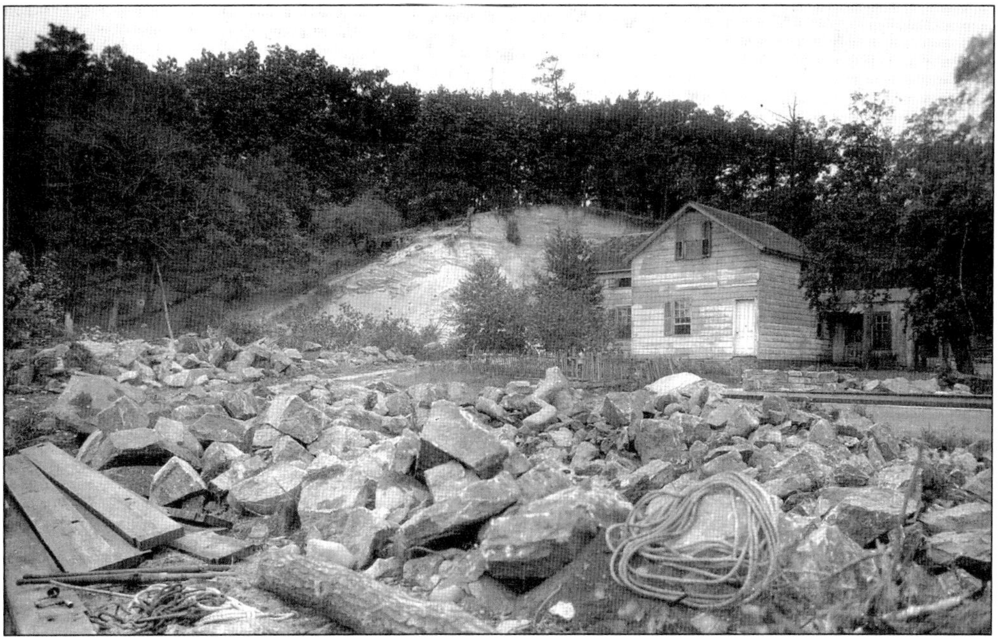

Home of Everett and Celia Hawkins, Setauket Millpond, Built c. 1870. The one-and-a-half-story extension of the house in the foreground has been removed. The remaining portion of this house is now known as the Gardener's Cottage at Frank Melville Memorial Park. This photograph was taken August 26, 1936. The mill was last operated by Everett Hawkins and his pipe-smoking wife, Celia.

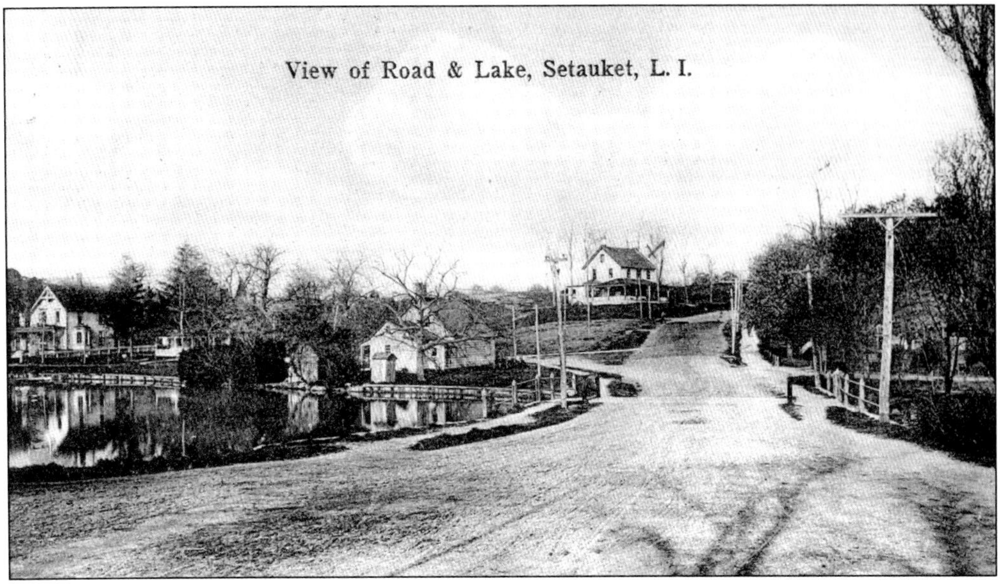

OLD FIELD ROAD AND LAKE STREET, C. 1905. The Elbert (Bert) Wells House, built around 1890 at 6 Old Field Road, is seen here at the top of the hill. The porch ceiling of the Wells House is painted the traditional sky blue to help repel mosquitoes. On Lake Street, from left to right, are the Preston Lyon-Reilly House, built around 1872 (36 Lake Street); the Jesse Wells House, built about 1780 (38 Lake Street, among the trees); and the Hawkins-Tyler House, built by Ralph Hawkins around 1780 (35 Lake Street, on the southeast corner of Lake Street at the Millpond Bridge). Note the outhouse of the Hawkins-Tyler House on the edge of the millpond.

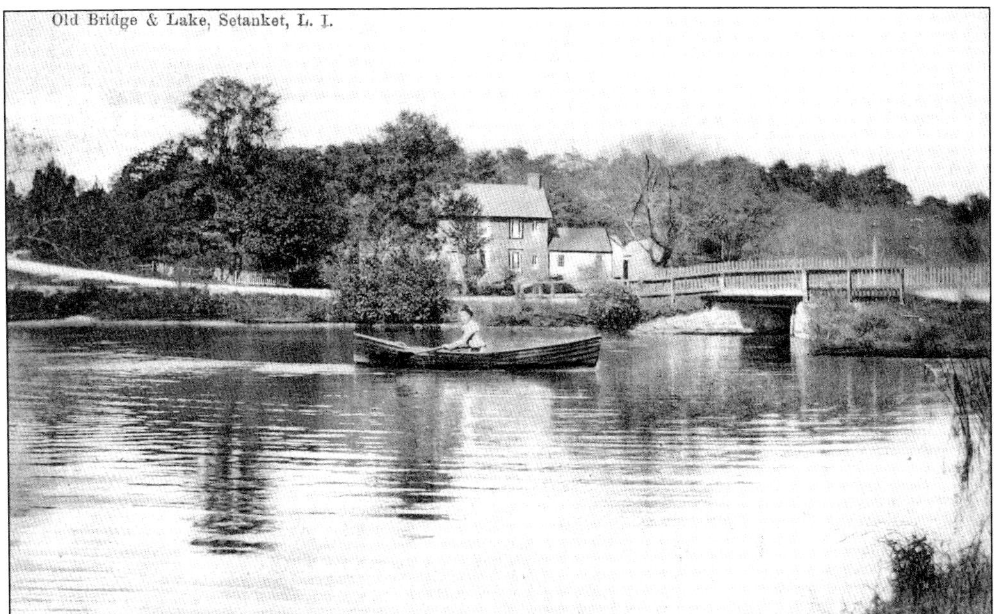

THE OLD WOODEN BRIDGE AT SETAUKET MILLPOND, C. 1895. At the left is the 17th-century Satterly-Jergenson House. Mary Jergenson lived in the house until her death in 1966. The house was purchased by Ward Melville in 1967. The boat in the photograph was owned by Israel (Izzy) Hawkins; his wife, Ida, is rowing.

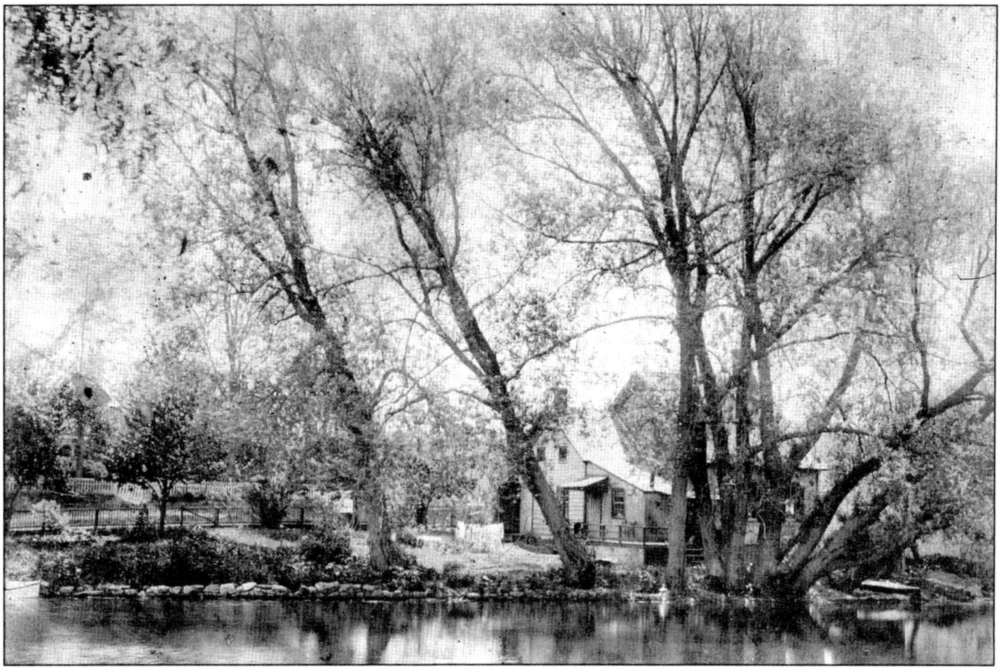

THE RYDER-JOHNSTON HOUSE, 90 MAIN STREET, BUILT C. 1812. This *c.* 1890 photograph is believed to have been taken by Sadie Lyon, who lived across the pond at 36 Lake Street. In the 1890s, the barn on this property housed 10 horses and a cow. The horses were used to transport the guests from the Elderkin Hotel, now the Neighborhood House, to the railroad station. The picket fence in front of the house lines Main Street, then a gravel road. (Courtesy of Preston Pautch.)

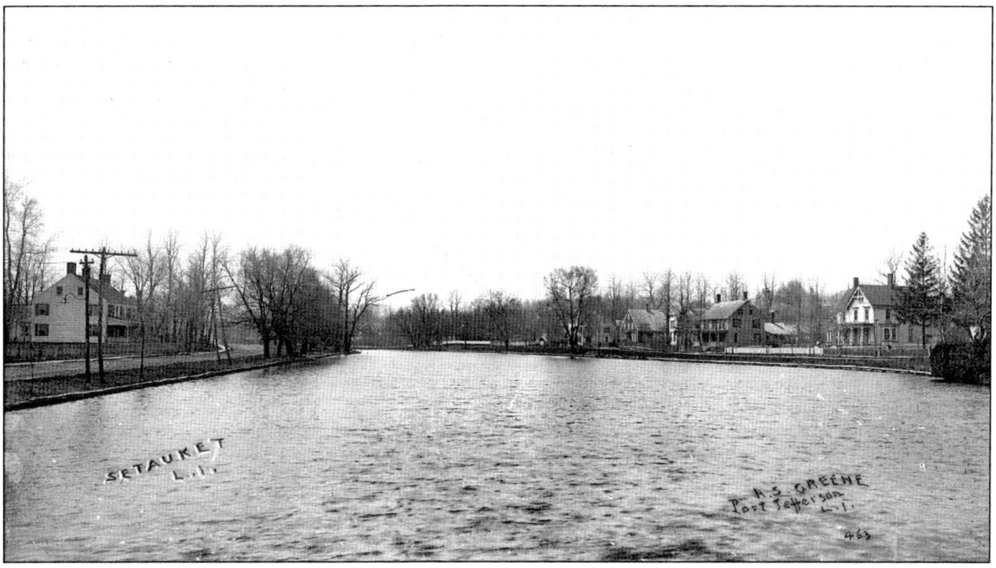

WILLOW LAKE, C. 1900. This photograph by Arthur Greene shows the Setauket Millpond with the Neighborhood House (on the left). The original part of the Neighborhood House was moved from Conscience Bay to this location in 1820, and after additions to both ends, it became Ye Old Elderkin Inn. In 1918, Eversley Childs purchased the property and donated it to the community with funds to build the ballroom that was later added. Lake Street is at the right.

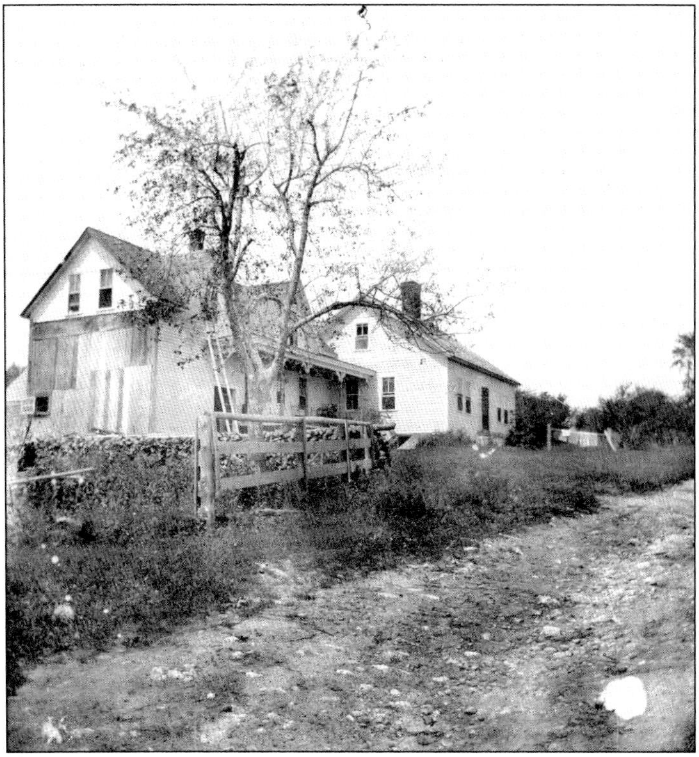

Main Street, c. 1885. This photograph shows what is now 65 Main Street in the foreground. Subsequent to this photograph, the house was moved north and rotated 90 degrees. The building to its right is the Tyler-Jayne Tavern, built around 1750, before it was moved to the top of the hill by Edward G. Acker in about 1890. The tavern, including a boardinghouse and general store, was the site of a minor skirmish during the American Revolution that resulted in four deaths.

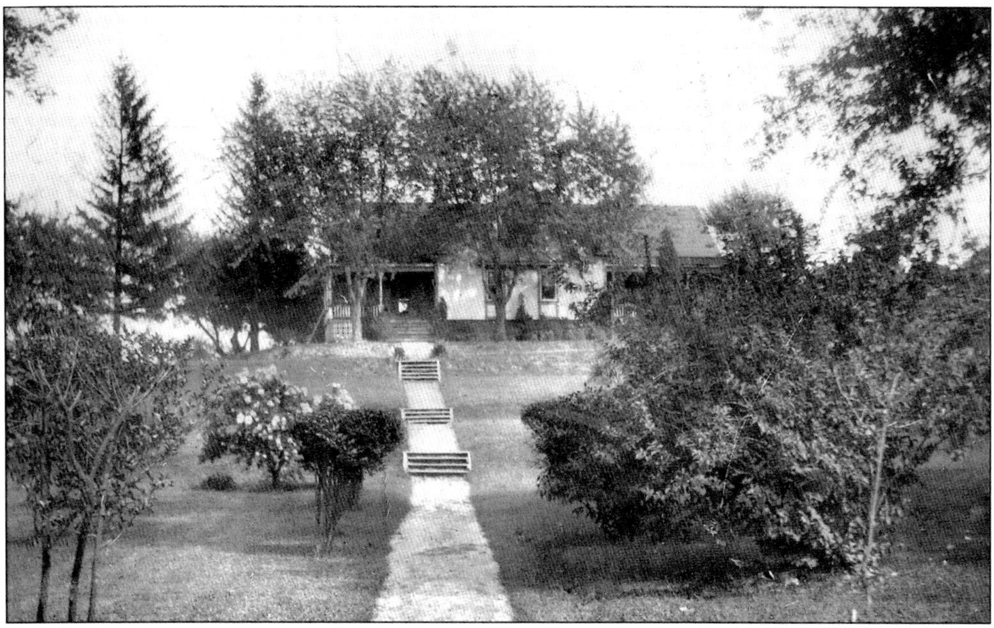

Tyler-Jayne Tavern, 1 Tavern Way, Built c. 1750. This photograph, taken around 1920, shows the Tyler-Jayne Tavern after Edward G. Acker moved it up the hill in about 1890. Acker, who owned the sand and gravel works and oil-tank farm in Port Jefferson, had "Victorianized" the tavern with a dormer and end porches. This conversion was subsequently removed in 1942 and more dormers were added later. (Courtesy of Michael O'Dwyer.)

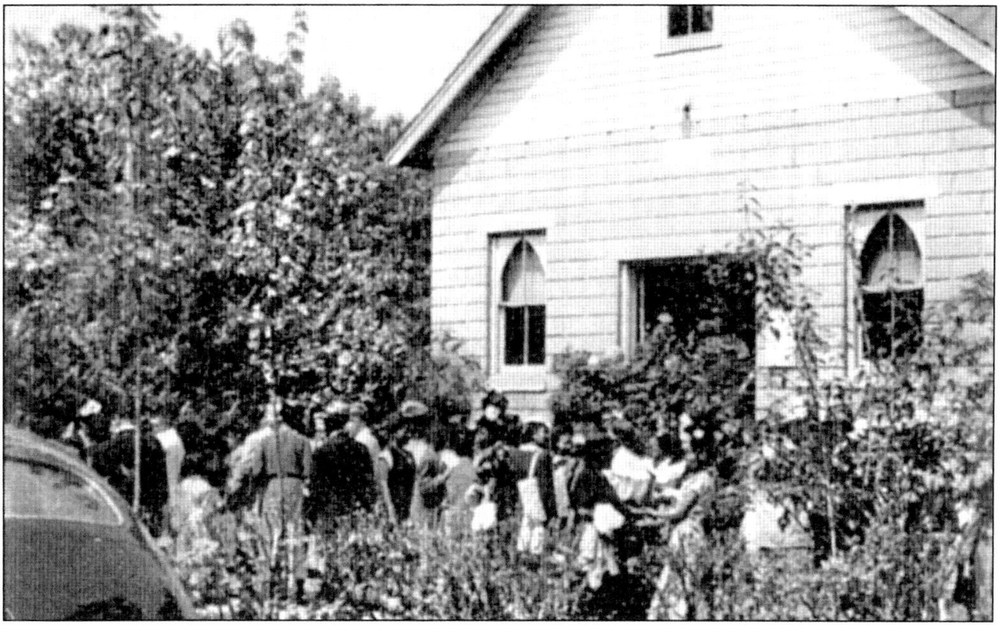

BETHEL AFRICAN METHODIST EPISCOPAL CHURCH, 33 CHRISTIAN AVENUE, BUILT 1909. This church was founded in 1850. Its original church was located on Woodfield Road (originally Webber Street) at Christian Avenue. The congregation's second church was built at 33 Christian Avenue, which burned in 1908 and was replaced with the present building, seen here in about 1948. (Courtesy of Pearl Lewis Hart.)

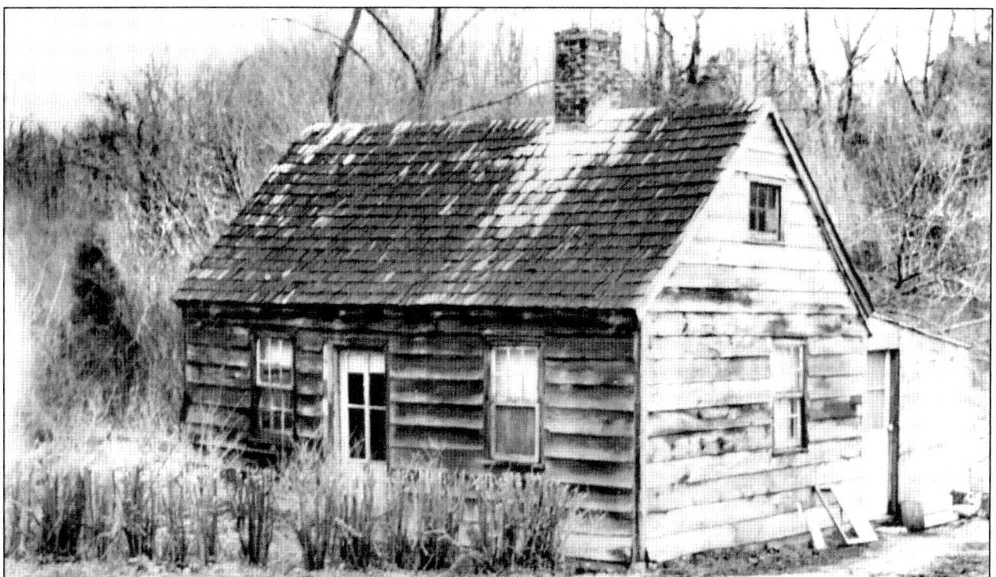

HANNA HART HOUSE, BUILT C. 1700. The house in this *c.* 1920 photograph was on the southwest corner of Lake and Main Streets before its demolition. The address was approximately 2 Lake Street. Early in the 20th century, Hanna Hart (1860–1921) lived in this house with her children Jacob, James, Martha, Anna, Minnie (Sanford), Lucy (Keyes), Ernest, Julia (Smith), and Hannah (Sells). The house was last occupied by her son Ernest. In November 1985, Lucy Hart Keyes died from a fall into an old well across from the African Methodist Episcopal church on Christian Avenue.

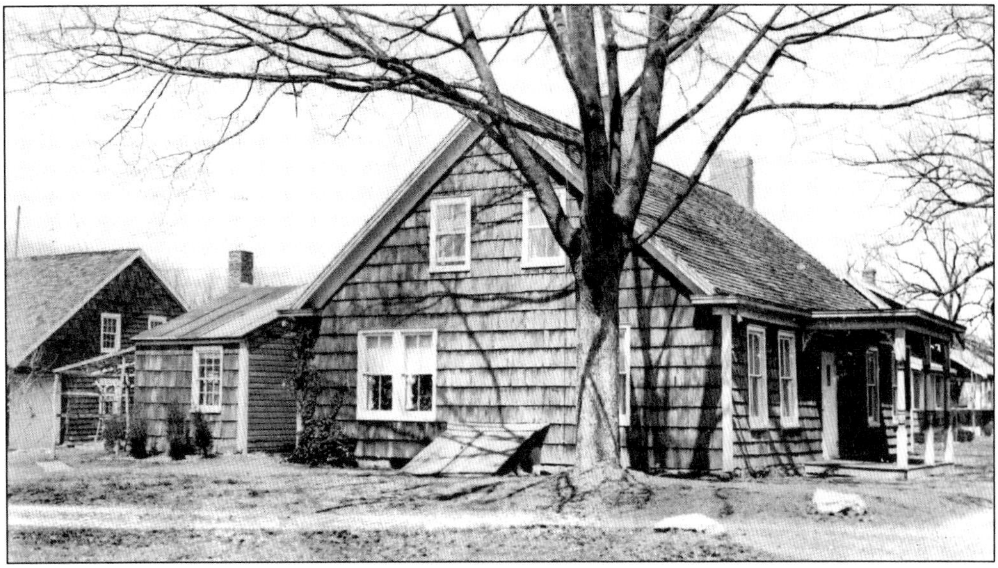

BREWSTER-HOWELL HOUSE, 34 MAIN STREET, BUILT C. 1750. This house, shown here around 1920, is at the corner of Brewster Hill Road. In about 1860, a "Dutch" upsweep was added at the edge of the roof. (Courtesy of John Wastiewicz.)

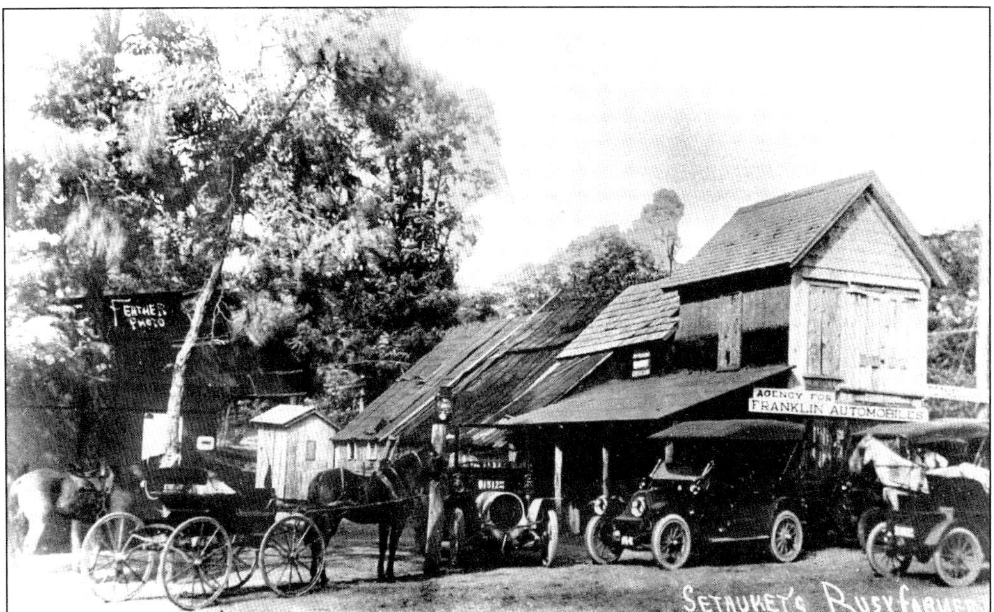

PFEIFFER'S CORNER, RIDGEWAY AVENUE AND NORTH COUNTRY ROAD, C. 1910. Among the many enterprises on this corner, Adolph Pfeiffer operated an official Franklin Automobile "showroom" and a butcher shop. In about 1920, in the area behind the buggy (fronting North Country Road), Frank Gumbus rented a house, which he operated as a general store and gas station. Harry Reilly took over the operation in about 1950. The building then became Thy Oriental Foods and, finally, Larry Roberts Great Escapes Restaurant in the late 1970s. The building burned in the 1980s.

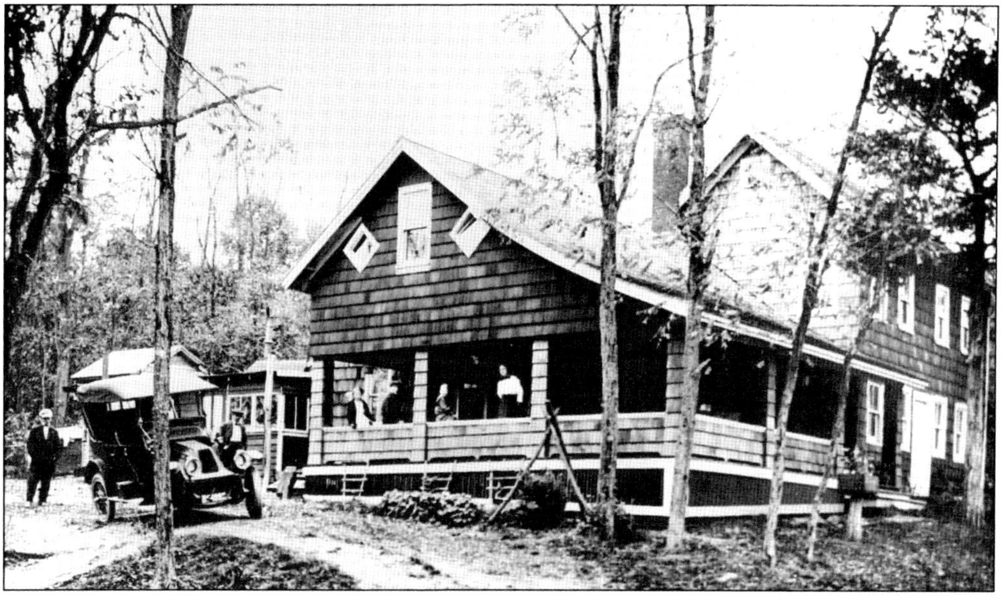

GRIFFIN HOUSE, BUILT c. 1750. Pfeiffer acquired the Griffin House at 70 Ridgeway Avenue around 1910 and attached a building that he moved from Stony Brook to provide more bedrooms since he had 10 children. In this c. 1910 photograph are, from left to right, Robert Emery Pfeiffer (son, 1895–1952); Adolph Pfeiffer (father) standing next to a 1907 air-cooled Franklin; and, on the porch, Pfeiffer children Alice, Theodore (1898–1965), Reginald (1905–1956), and Eva or Fanny.

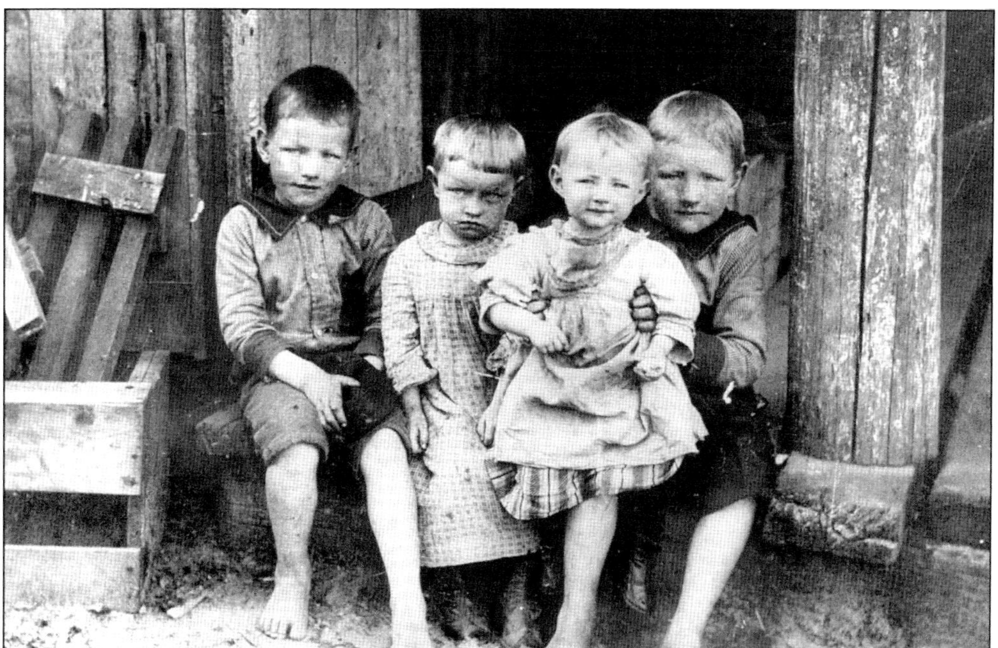

THE FIRST FOUR CHILDREN OF ADOLPH AND MARTHA (CRAWFORD) PFEIFFER. From left to right are the following: William (1887–1955), Fannie Viola (1892–1960), Eva May (1894–1925), and Reed Benedict (1889–1962). The photograph dates to about 1896.

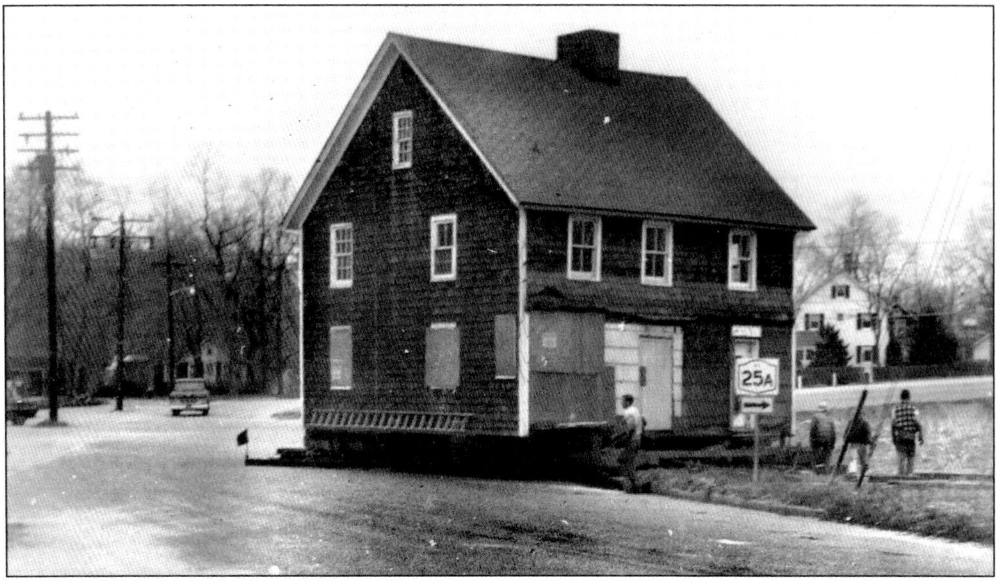

BAYLES-SWEEZY HOUSE, BUILT C. 1800. Originally located at 65 North Country Road, this building was donated by the New York Telephone Company to the Society for the Preservation of Long Island Antiquities and was moved to its present location at 93 North Country Road in May 1961. In May 1998, the Three Village Historical Society purchased this building for its headquarters and history center with a Community Enhancement Facilities Assistance Program grant from New York State, arranged by assemblyman Steven Englebright. Note that at the time of this photograph, Route 25A followed Ridgeway Avenue to Pfeiffer's Corner and thence south on North Country Road, turning west toward Wood's Corner.

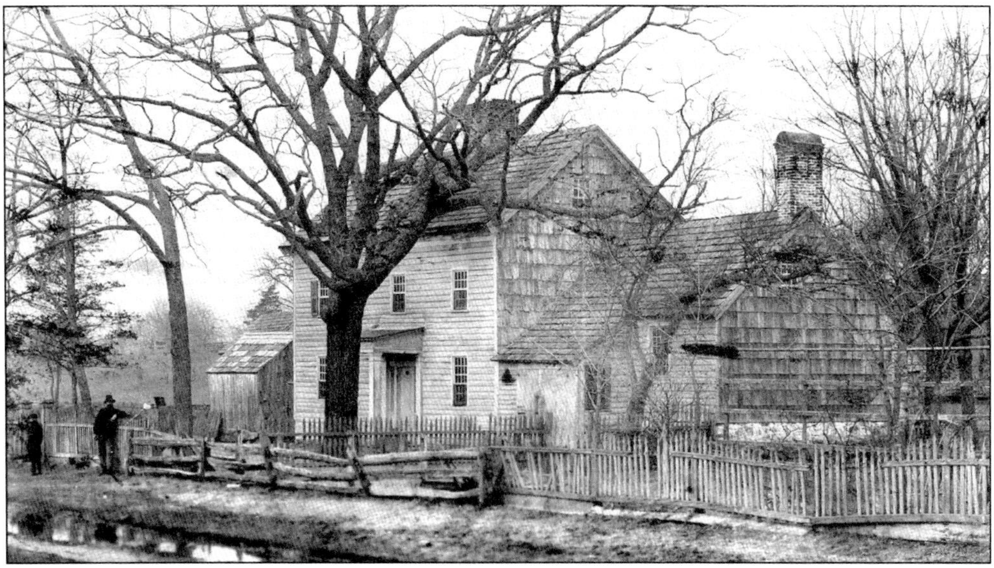

THOMPSON HOUSE, BUILT C. 1700. Benjamin Franklin Thompson (1784–1865) was born and raised in Setauket. A doctor and lawyer, he wrote the first comprehensive history of Long Island in 1839 and carried it through two editions. This property, located at 89 North Country Road, remained in the Thompson family until 1887. It is now owned by Ward Melville Heritage Organization and interpreted by Society for the Preservation of Long Island Antiquities as an 18th-century residence.

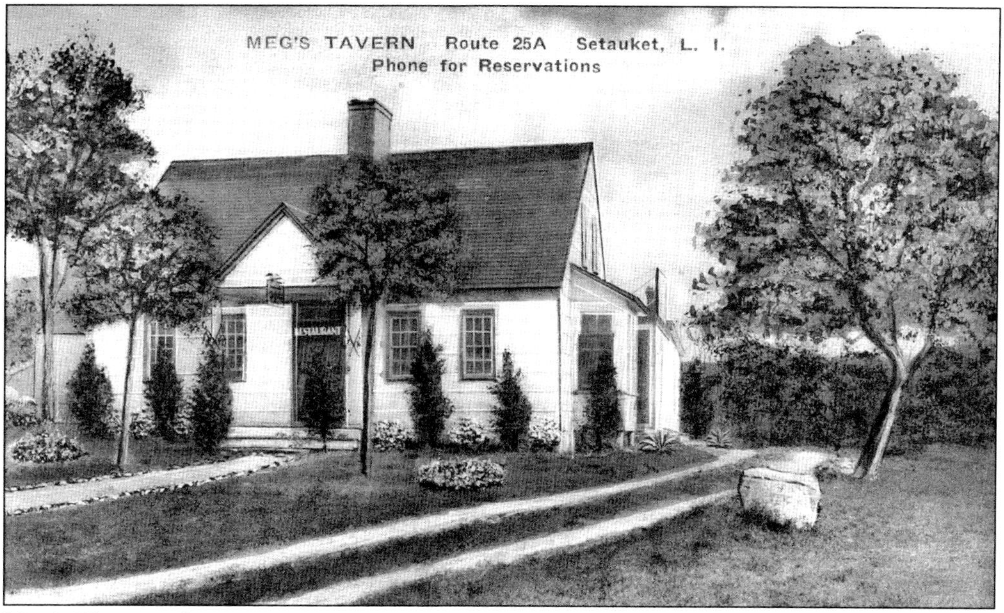

MEG'S TAVERN, SOUTHWEST CORNER OF BENNETTS ROAD AND ROUTE 25A, BUILT C. 1750. Shown here in about 1910, Meg's Tavern became a roadhouse and speakeasy during the Prohibition era. After the law's repeal in 1933, it returned to use as a legitimate tavern. It was later the site of the Schmeelk Family Farm Stand.

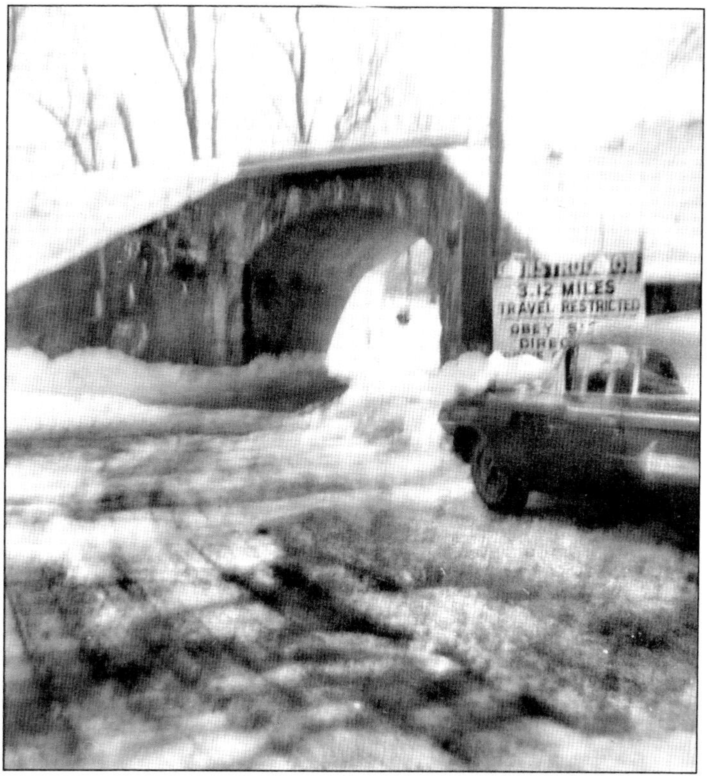

SHEEP PASTURE ROAD OVERPASS, 1961. This overpass, the two stone railroad overpasses in Setauket at Bennetts and Gnarled Hollow Roads, and the iron bridge at Old Town Road were constructed when the Long Island Railroad completed its North Shore division to Port Jefferson and Wading River in 1873. Due to a lack of riders, the section between Port Jefferson and Wading River was removed in 1938. The construction of Nicolls Road eliminated the need for this overpass, and it was demolished. (Courtesy of Beatrice and Susan Jayne.)

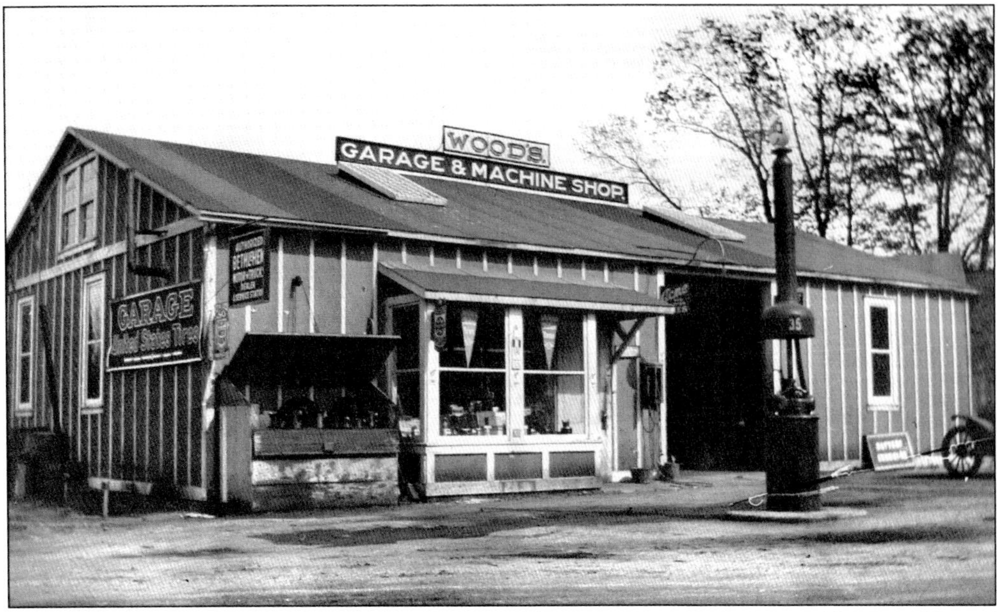

Wood's Garage and Machine Shop, 1920. This garage, at the corner of Route 25A and Sheep Pasture Road, gave Wood's Corner its name. The building operated as a garage and machine shop for over 70 years. During Chester Wood's tenure as owner, there was always a cold beer available for the customer. Chester Wood made the mechanism for the eagle's wings on the Stony Brook Post Office. The Sheep Pasture Road overpass is behind the machine shop in this photograph. A Model T Ford stands out front. (Courtesy of James McNamara.)

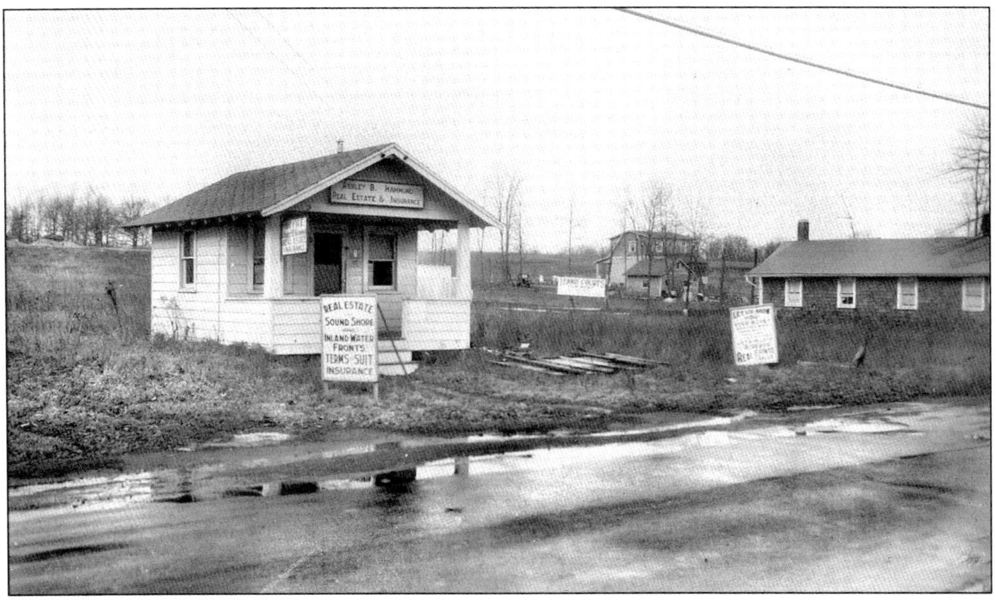

Ashley B. Hammond Real Estate and Insurance, 1009 Route 25A, c. 1935. The signs in this image read "Real Estate, Sound Shore and Inland Water Fronts, Terms to Suit, Insurance," "Tennis Courts for Rent," and "Let us show you good buys, Lots, plots, acreage, Real Estate." In about 1940, Thelma Diebel purchased this property for her real estate office. The building is still standing at this location.

Three

Old Field and West Meadow

Old Field was allocated for early grazing rights. It was far removed from the center of village activity and, therefore, never developed a concentration of population. In addition, the high bluffs along much of the Long Island Sound margin made direct water access difficult. Except for one shipyard on the narrows of Conscience Bay, there was little commercial activity. The lighthouse at the point was built in 1823 as an aid to navigation and became a landmark in the area. The Old Field Inn, a summer hotel, was built near the lighthouse in the late 19th century but burned after a short existence. Wealthy summer visitors were attracted to the high bluffs overlooking the sound, and the future character of the village, incorporated in 1927, was determined.

Flax Pond extends into central Old Field from Long Island Sound. In the early years of settlement, the pond was used to ret flax, hence its name. Eversley Childs purchased most of this area as well as the peninsula to the south, West Meadow Beach. He donated the beach to the town, and the Stony Brook Community Fund, now the Ward Melville Heritage Organization, purchased most of the marsh behind the beach.

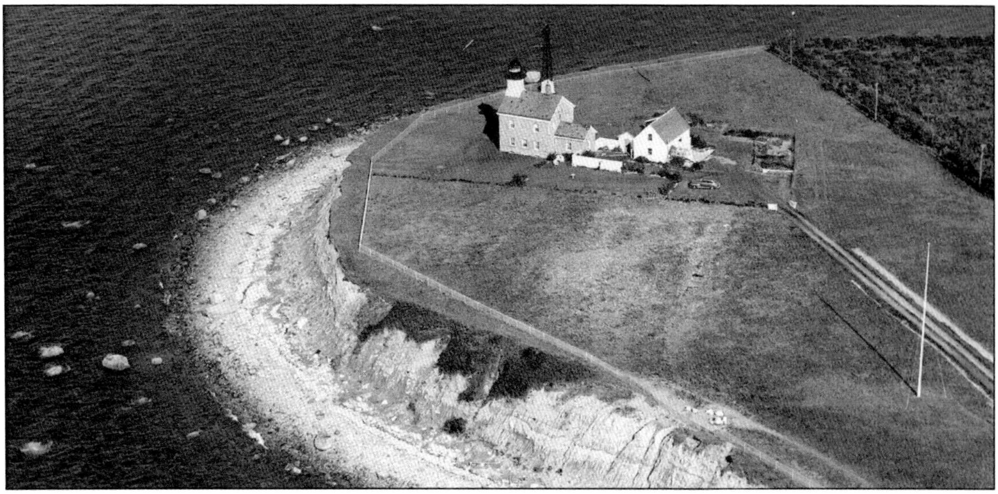

OLD FIELD POINT AND LIGHTHOUSE, BUILT 1868. This 1941 photograph shows the lighthouse, the 1824 keeper's house, at the right, and the generator building attached to the rear of the lighthouse. The original Old Field Light was established in 1823 and replaced by the present building in 1868. The light was deactivated between 1933 and 1991. The building now serves as Old Field Village Hall.

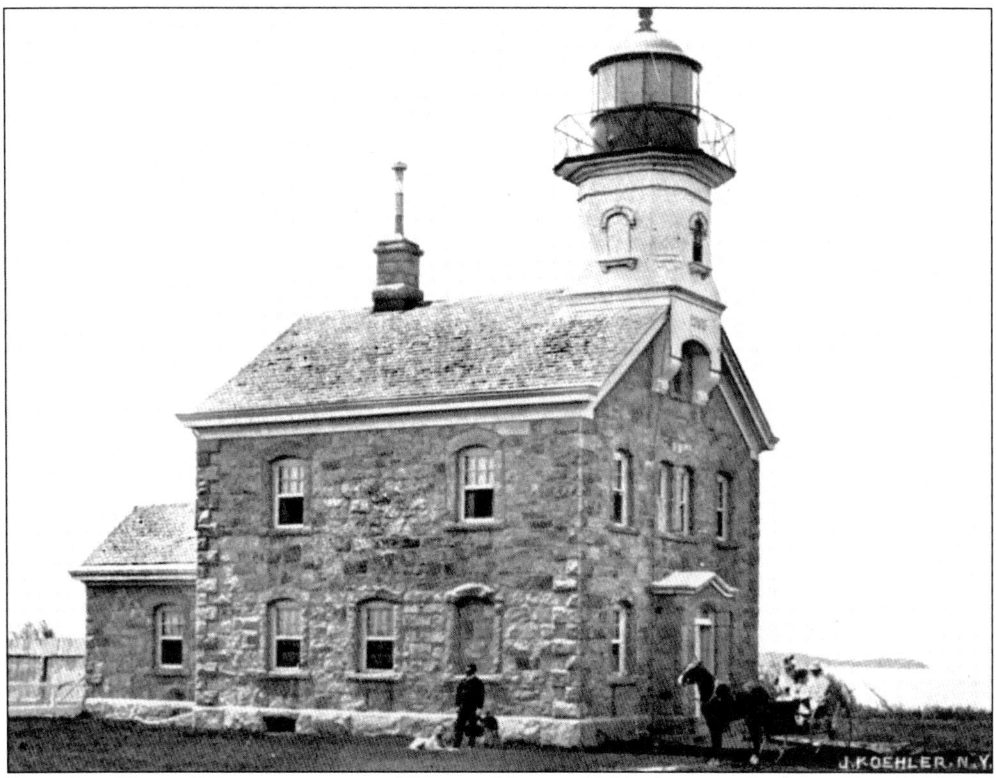

THE OLD FIELD LIGHTHOUSE AND KEEPER. This c. 1910 photograph shows the Old Field Lighthouse with the keeper Richard Edwin Day and his dogs at the side of the building. Walter Smith was keeper between 1827 and 1830. At his death, Elizabeth, his wife, took over until 1856. In 1840, she witnessed the burning of the steamship *Lexington* from this location.

THE *HARD CHANCE* MONUMENT, C. 1905. This monument, erected around 1900 on the Rt. Rev. James Henry Darlington property at Old Field Manor, reads, "The *Hard Chance* of Salem Massachusetts. Captain Weeks, All lost November 27, 1898, Ashore in Blizzard." The blizzard was of hurricane proportions and arrived the Saturday after Thanksgiving. The *Hard Chance* went ashore about 1,000 feet west of the Old Field Light. Captain Weeks, his brother, and a crewman perished in the wreck. The *Hard Chance* was built in Gloucester, Massachusetts. Its cargo capacity was 75 tons, and it was 73 feet long and 23 feet wide.

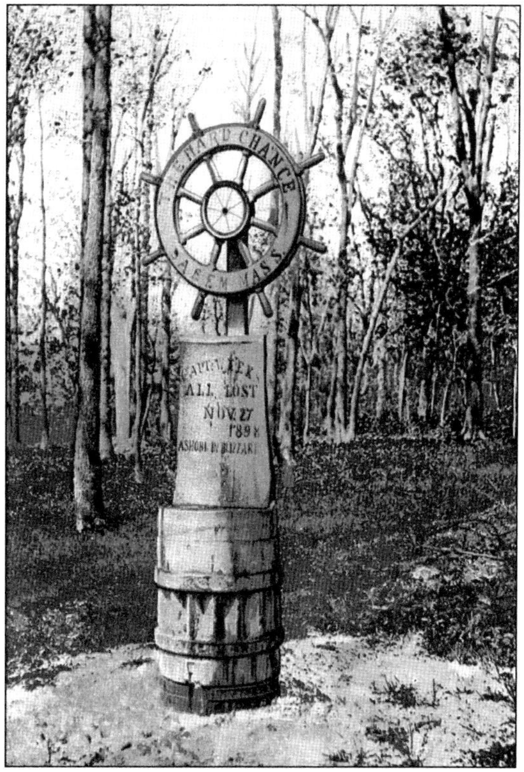

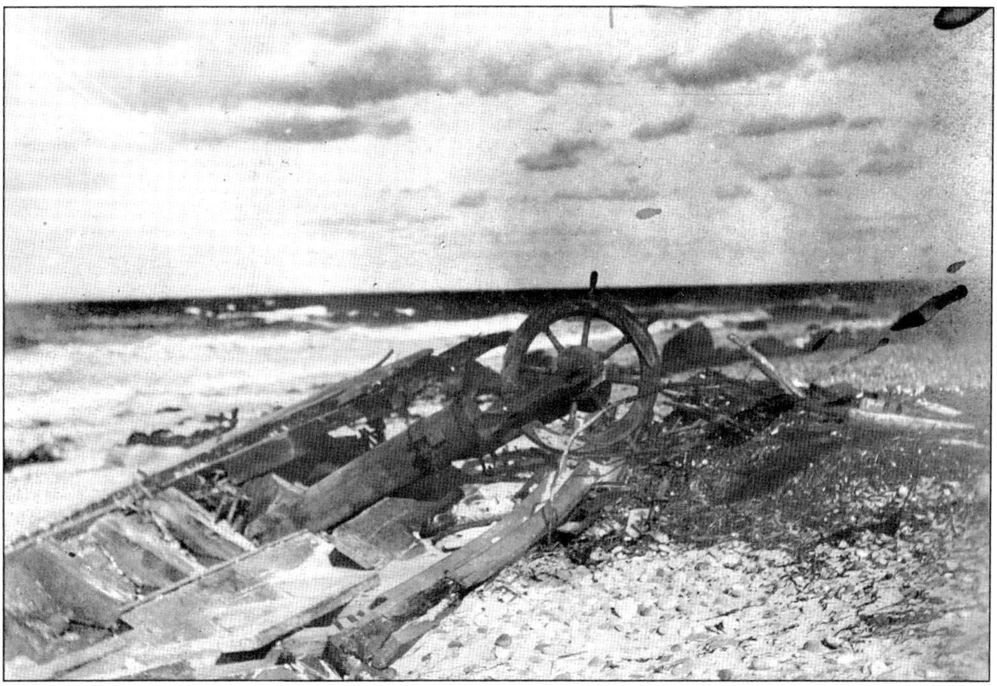

THE WRECK AT OLD FIELD POINT, C. 1915. This wreck is believed to be the *Hard Chance*. In 1908, Hanford Twitchell and his brothers explored what was left of the wreck, and he reports that by the time of World War I it was covered with sand.

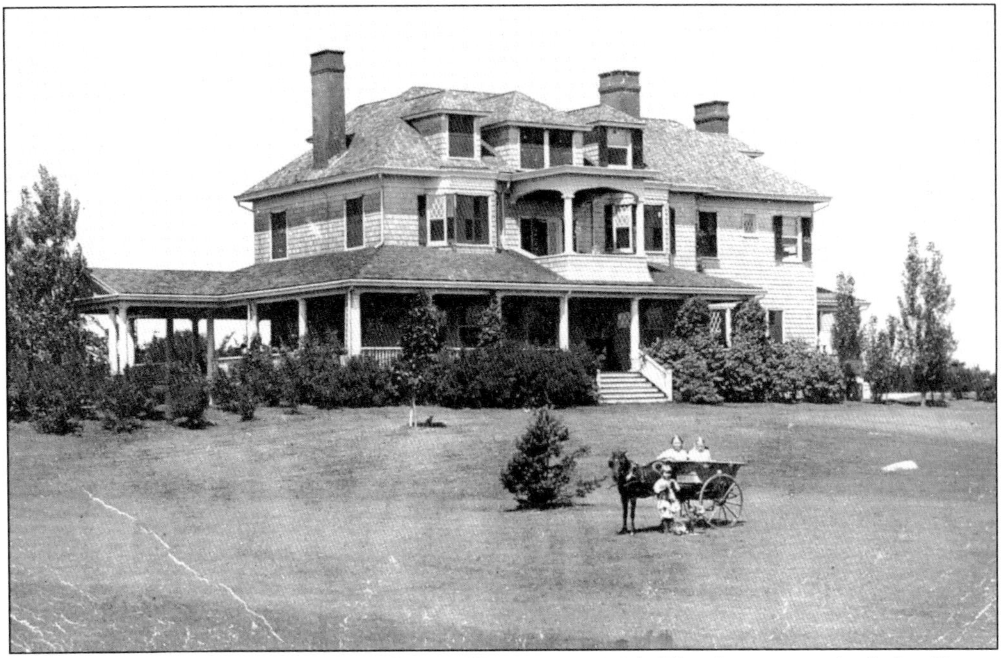

THE KENYON HOUSE, OLD FIELD ROAD, BUILT C. 1895. This house was built by Trevor Kenyon Sr. In this photograph, taken around 1900, are three children thought to be Kenyons and their dogs by their pony cart.

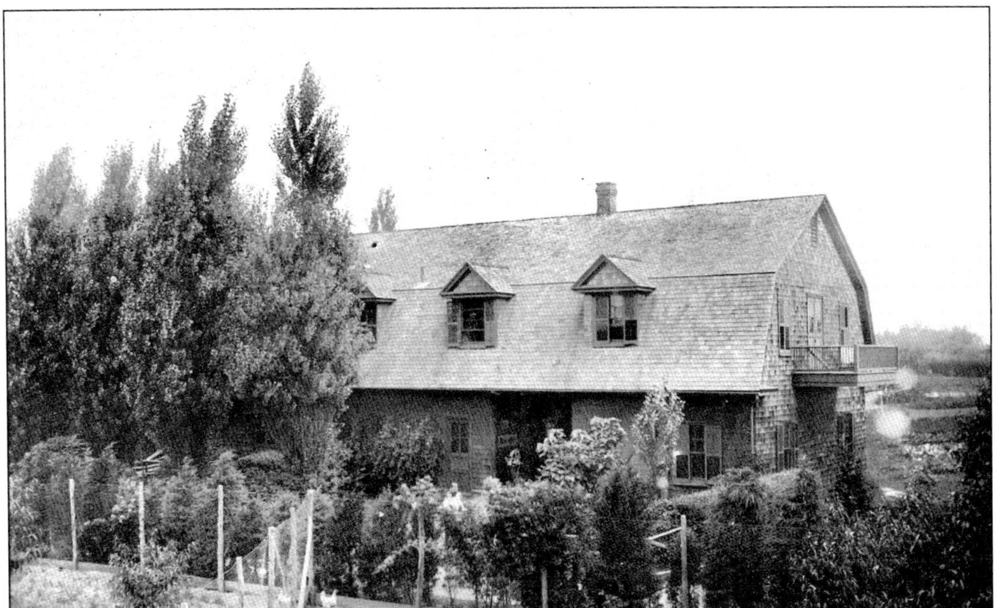

THE KENYON BARN, 1903. In about 1920, Trevor Kenyon Sr. cut this *c.* 1895 barn in two. The halves became the base for the houses of Trevor Jr. and Doris, his children.

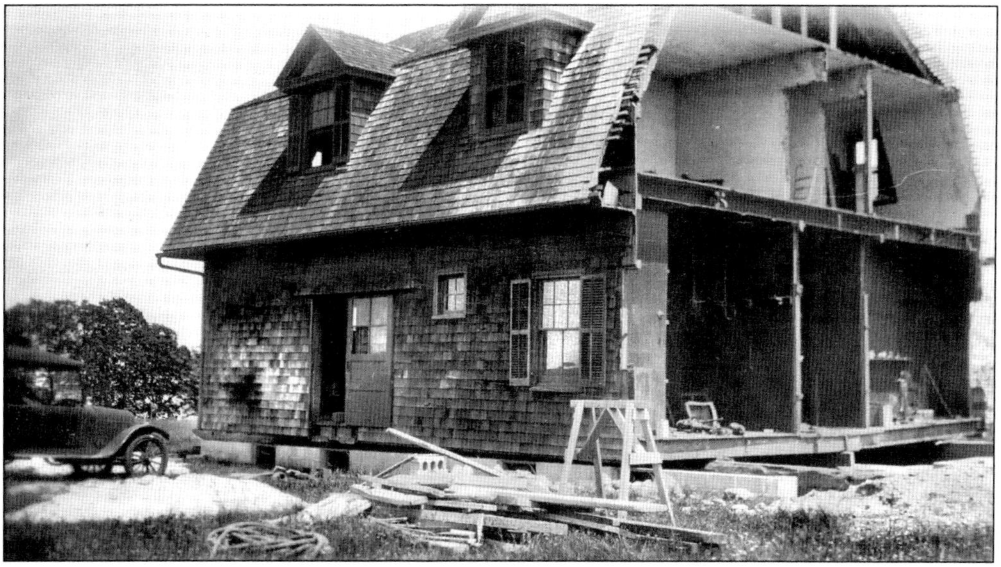

HALF OF THE KENYON BARN, C. 1920. Both halves of the *c.* 1895 barn were moved to new locations on the estate and converted into individual houses.

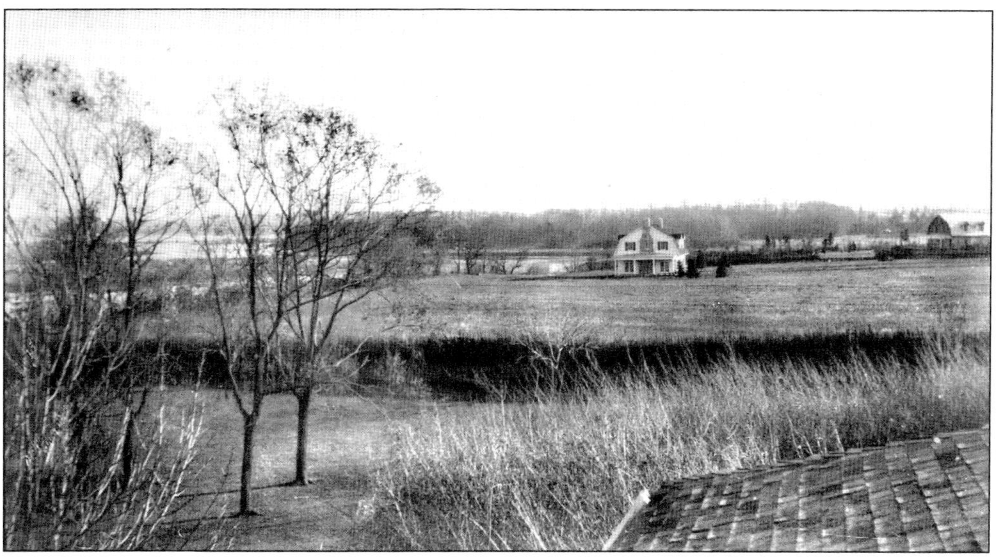

THE KENYON BARN HALVES. This *c.* 1920 photograph shows the house of Trevor Kenyon Jr. (at the center) and that of Doris Kenyon Gillespie at the far right. The Narrows and Whitehall Beach are at the left, and Strong's Neck is in the background.

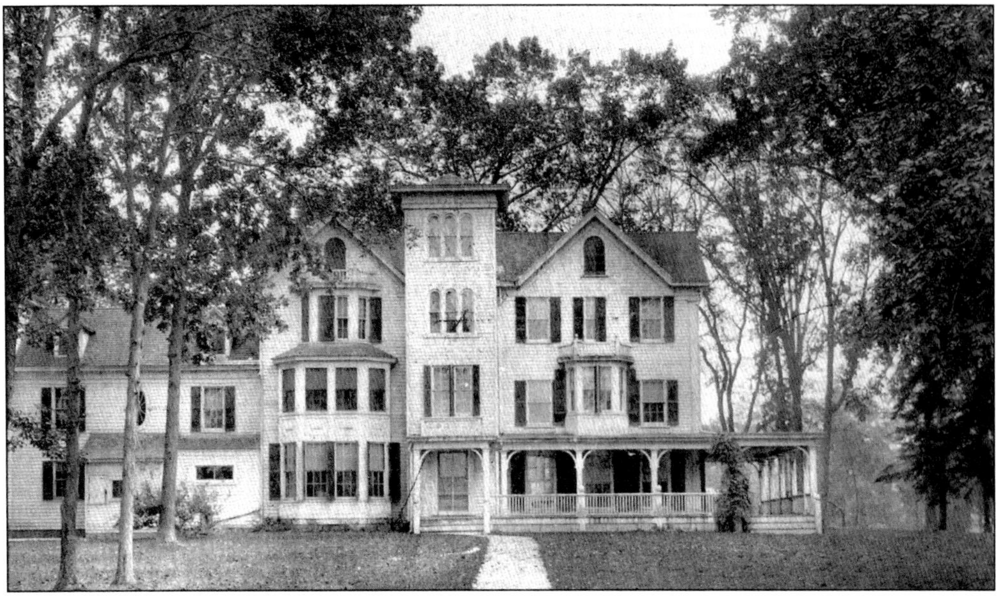

OLD FIELD MANOR, OLD FIELD ROAD. Renamed Widewater by J. Ward Melville, Old Field Manor is shown here when he first purchased the property in 1924. The oldest part of the house is reputed to have been built around 1835. At the mid-19th century, it was owned by Alexander Hamilton's grandson. Elizabeth Beebe of New York City subsequently built the mansion around the original house. J. Ward Melville purchased the property from the Rt. Rev. James Henry Darlington, Episcopal bishop of Harrisburg, Pennsylvania.

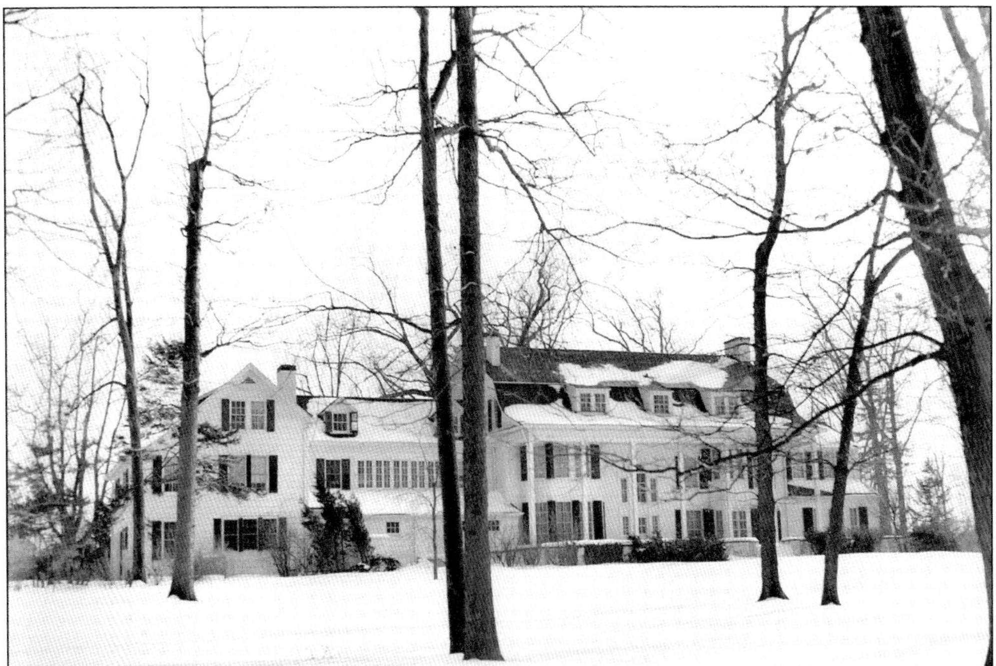

WIDEWATER. This 1945 photograph shows Widewater after J. Ward Melville extensively altered the Beebe mansion to portray Colonial origins.

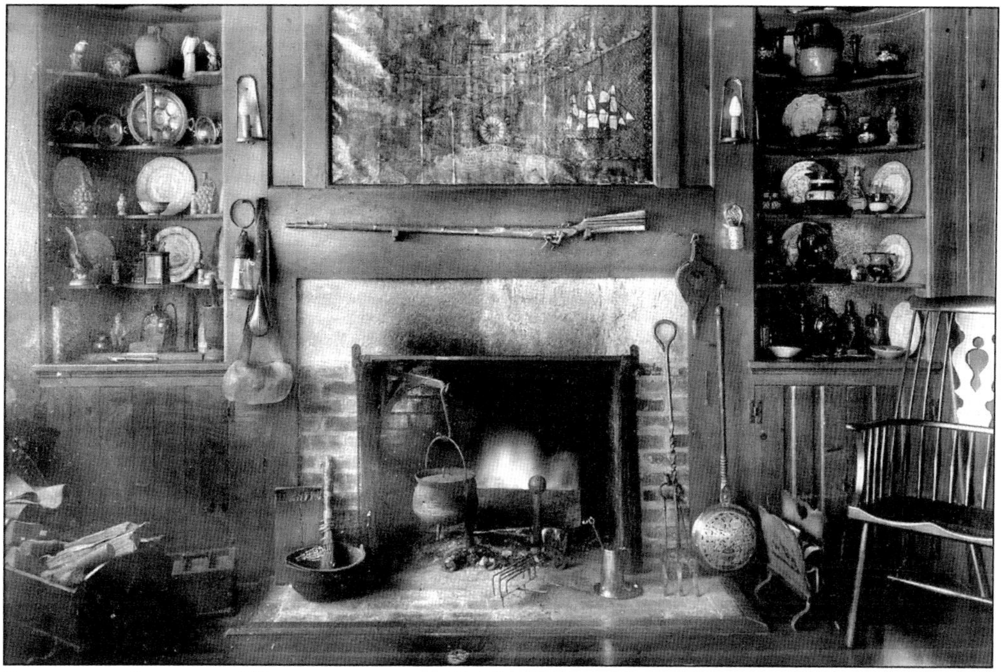

Breakfast Room at Widewater in 1945. This is the oldest room in the house.

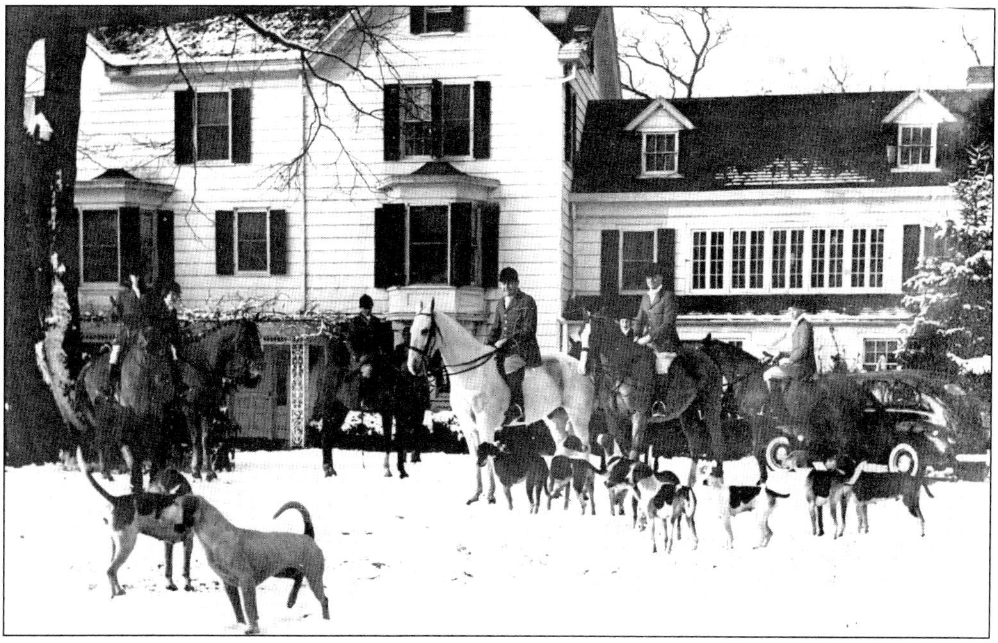

The Smithtown Hunt at Widewater, c. 1940. Gus Mollet, seen mounted on the white horse, was Melville's stable master and "master of the hunt." He lived in the gatehouse at Widewater. The dogs were known as "the Meadow Brook hounds" and were housed at the Widewater kennel.

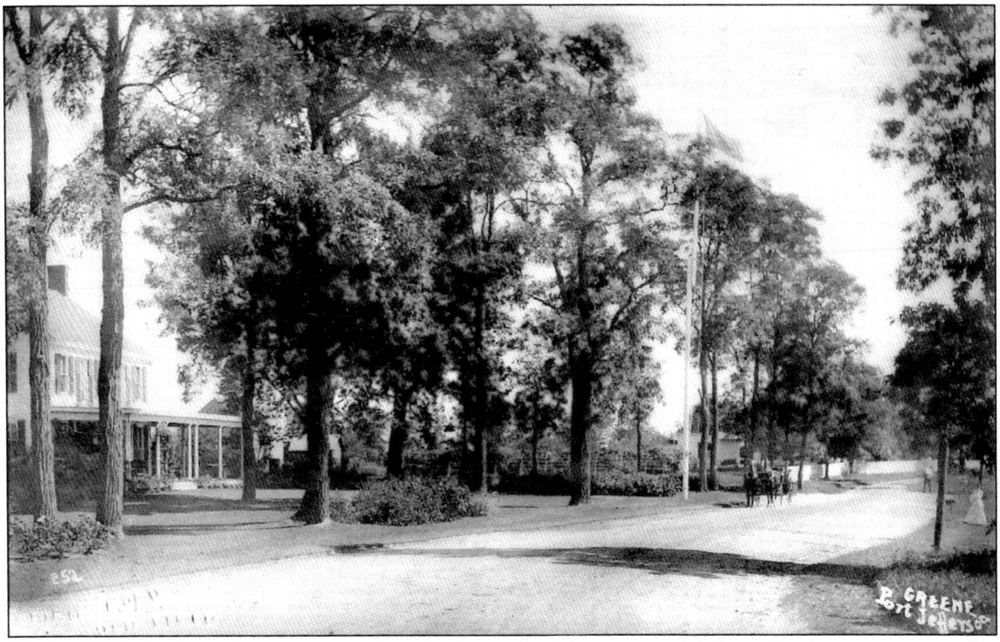

VINCENT T. DICKERSON HOUSE, BUILT C. 1850. Vincent and Miner Dickerson operated a shipyard across from the V. T. Dickerson home at 154 Old Field Road. They built nine vessels of record. This photograph from about 1910 shows the house when it was in possession of Clinton L. Rossiter. The Rossiters sold the house to Mr. and Mrs. Peter Costigan after their daughter drowned in the pond on the west end of their property. (Courtesy of Victoria Costigan.)

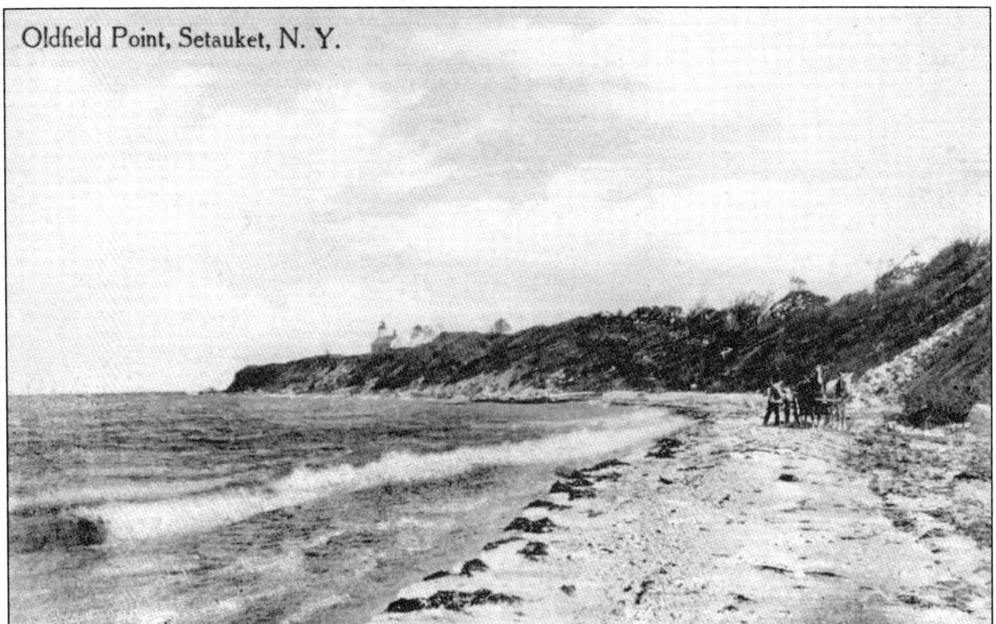

OLD FIELD POINT, C. 1915. The farmer on the beach is gathering seaweed as fertilizer for his fields. The Old Field Lighthouse is at the left. (Courtesy of Beverly and Barbara Tyler.)

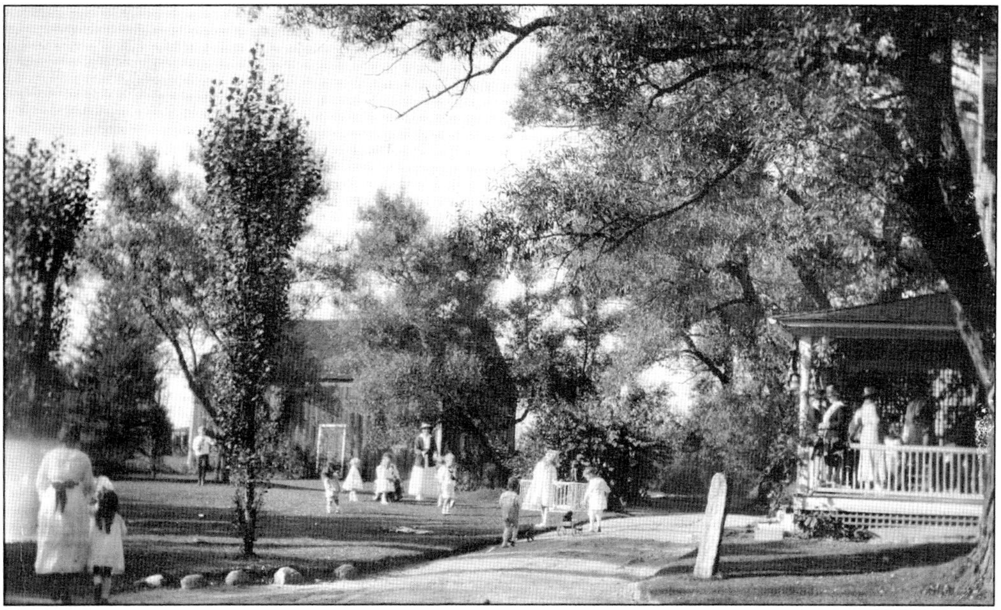

BRAMBLETYE FARM, BRAMBLETYE AND OLD FIELD ROADS, BUILT PRIOR TO 1875. This photograph, taken around 1920, shows a James McLaren family summer gathering. McLaren owned, farmed, and leased land all the way to Flax Pond. Thomas Hodgkins, the previous owner, built and donated the Emma S. Clark Memorial Library in memory of his niece.

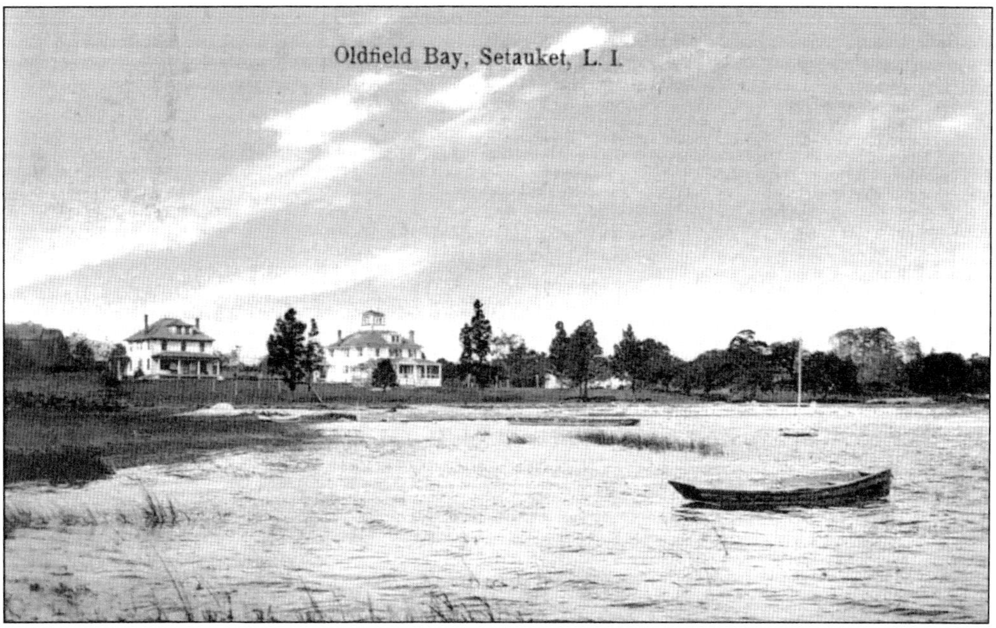

OLD FIELD BAY WITH THE DAUPHINOT AND KIENDL HOUSES. The house on the right was built about 1900 as a summer home for the Kiendl family and was enlarged in 1912. The Dauphinot house at the left was built about 1912, following the basic design of the Kiendl house.

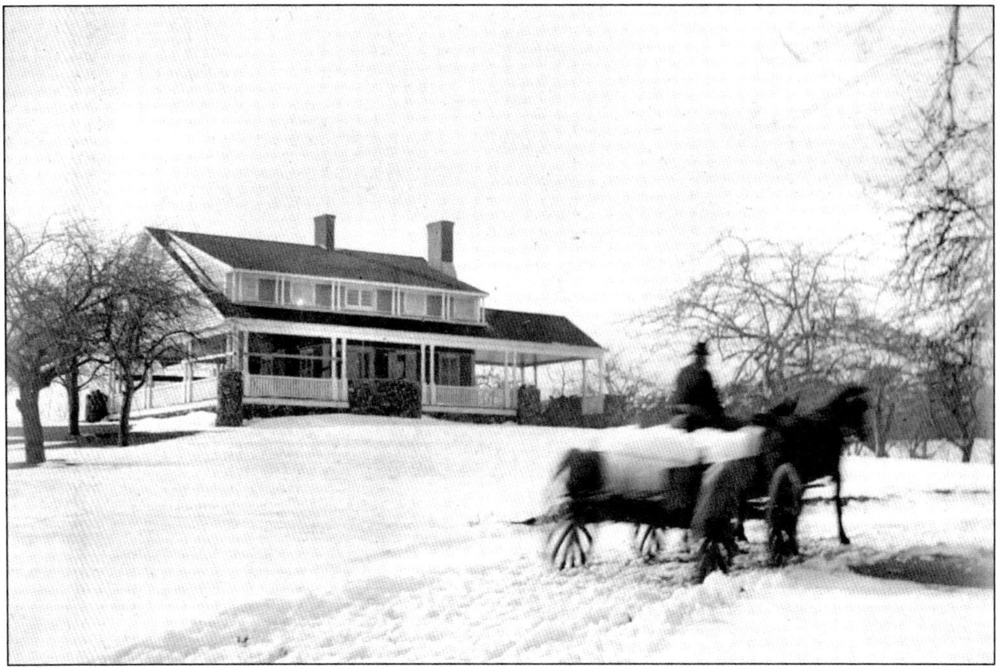

RED ROOF, 98 OLD FIELD ROAD, BUILT PRIOR TO 1858. Purchased in 1900, this was the first home of Frank and Jennie Melville in the area. The photograph was taken on February 23, 1903.

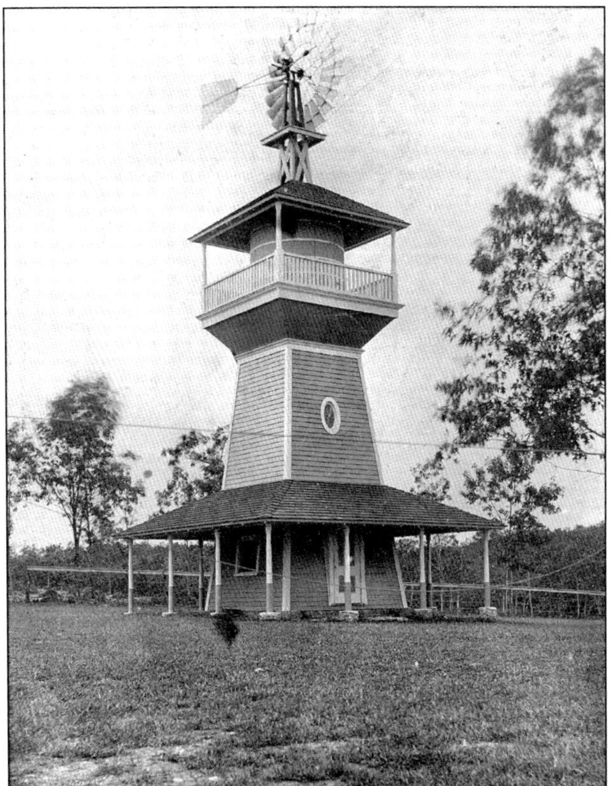

WINDMILL AND WATER TOWER AT RED ROOF. At the time of this 1905 photograph, this windmill and water tower supplied running water to the Frank Melville family at Red Roof. After Melville built Sunwood, Red Roof became the home of Dr. Charles Gerstenberg.

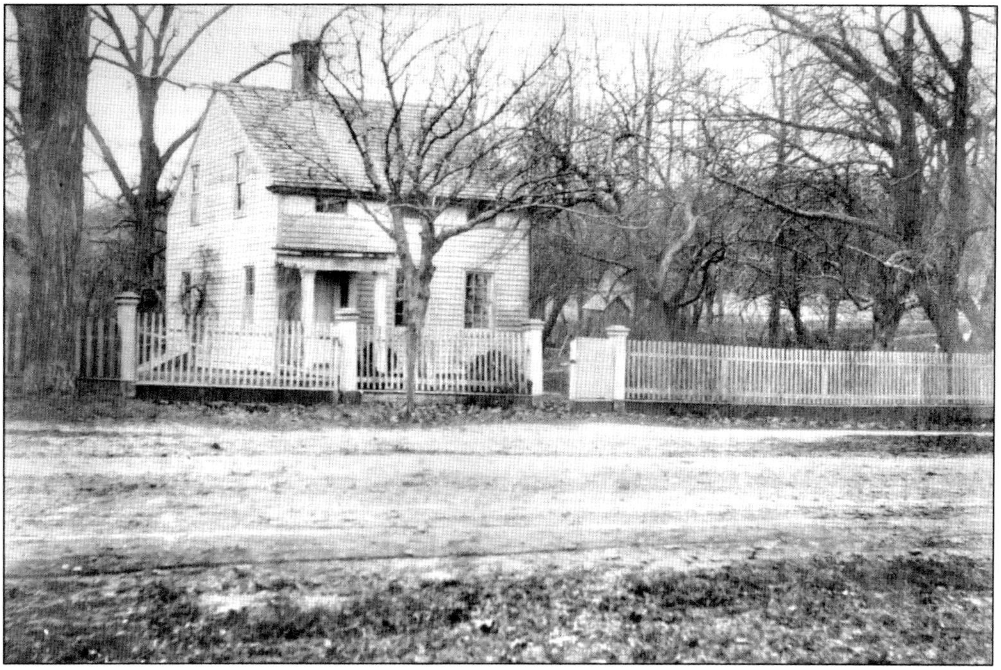

OAKDENE, 81 OLD FIELD ROAD, BUILT IN THE EARLY 19TH CENTURY. The original house was moved and turned 90 degrees to become the south wing of the present house.

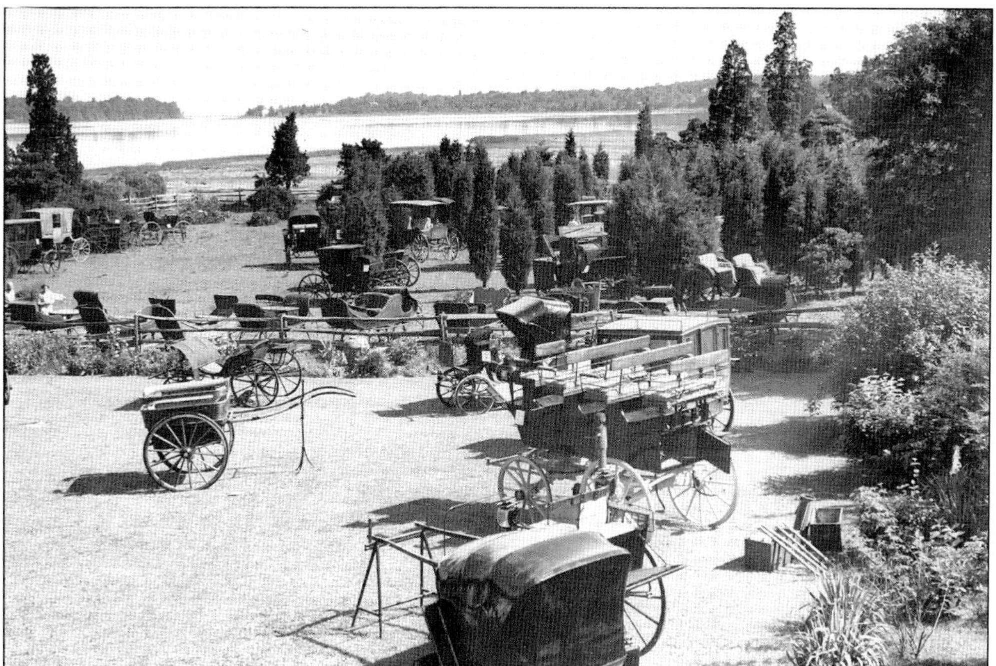

CARRIAGE COLLECTION OF J. WARD MELVILLE. On September 10, 1950, J. Ward Melville invited the public to view his carriage collection in the field behind the Crawford-Dominick Barn at Old Field Road and Quaker Path. The event was a fund-raiser for the founding of the Society for the Preservation of Long Island Antiquities.

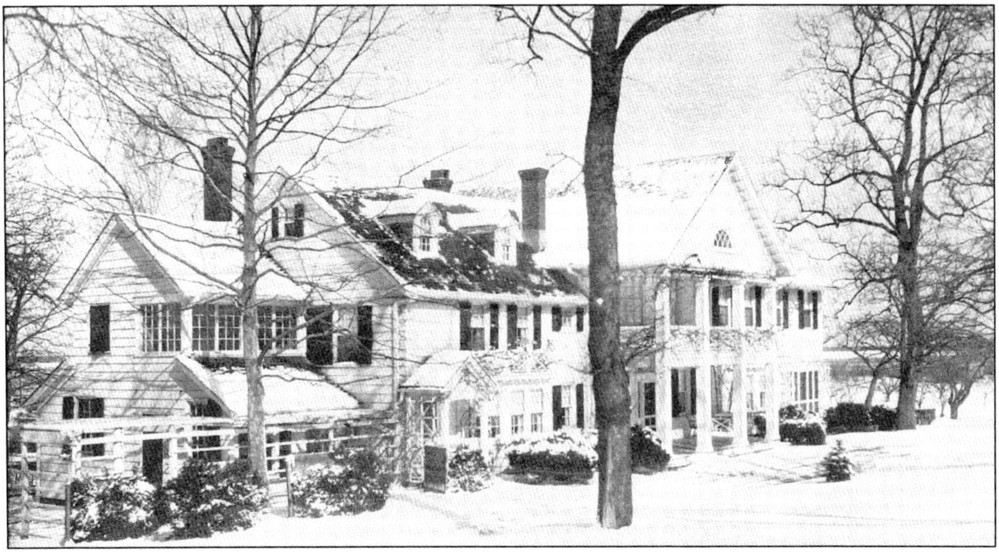

THE CHILDS MANSION, SHORE DRIVE. The Eversley Childs mansion was built during at least three different time periods: between 1786 and 1797, before 1836, and after 1901. Its appearance as a Long Island farmhouse was converted to Colonial Revival during the last addition. Stony Brook University took title to the mansion in 1958. After a period of initial use, the building remained empty for several years. Funds for its restoration were provided by a series of discretionary grants from assemblyman Steven Englebright and from the university president, Shirley Strum Kenny.

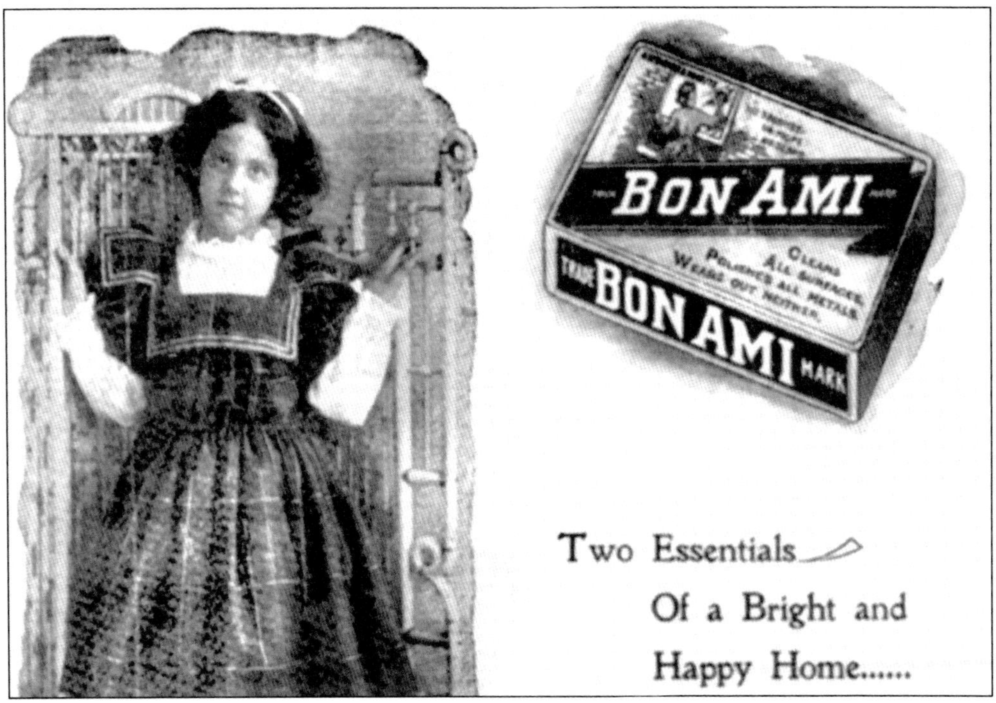

BON AMI ADVERTISEMENT, C. 1895. Dorothy, daughter of Eversley and Mary (Shubrick) Childs, appears as a young girl in this family business advertisement. (Courtesy of Margherita Abbey Childs Fidao.)

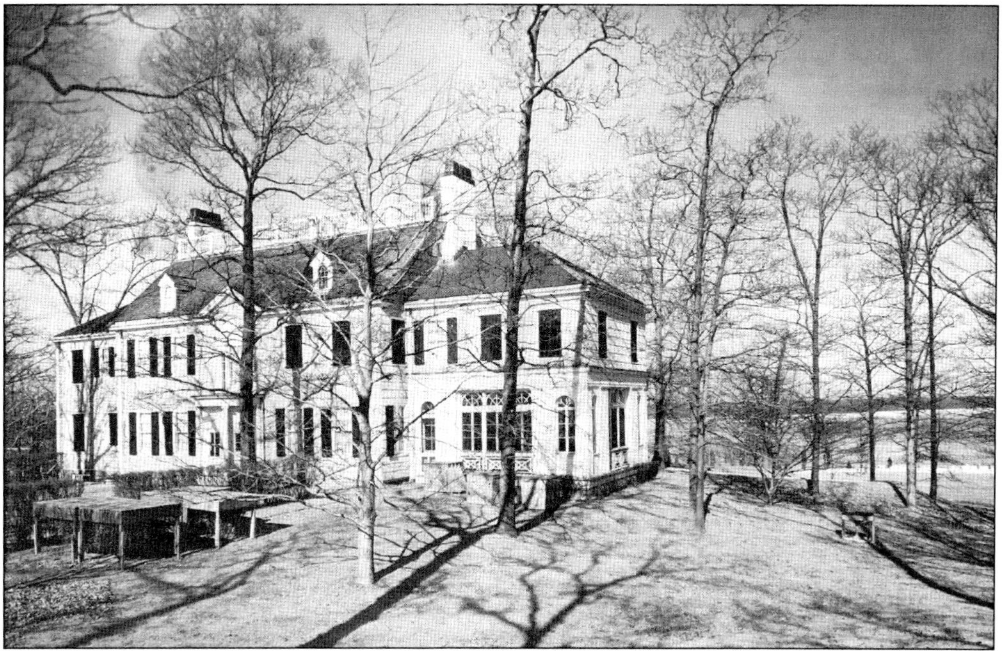

HOME OF DOROTHY SHUBRICK CHILDS MCLAREN, C. 1920. This home was a gift from her parents on her wedding day in 1912.

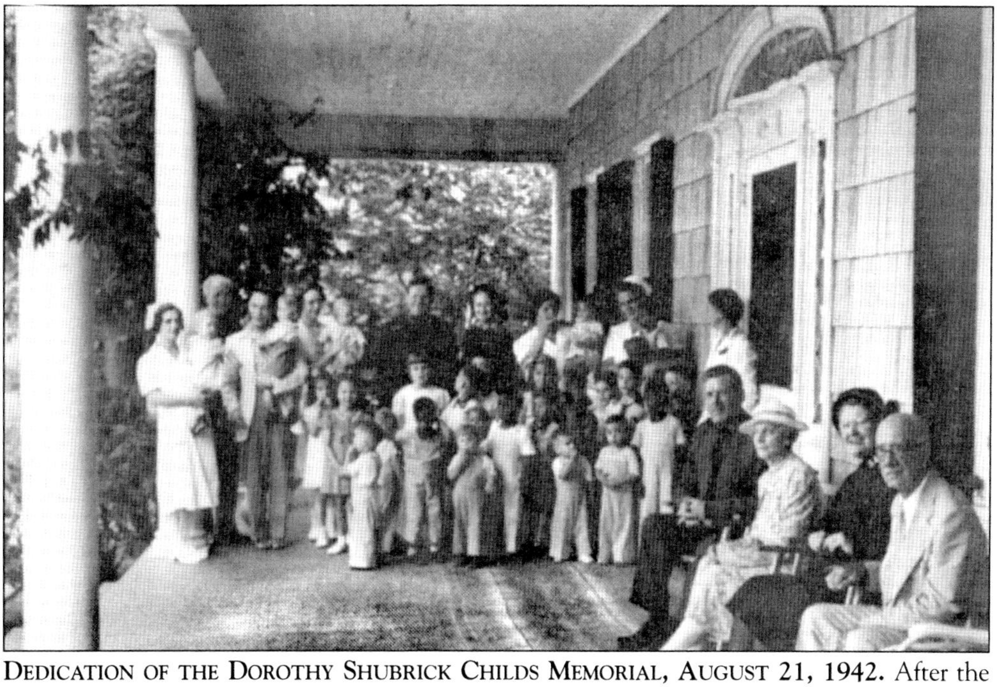

DEDICATION OF THE DOROTHY SHUBRICK CHILDS MEMORIAL, AUGUST 21, 1942. After the death of their daughter, Mr. and Mrs. Eversley Childs Sr. donated her former home to the Salvation Army. It served as the summer home of the Brooklyn Nursery and Infants' Hospital. Eversley Childs Sr. and his wife Mary (known as Minnie) are at the right. (Courtesy of Margherita Abbey Childs Fidao.)

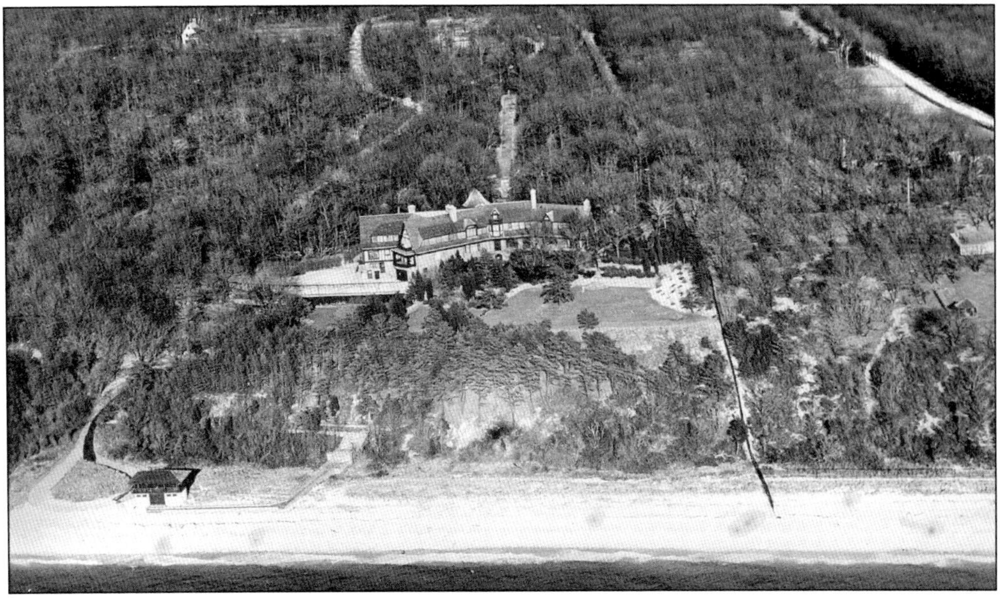

SUNWOOD, MARCH 1942. This mansion was designed by Katherine Budd in 1919, and the gardens were designed by Jennie Melville. It remained the home of Frank and Jennie Melville until their deaths in the late 1930s.

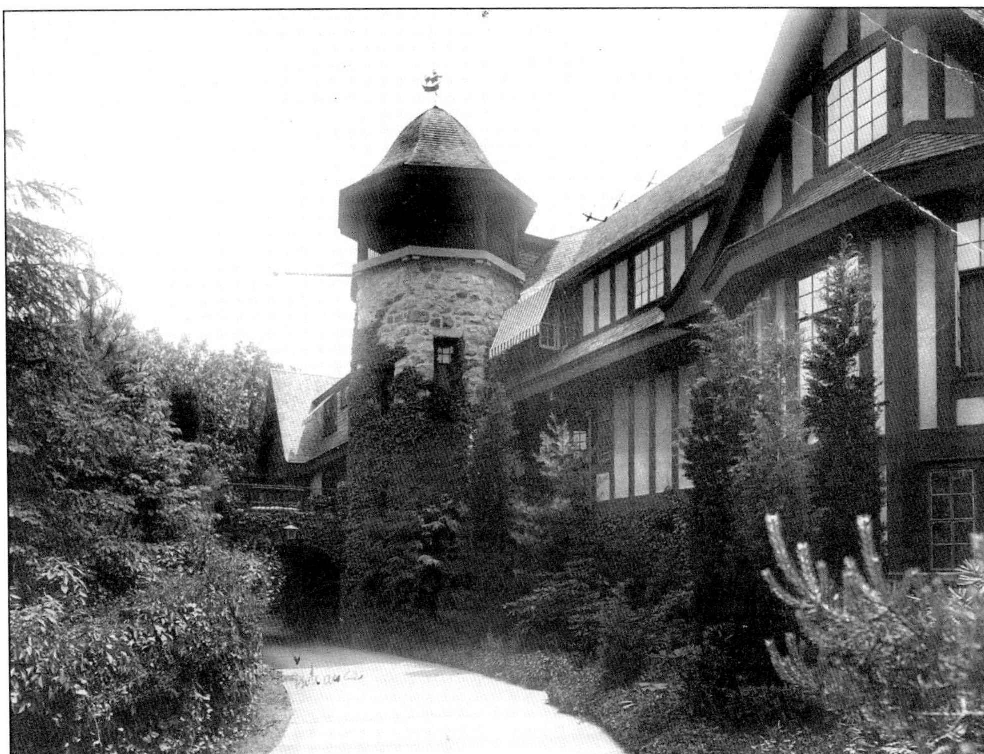

THE DRIVEWAY APPROACH TO SUNWOOD, C. 1930. The main entrance to Sunwood was under the bridge next to the turret.

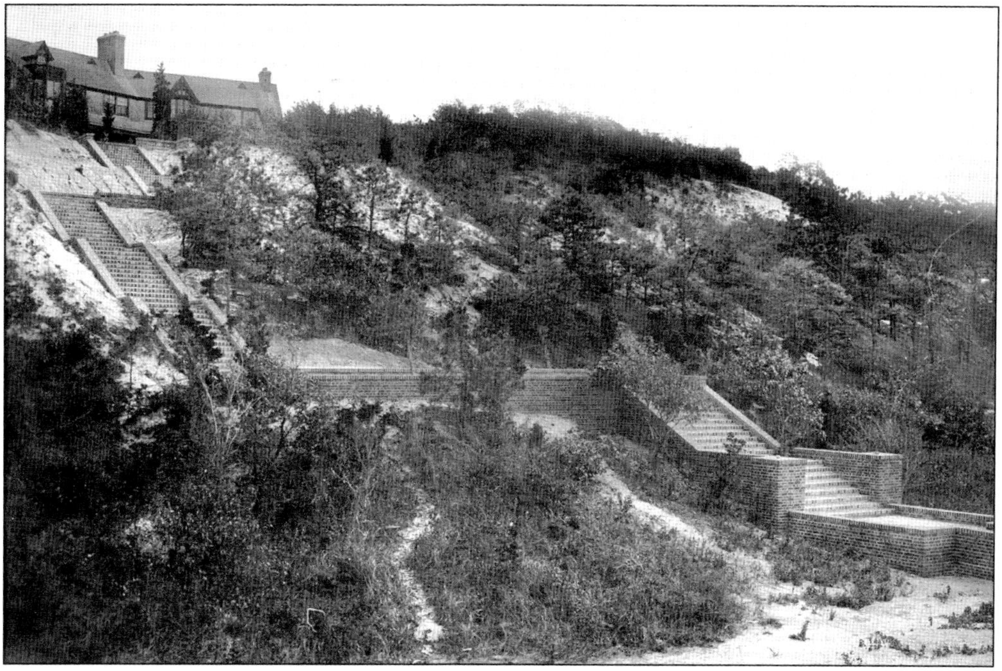

SUNWOOD, STEPS TO THE BEACH, 1919. In 1959, J. Ward and Dorothy (Bigelow) Melville donated this property to Stony Brook University for use as a conference center. The mansion was consumed by a fire in March 1986.

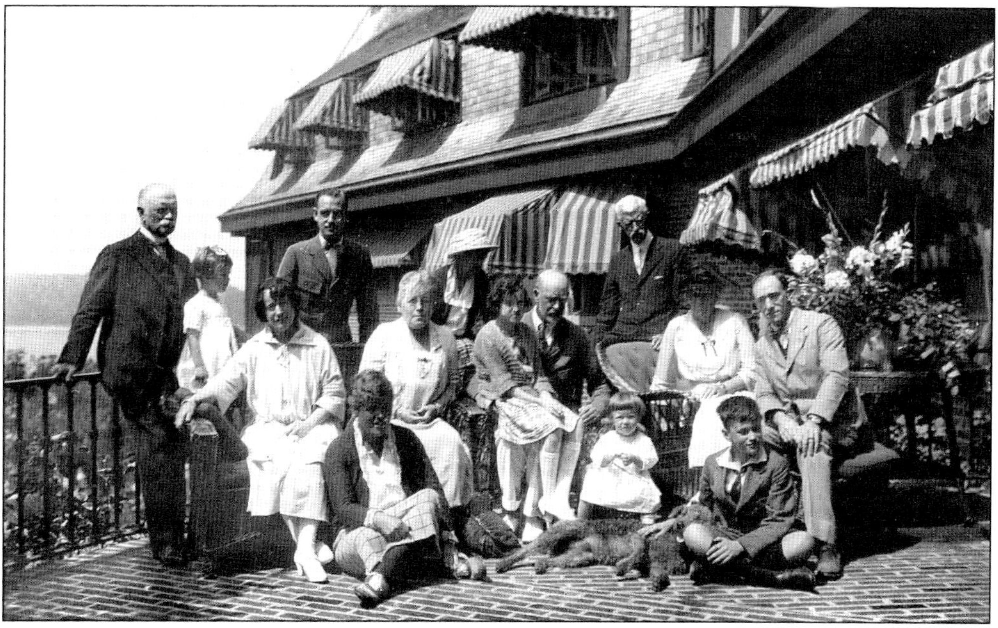

THE MELVILLE FAMILY AT SUNWOOD, C. 1922. From left to right are the following: (first row) Dorothy Melville, Ruth Melville, and Jan W. Liszniewska; (second row, seated) Marguerite Melville Liszniewska, Mrs. Charles E. Bigelow, Josslyn Liszniewska, Frank Melville, Mrs. William C. Beecher, and Karol Liszniewska; (third row, standing) Charles Bigelow, Margaret (Peggy) Melville, John Ward Melville, Jennie Melville, and William C. Beecher.

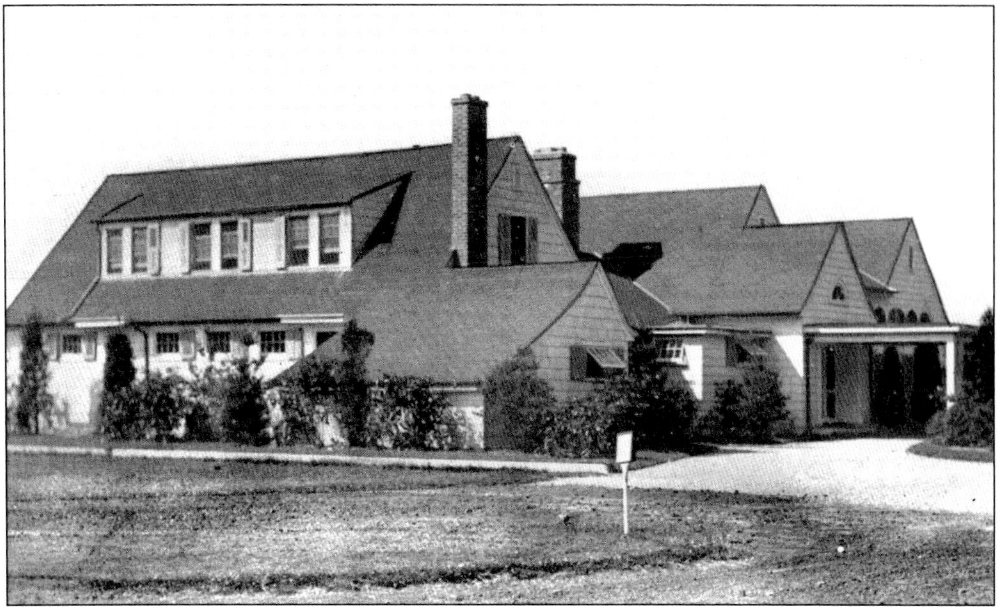

OLD FIELD CLUB, C. 1930. This tennis/beach club was founded in 1929 to provide a social and athletic atmosphere.

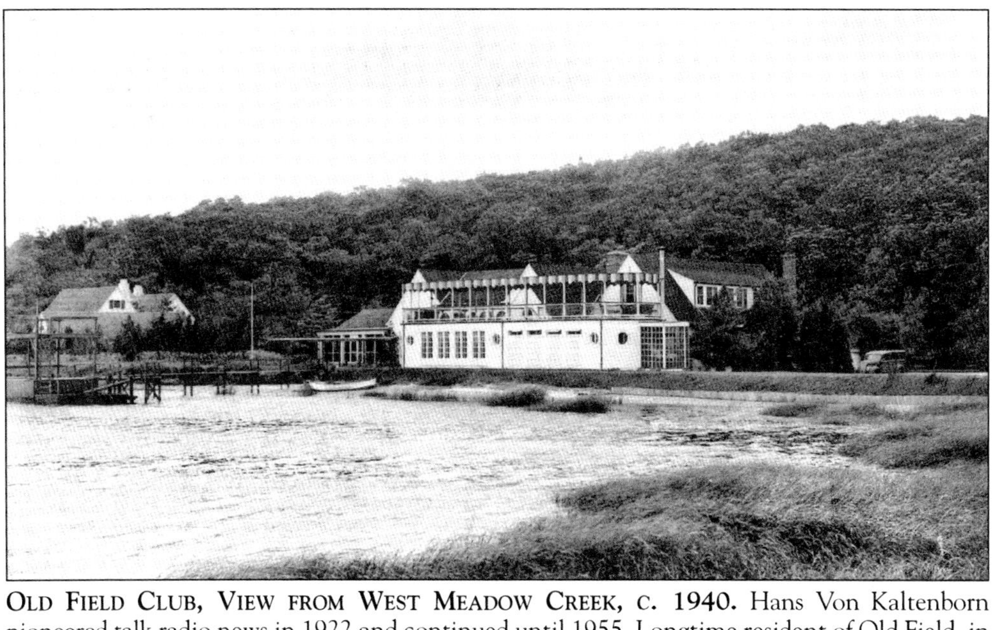

OLD FIELD CLUB, VIEW FROM WEST MEADOW CREEK, C. 1940. Hans Von Kaltenborn pioneered talk radio news in 1922 and continued until 1955. Longtime resident of Old Field, in 1950, he donated Kaltenborn Commons to the Village of Old Field. Kaltenborn's 1940 Dodge "woody" station wagon is seen at the right.

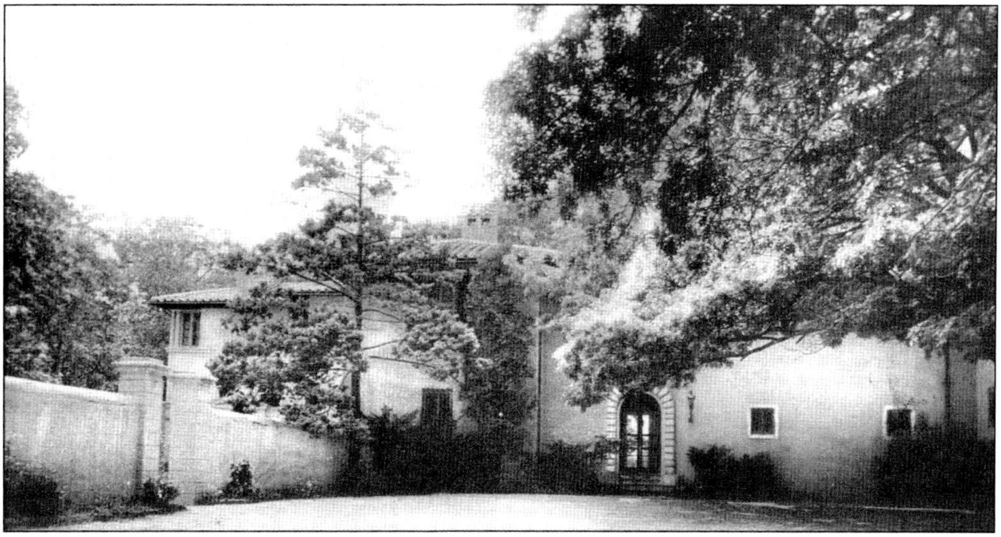

MARYVILLE CONVENT, BUILT 1917. Frederick L. Steenken, a noted scientist, built this home at 7 Dodge Lane to resemble a villa overlooking the Bay of Naples. Frederick W. Gurney, the inventor of roller bearings, bought the home in 1920 as a summer residence. He added a 20-by-50-foot addition for his son John, who performed concerts at the Metropolitan Opera House in New York. Gurney called it the Villa del Canto. Olga Petrova, a star of the silent screen, vaudeville, and Broadway, purchased the property in 1946. She renamed the house Casa Mia and lived there for six years. The house was occupied by the Apostalate Pallotine, an order of Catholic sisters, from 1951 to 1973.

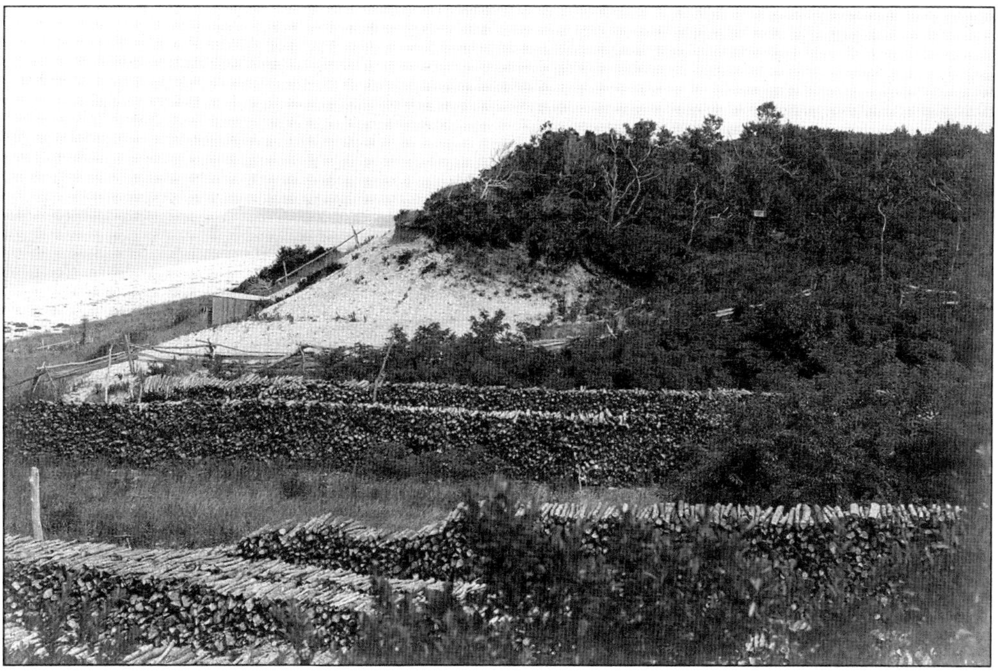

CORDWOOD AT THE NORTH END OF WEST MEADOW BEACH, C. 1885. In this image, cordwood is ready for loading on schooners that will transport it to brick kilns on the Hudson or in Connecticut. The cabanas for the Old Field Club now occupy this site.

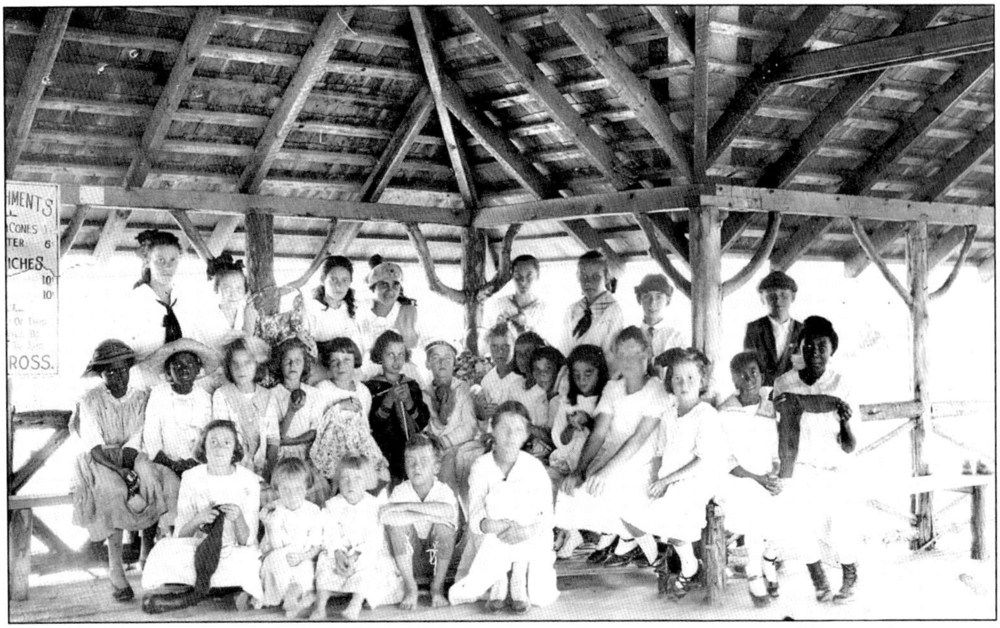

THE JUNIOR RED CROSS, WEST MEADOW BEACH, AUGUST 29, 1918. This is the annual picnic of the Junior Red Cross of the Setauket Union Free School at the West Meadow Beach pavilion. Mrs. Van Brunt was the chairperson.

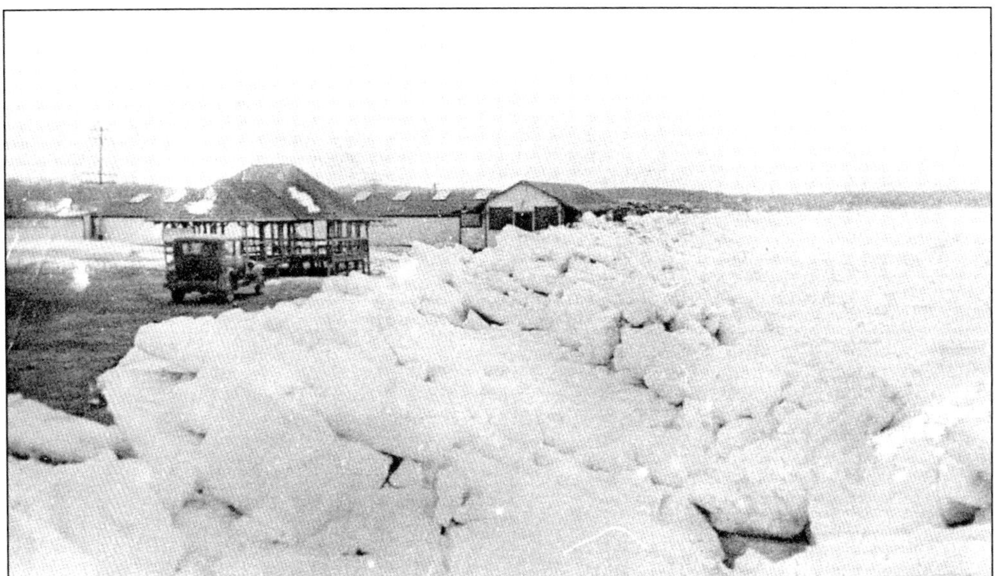

PACK ICE, WEST MEADOW BEACH, FEBRUARY 17, 1934. The beach pavilion is in the foreground by the car. Gus Gokomeir's Luncheonette and the L-shaped bathhouse are at the center of the photograph.

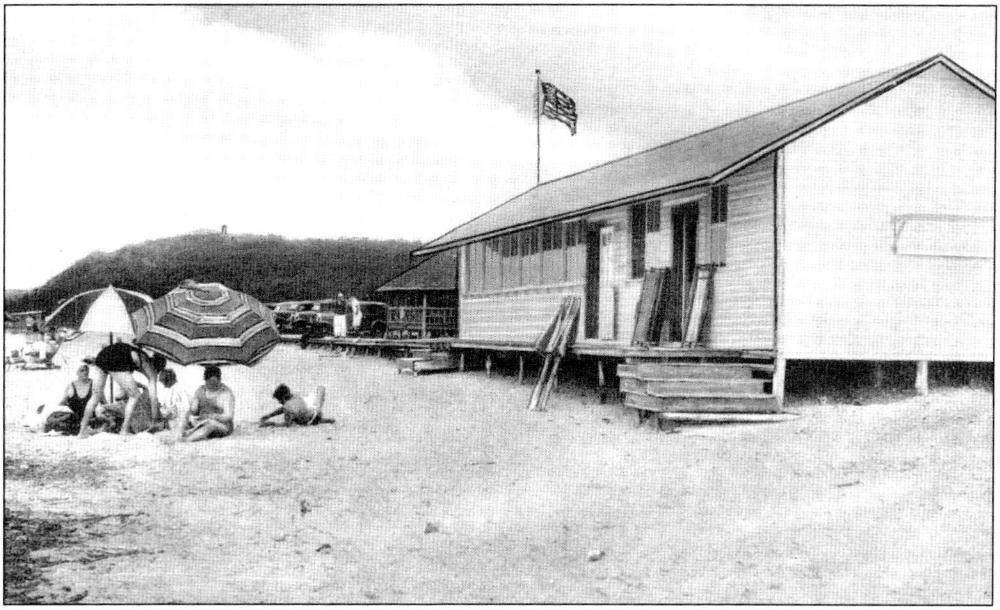

REFRESHMENTS AT WEST MEADOW BEACH, C. 1935. This photograph shows Gus Gokomeir's Luncheonette and Concession.

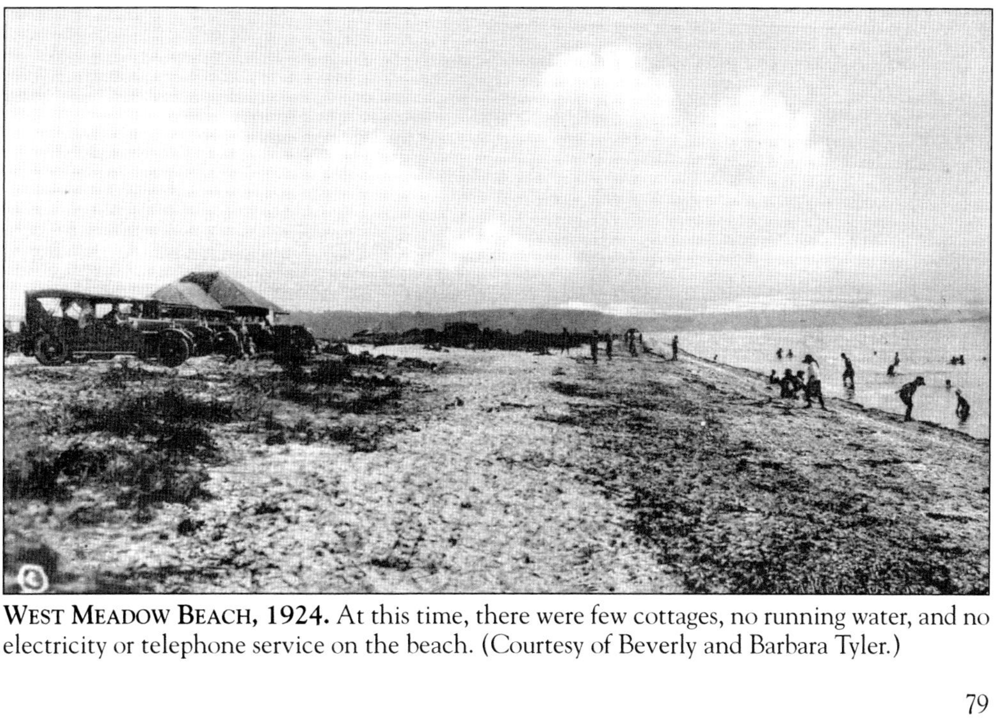

WEST MEADOW BEACH, 1924. At this time, there were few cottages, no running water, and no electricity or telephone service on the beach. (Courtesy of Beverly and Barbara Tyler.)

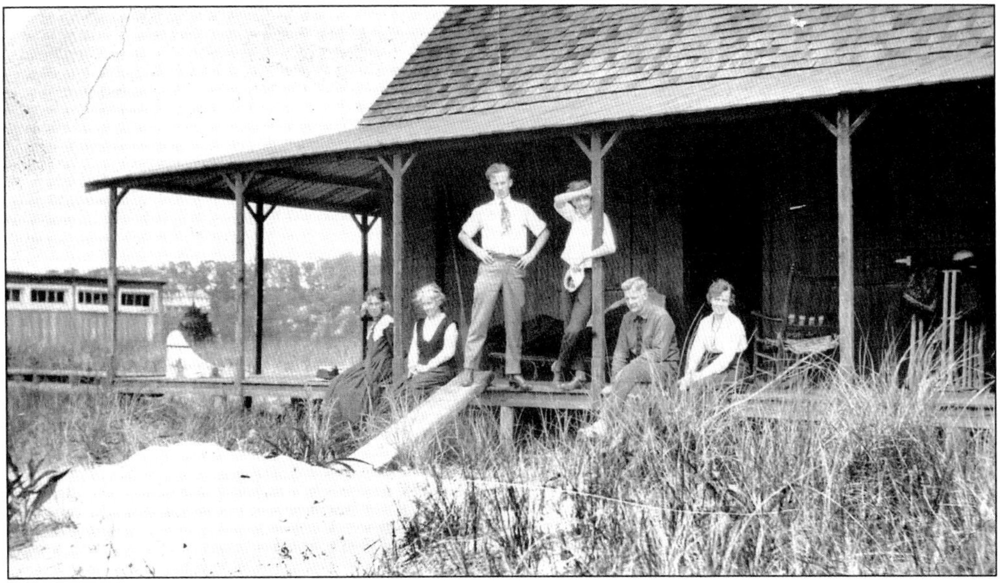

THE COTTAGE AT 73 TRUSTEES ROAD, C. 1927. This is one of the many cottages that lined West Meadow Beach. The Brookhaven Bathing Association, Inc., beach house, built in 1924, is seen at the far left. The portion visible is the women's changing side of the building. The men's side burned down in 1981. The Trustees Road cottages, as well as the association's beach house, were demolished in the winter of 2004–2005. (Courtesy of Beatrice and Susan Jayne.)

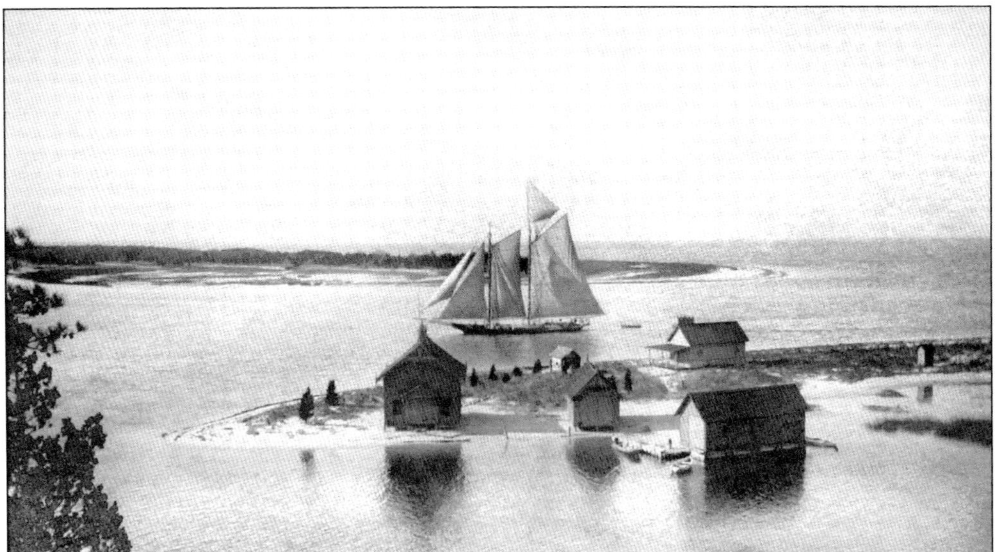

SHIPMAN'S POINT, WEST MEADOW BEACH, C. 1890. Gamecock Cottage is at the center of this image. This cottage was originally built as an aviary on the William Shipman property at 92 Cedar Street, Stony Brook. It was moved across West Meadow Creek on a raft, and Shipman converted it into a boathouse for racing shells. Jennie Melville purchased the cottage and made it a rental summer residence. Later she transferred the cottage to the Three Village Inn. It is now owned by the Town of Brookhaven. The *Sarah Maria* is seen in the channel heading for Stony Brook. Its homeport was Port Jefferson. Built in 1869 at Cold Spring, New York, it was 48 tons burthen with a crew of two. (Courtesy of Susan White Pieroth.)

Four

NASSAKEAG AND SETAUKET SOUTH

The region south of the Long Island Railroad tracks was sparsely populated. It was used for cordwood cutting, and where the soil was good enough, there were individual family farms. This portion of Setauket is close to the crest of the Harbor Hill moraine, and, as a result, the soil can be quite rocky. It was far enough removed from the main village that it had its own schoolhouse, church, and burying ground.

Throughout the 19th century, apple orchards tended to dominate farm production in this area. A long series of cider mills were built to process the fruit. In 1841, William Sidney Mount depicted the area in his work *Cider Making on Long Island.* This painting shows a cider mill, the Hawkins house and pond. It is also a political commentary on the evils of drink.

In the early 20th century, one of the farms, originally a Hawkins farm but later owned by the Williamson family, became the St. George's Golf and Country Club. Where the soil could not support row crops, dairy cattle had ample grazing, and the Hawkins and Lewis Dairy developed. The area between Pond Path and the golf course remained heavily wooded and almost impenetrable. In the 1930s, this became an ideal location for moonshine operations. These operations were large enough to cause at least one local resident to spend time as a guest of the federal government.

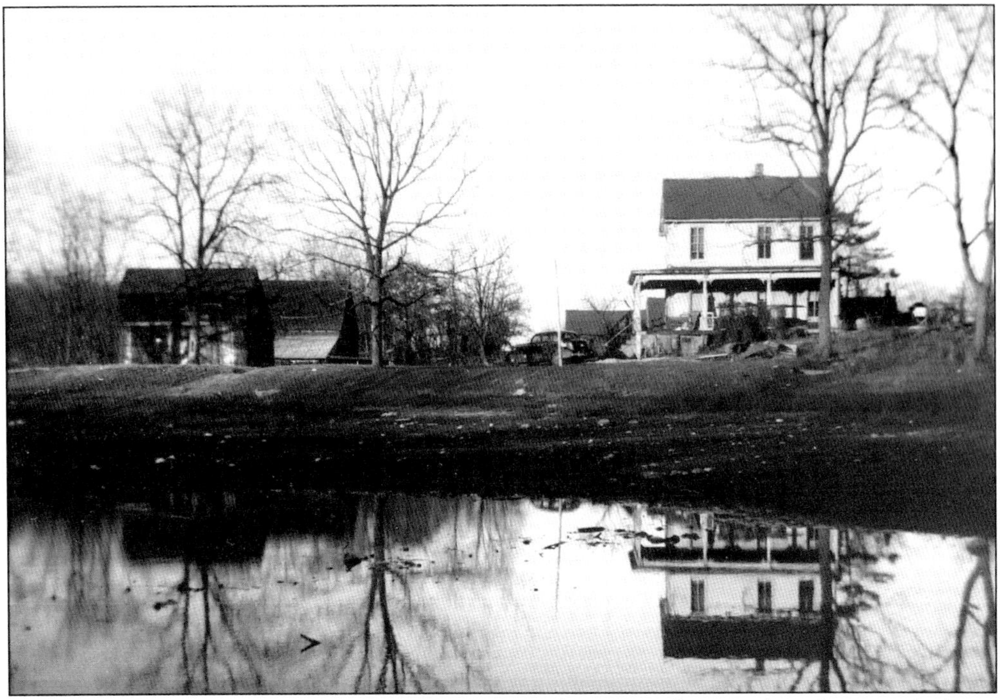

HAWKINS HOUSE, HUB ROAD, BUILT C. 1830. Taken around 1936, this photograph shows the Hawkins and Lewis Dairy. Thomas and Chester Hawkins operated the dairy throughout the 1930s and 1940s with about 20 cows. Clifford Lewis then took over the management. The dairy operated until the late 1950s. (Courtesy of Ken Tuck.)

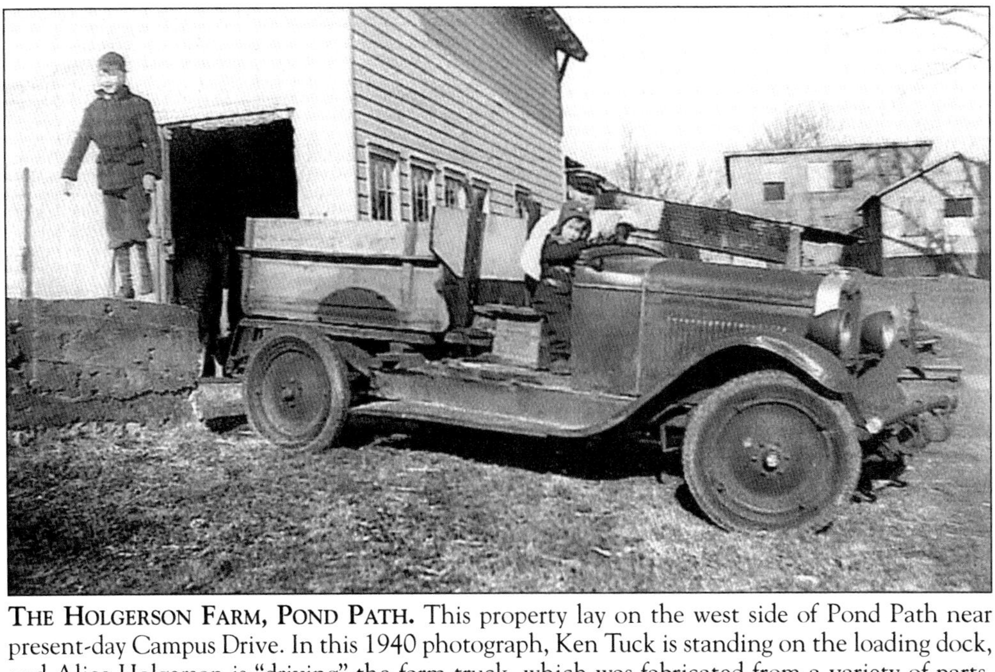

THE HOLGERSON FARM, POND PATH. This property lay on the west side of Pond Path near present-day Campus Drive. In this 1940 photograph, Ken Tuck is standing on the loading dock, and Alice Holgerson is "driving" the farm truck, which was fabricated from a variety of parts. (Courtesy of Ken Tuck.)

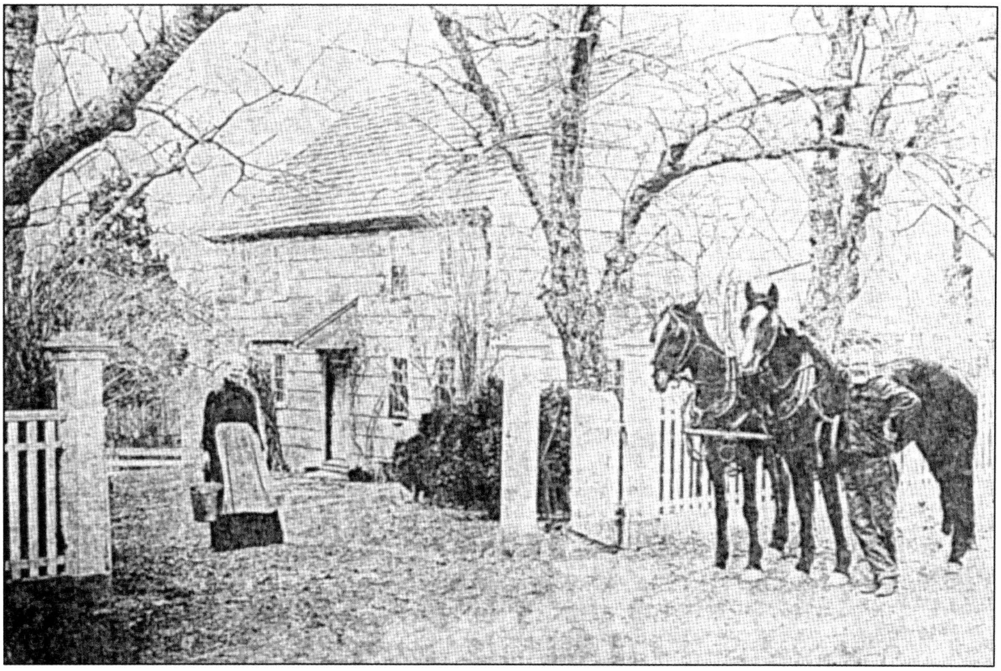

MERRITT HAWKINS HOMESTEAD, 512 POND PATH, BUILT 1802. Ethelbert Selleck (1838–1926) and Hester Ann Hawkins Selleck (1839–1905) are pictured in front of their home around 1900. (Courtesy of Ruth Rothermel.)

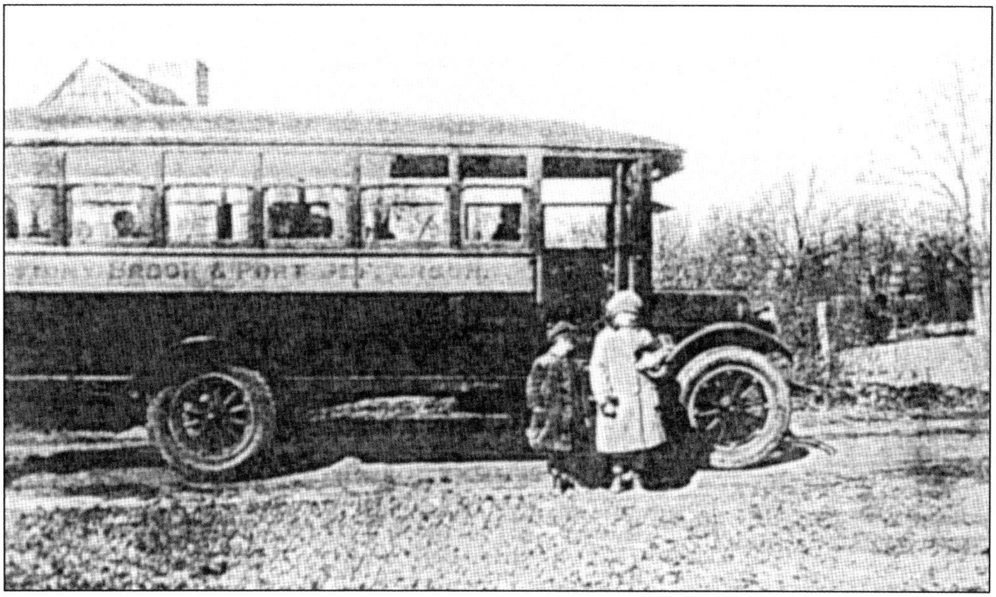

GOING TO SCHOOL, 1927. Muriel (first grade) and Merle Selleck (second grade) are pictured boarding the school bus heading for the Setauket Union Free School. Russell Darling regularly drove this school bus. Later he worked as a driver for Joseph (Jes) Eikov's buses. (Courtesy of Ruth Rothermel.)

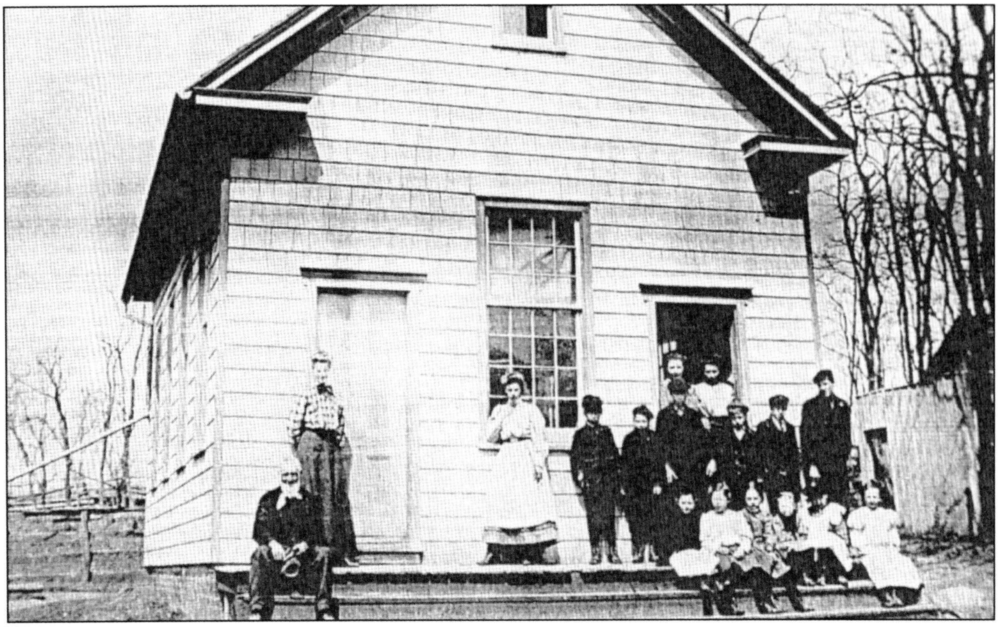

The First Nassakeag School, Built 1877. This Nassakeag school stood opposite the entrance to St. George's Golf and Country Club at approximately 155 Lower Sheep Pasture Road. Shown here in 1907, Ethelbert Selleck (1838–1926), school trustee, is seated on the steps at the left. The schoolhouse was moved to the grounds of the Long Island Museum of American Art, History and Carriages, Stony Brook, in 1952. (Courtesy of Ruth Rothermel.)

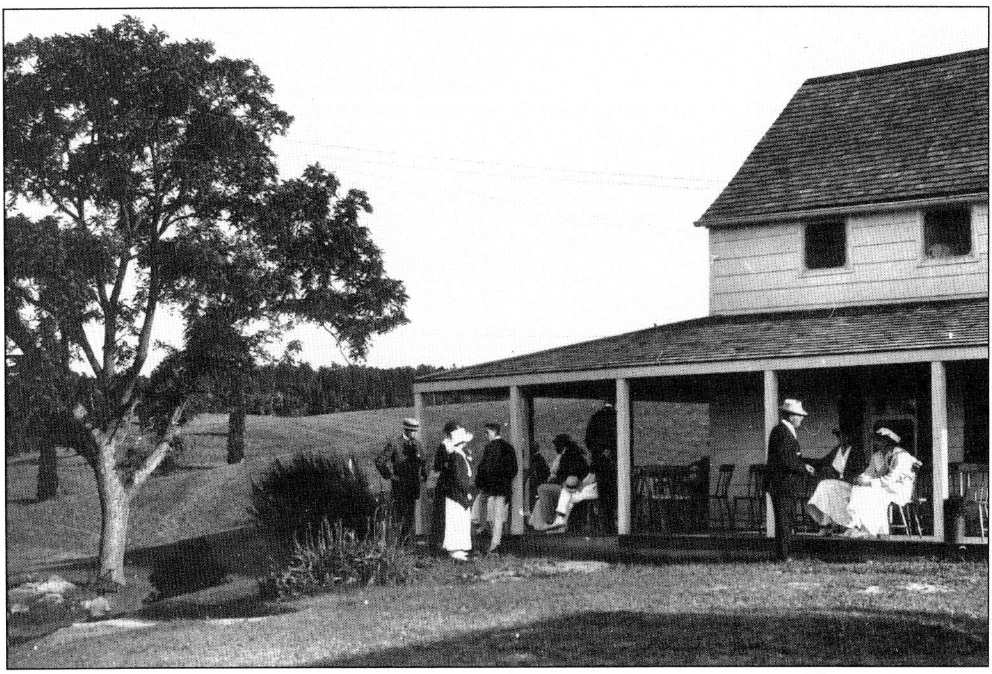

First Clubhouse, St. George's Golf and Country Club, c. 1920. The 18th-century Williamson farmhouse was converted into the first clubhouse when the country club was founded in 1918. It served the members from 1919 to 1929.

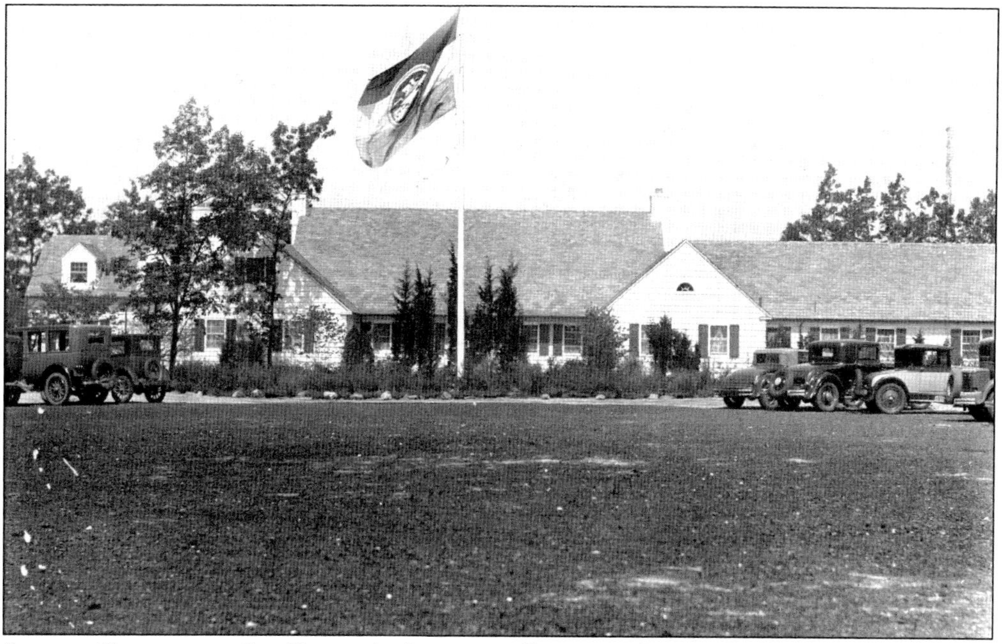

SECOND CLUBHOUSE, ST. GEORGE'S GOLF AND COUNTRY CLUB, C. 1935. This building was the center of club activity beginning in 1930. Only the chimneys and foundation remained after a fire that destroyed the building on January 12, 1953. On February 14, 1969, the third clubhouse was also destroyed by fire and was replaced by the present building.

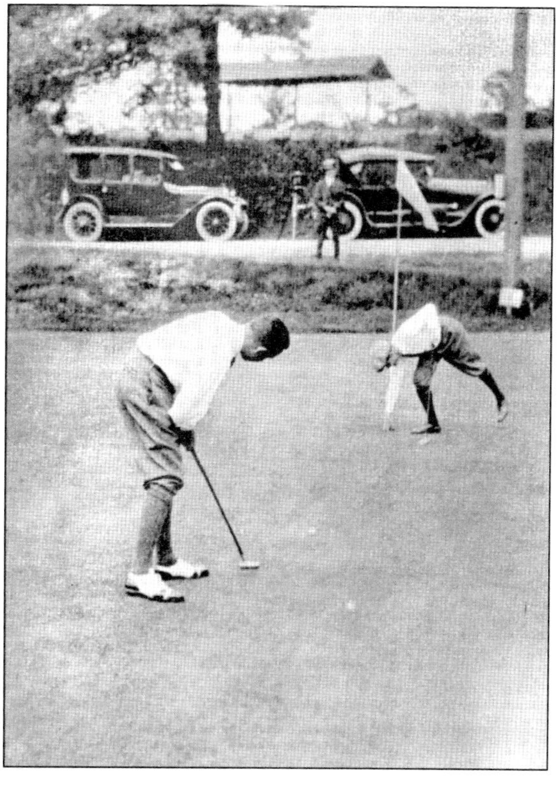

MAKING HIS PUTT. Jerome D. Travers, the 1915 U.S. Open champion, is at the left and Gardiner White is at the right in this 1919 photograph. In the background are a 1919 Cadillac (left) and a 1919 Lincoln (right). (Courtesy of St. George's Golf and Country Club.)

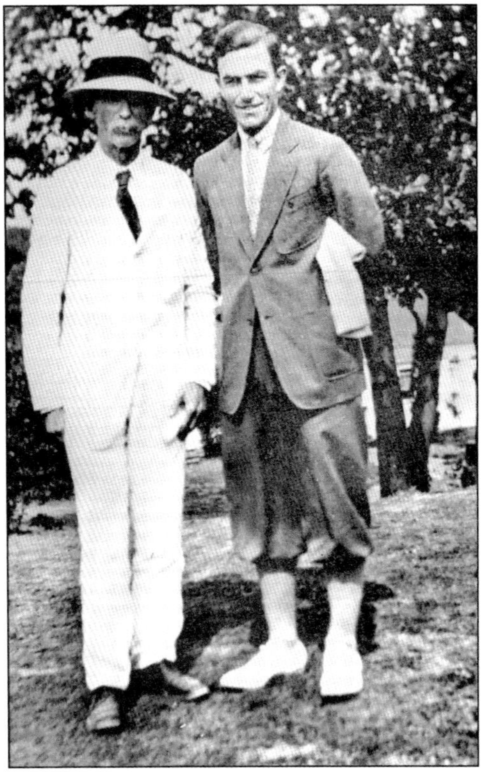

THE CLUB DESIGNER. Taken about 1920, this photograph shows Devereux Emmet, designer of the St. George's Golf Course and a Stony Brook resident, at the left. Standing next to him is Johnny Farrell, later the 1928 U.S. Open champion. (Courtesy of St. George's Golf and Country Club.)

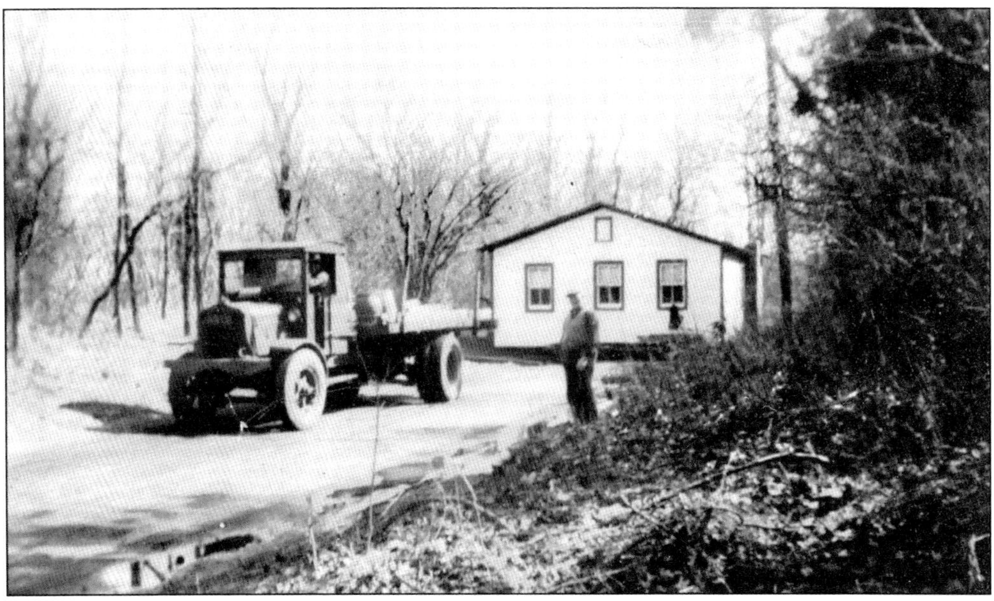

LYONS-TURANO HOUSE, BUILT C. 1918. Originally built as the caddy shack at St. George's Golf and Country Club, this house was converted to a private home and then sold. In this 1940 photograph, the house is being moved to 62 Bennetts Road by William (Bill) Winters, who is driving the truck. (Courtesy of Frank Turano.)

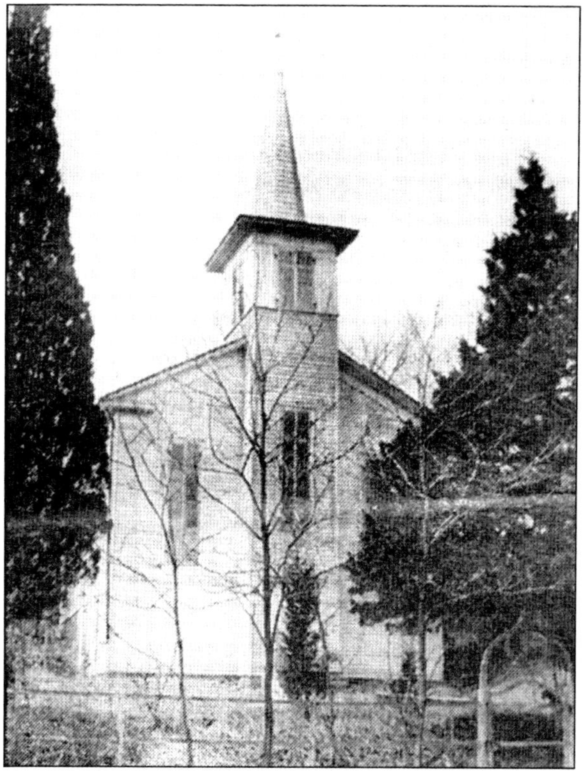

South Setauket Presbyterian Church, 60 Bennetts Road, Built c. 1860. This church was active from about 1860 to 1920. Ethelbert Hawkins Selleck and Elsie Burnell, who married on October 17,1889, were the only couple to wed in this church. In the late 19th century, the pastor's annual salary was $2. The church was torn down in 1967 and replaced with a residence. (Courtesy of Ruth Rothermel.)

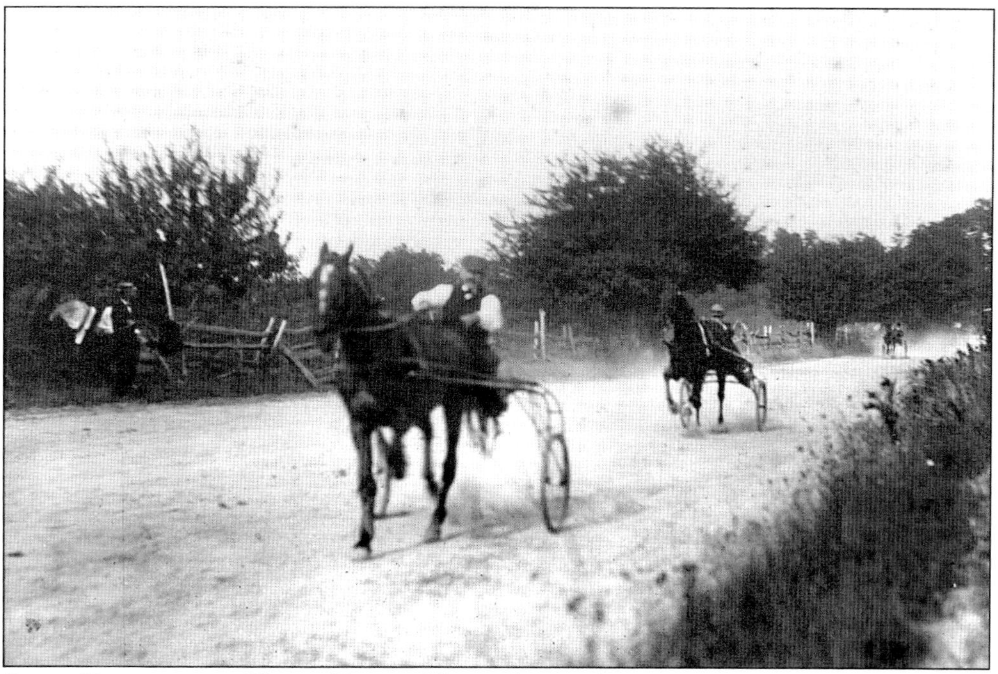

Sulky Race at the Hulse Track. The Hulse Track was located on Hulse Road at the junction of Old Post Road, north of the railroad tracks. The first driver is Frank Jayne; the second is Bob Davis, driving "Sportin' Bill."

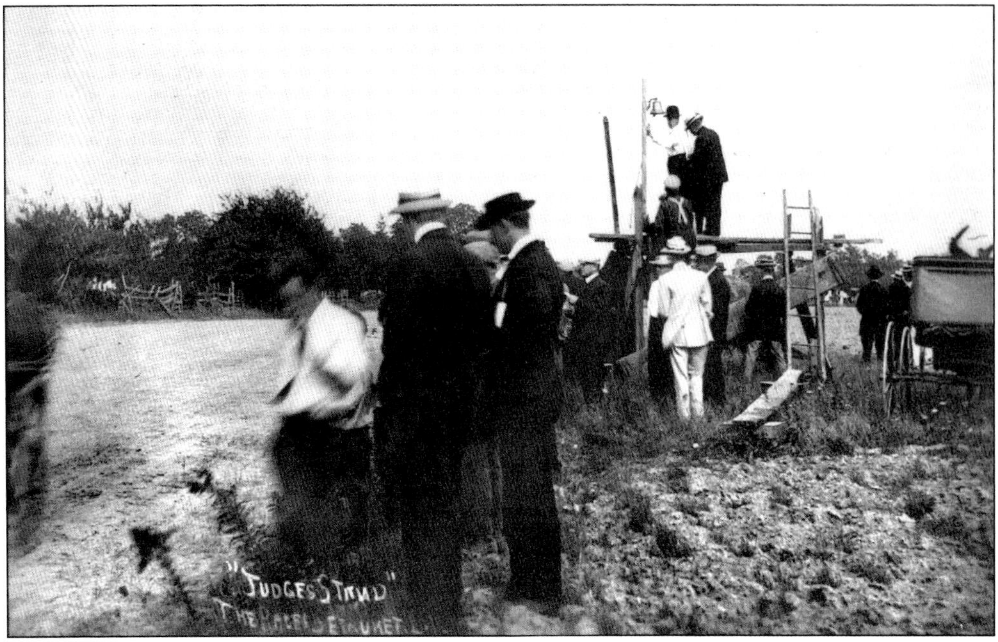

THE JUDGE'S STAND, HULSE ROAD RACE, C. 1910. The long-standing local tradition of trotting was maintained in the 1940s by Herman (Hymie) Golden. Golden owned, trained, and drove trotters at Roosevelt Raceway, as well as keeping score for local betters.

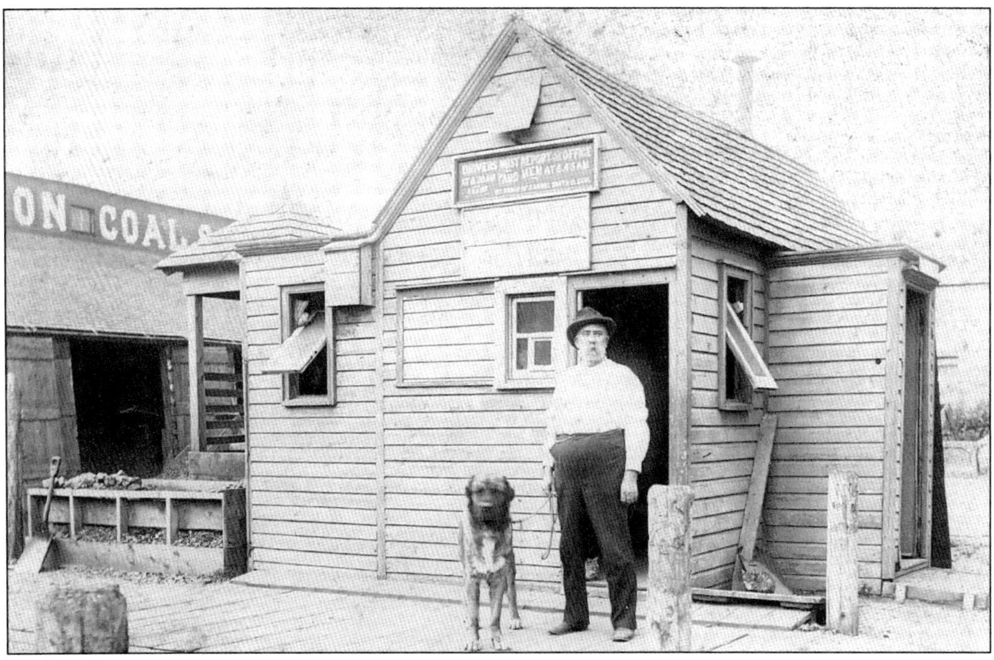

SAMUEL SMITH AND SON COAL YARD, C. 1910. Samuel Smith is pictured at the door of his coal yard office, north of the Setauket Railroad Station at 86 Gnarled Hollow Road. Shown here in about 1910, the sign reads: "Drivers must report to the office at 6:30 a.m. sharp and yard men at 6:45 a.m. by order of Samuel Smith and Son." William Sells, the night watchman and the son of Aunt Sara Sells, froze to death in the coal yard one night in the winter of 1940.

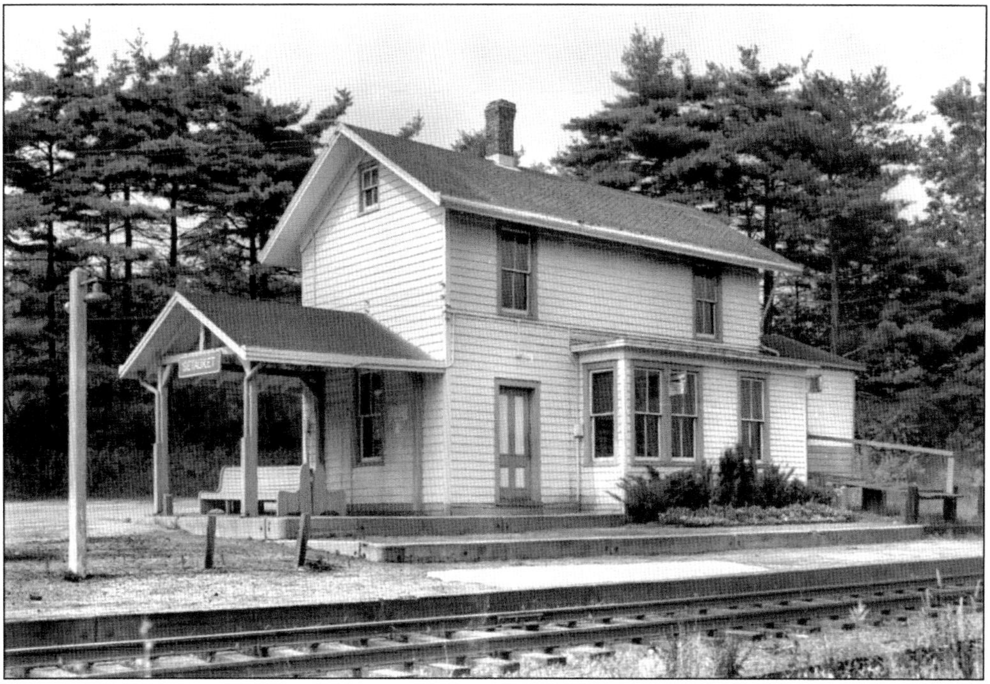

SETAUKET RAILROAD STATION, GNARLED HOLLOW ROAD, 1953. This station was established in 1873. In the summer of 1934, at about 4:00 a.m., there was a dynamite explosion in a barn at 94 Gnarled Hollow Road, southwest of the Setauket Railroad Station. The barn was isolated enough so that the barn and two sheep were the only casualties.

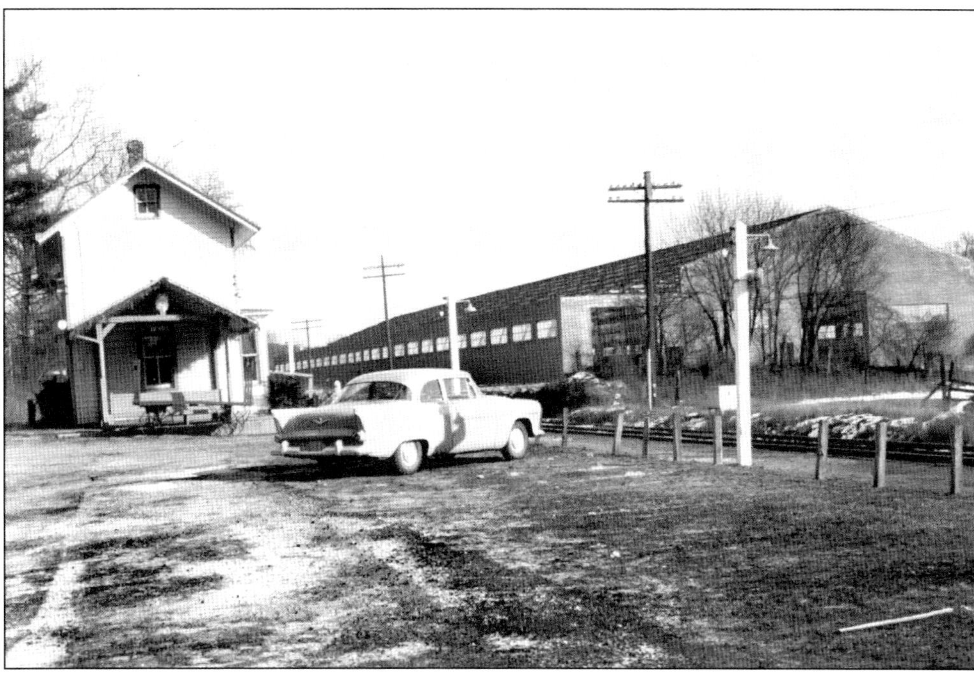

SETAUKET RAILROAD STATION AND THE AMERICAN FLAGPOLE FACTORY, 1956. This station was torn down in 1960. (Courtesy of Ken Tuck.)

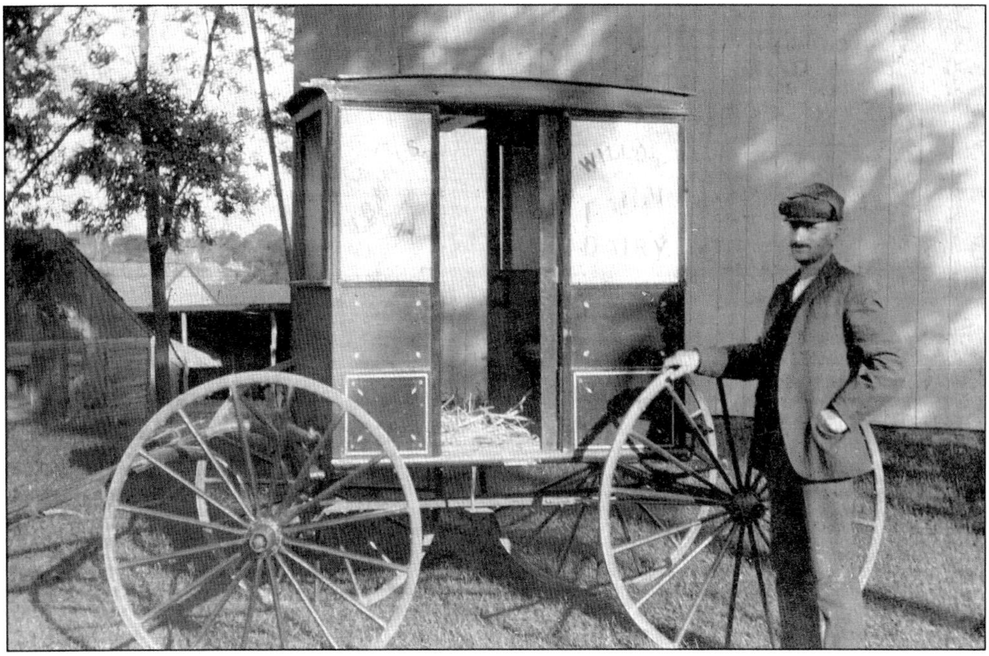

THE WILLOW FARM DAIRY DELIVERY WAGON, C. 1915. This dairy was located on Old Town Road, just south of the railroad trestle. In 1873, the property of 221 Old Town Road was owned by R. L. Terrell. This is known today as Walnut Tree Farm. (Courtesy of Beverly and Barbara Tyler.)

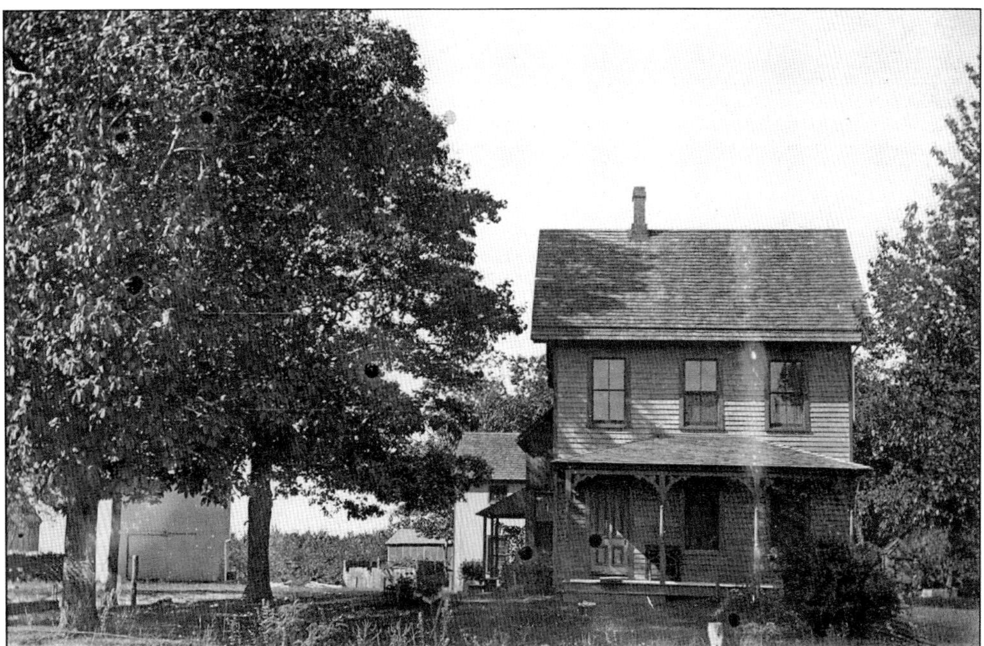

CHARLES HAWKINS HOMESTEAD, C. 1910. This house stood approximately 100 yards south of the Ward Melville High School property at about 400 Old Town Road. It was demolished in about 1975. (Courtesy of Betty Voss.)

Five

ON THE WATER

In the earliest days of settlement, Setauket was oriented toward the water, as it was the principal means of transportation and communication. Shipbuilding commenced as early as 1662 but became a major commercial enterprise for most of the 19th century. All of the Setauket ships were built along the shores of Setauket Harbor, mostly along Shore Road. Approximately 40,000 registered tons of shipping, or about 200 ships, were launched at Setauket. This does not include small-boat production and repair. At the height of activity, in about 1855, Setauket shipyards employed 90 to 100 men. Three vessels of particular note were built here: the *Adorna*, of 1,460 registered tons, is said to be the largest vessel ever completed in Suffolk County; the brig *Daisy*, which carried Robert Cushman Murphy on his first voyage to study pelagic birds; and the *Wanderer*, a 234-ton schooner-yacht that is referred to as the "last slaver." Just before the Civil War, this vessel landed 465 slaves at Jekyll Island, Georgia. Long Island Sound off Setauket was the temporary home for the North Atlantic Fleet in 1917 and the permanent home of the *Lexington*, which burned in 1840.

December 11, 1937, was one of the saddest days in the history of the Setauket School but one of the proudest testaments to the human spirit. Eleven-year-old Harry Lyons Jr. fell through the ice while skating on the millpond. His friend, fifteen-year-old William Leroy Sells, went to his aid, the ice giving way under him as well, and both boys drowned. Three would-be rescuers also fell through the ice but, after great difficulty, were able to get to shore. A plaque was erected in the Setauket High School in William Sells's honor. The plaque has been moved to the lobby of the Setauket Elementary School on Main Street.

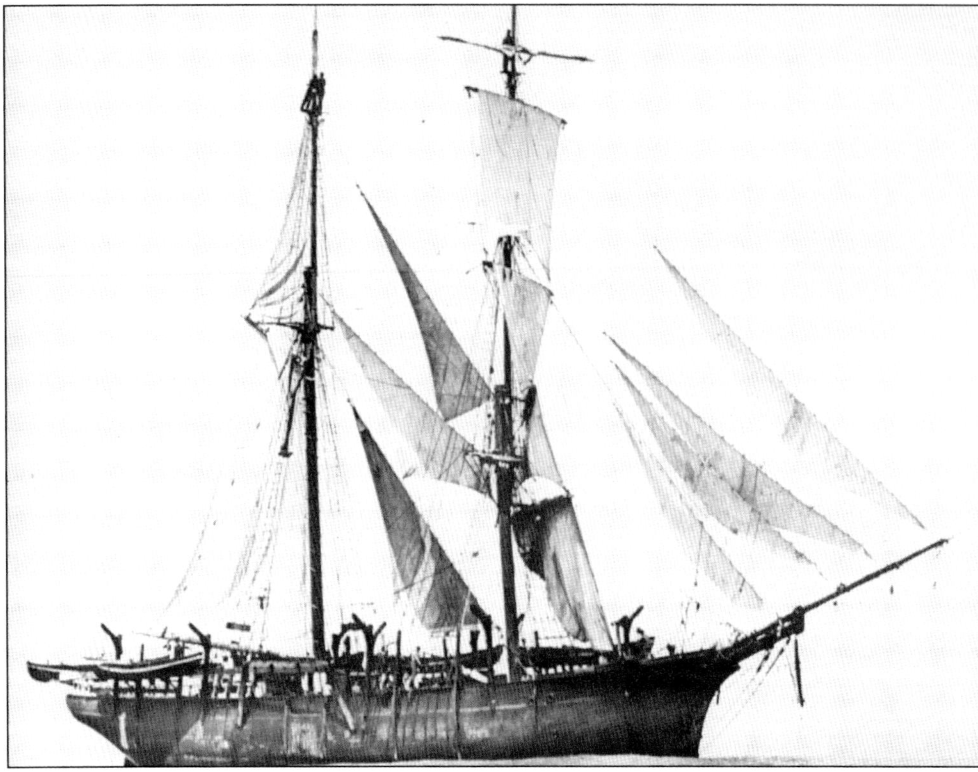

THE WHALING BRIG *DAISY*. This 1913 photograph by Robert Cushman Murphy shows the *Daisy* on the South Atlantic whaling grounds. The *Daisy*, built in 1872 at Setauket by Nehemiah Hand, was the 26th of 33 hulls he built between 1836 and 1882. It was 384 gross tons, 123 overall length, two decked, framed with white oak and chestnut, planked with longleaf pine, and copper fastened. It served first as a merchantman and then as a whaler, with Benjamin Cleveland of New Bedford as master and Dr. Robert Cushman Murphy as a passenger/naturalist. After the voyage with Murphy, it then went back into merchant service and was lost at sea in 1916. The silhouette of the *Daisy* appears in the logo of the Three Village Historical Society.

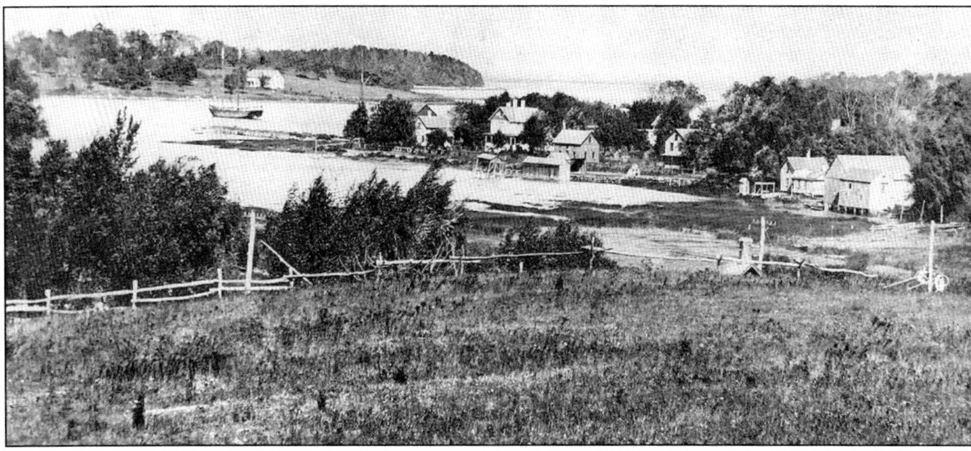

A VIEW FROM SCHOOLHOUSE HILL, C. 1890. This view shows the electric poles along Main Street at the base of the hill. Shore Road is at the center with Strong's Neck in the distance. (Courtesy of Beverly and Barbara Tyler.)

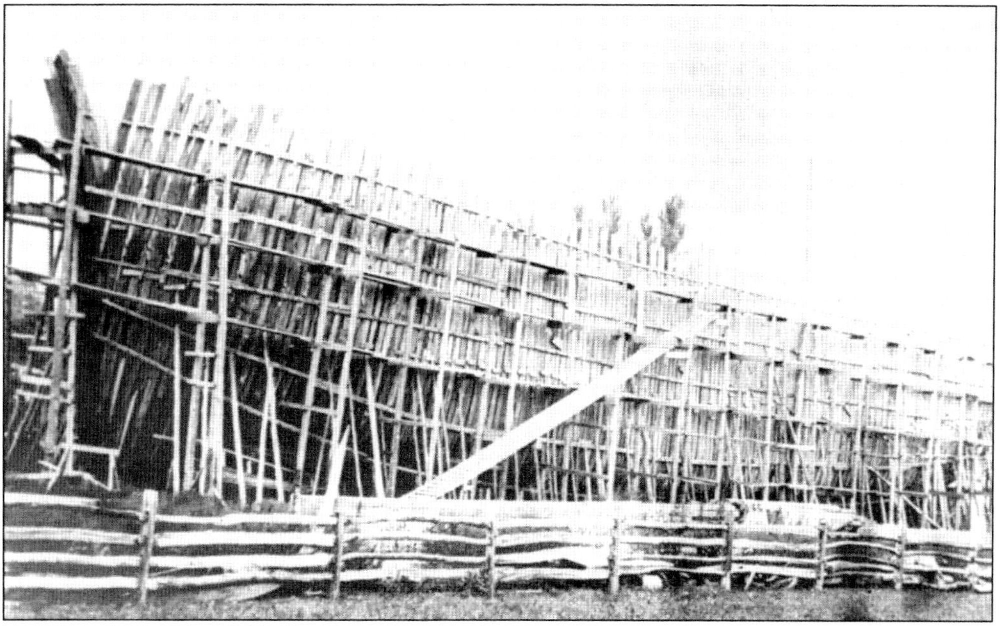

THE BIG SHIP. The *Wilkesbarre* was 240 feet long, 47 feet wide and scheduled to draw 34 feet. Building began in 1880 by David Bayles at his boatyard, which was opposite approximately 73 Shore Road. Financial reverses prevented the original owners from completing the ship. Other investors cut off the upper portion of "the big ship" and turned the remainder into a steam-propelled coal barge of 1,631 gross tons that drew 19.5 feet.

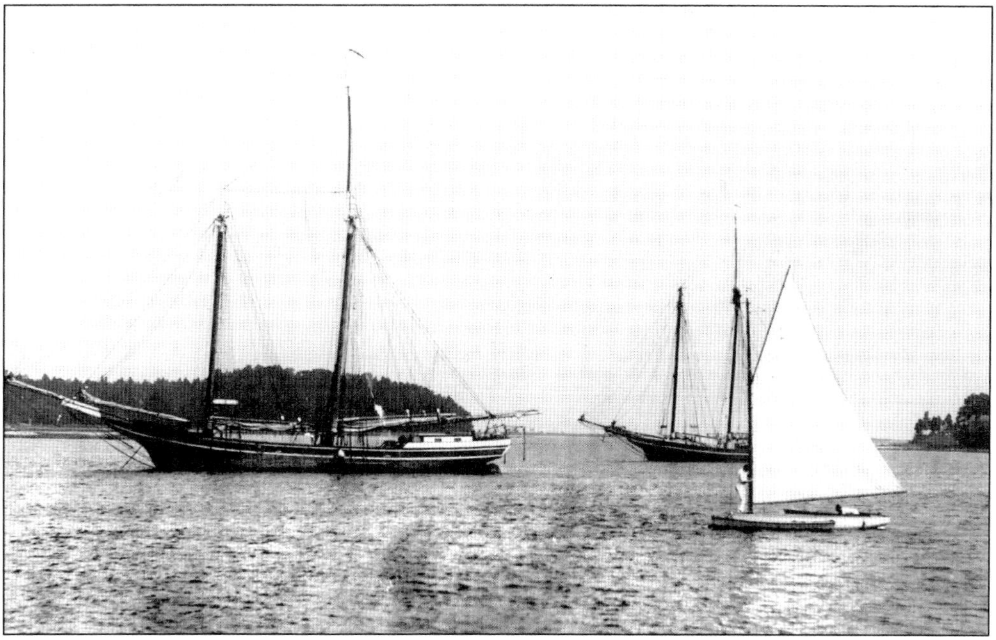

SETAUKET HARBOR, C. 1910. Strong's Neck is at the left and Tinker Point at the right in this image. The *H. V. Duree* is on the left and *Louise*, with Capt. Albert Nelson as master, is at the far right. The catboat in the foreground is unidentified. The *Louise* was towed to Scott's Cove and abandoned in 1920. (Courtesy of Betty Voss and Julia Oakes Darling.)

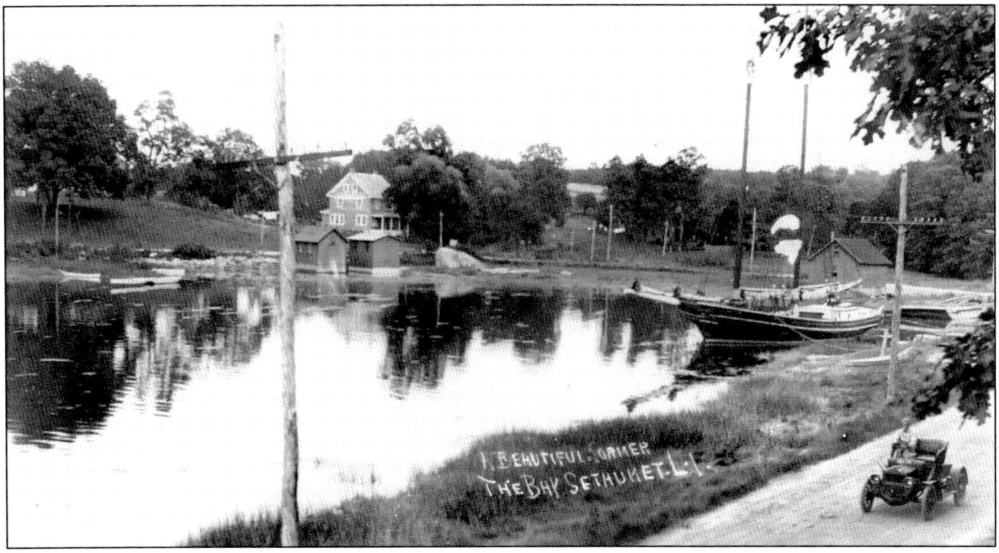

SCOTT'S COVE, C. 1911. The second Van Brunt Homestead is on the far shore at center. Two oyster shacks are on the shore in front of the home of James Van Brunt, at 45 Van Brunt Manor Road (built 1911). The schooner at the quay, possibly the *Deborah Hendrickson*, is likely to be unloading coal. Blue Point Oyster Company's oyster house is at the head of the cove beyond the schooner. The oysters were gathered in the harbor and shipped to New York City through Port Jefferson. The car at the right is a 1910 Reo. (Courtesy of Julia Oakes Darling.)

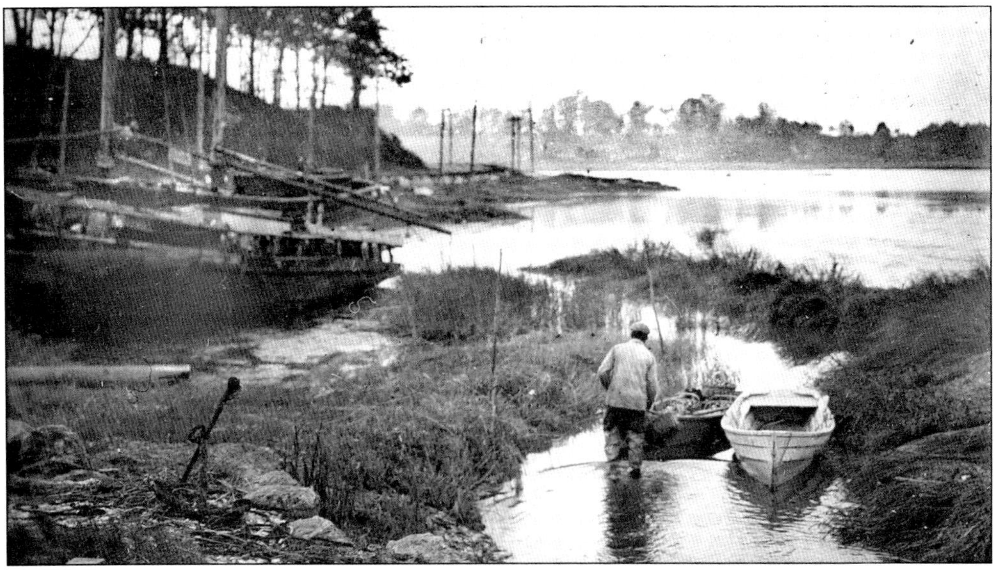

UNLOADING OYSTERS, SCOTT'S COVE, C. 1925. Photographer Edward L. Tinker captured this scene at Scott's Cove. The bayman in the foreground is preparing to unload his catch of oysters. To his left is the *Deborah Hendrickson* (28 gross tons), which was built at Keyport, New Jersey, in 1867. Capt. Willett Young of Stony Brook sailed it from Port Jefferson. Beyond the *Deborah Hendrickson* and closer to the shore lies the *Louise* (47 gross tons), which was built in Wilmington, North Carolina, in 1881. Capt. Alfred Nelson of Setauket also sailed it from Port Jefferson. Abandoned in 1920, it joined the already abandoned *Deborah Hendrickson*. The keel and ribs of these ships are still visible at low tide.

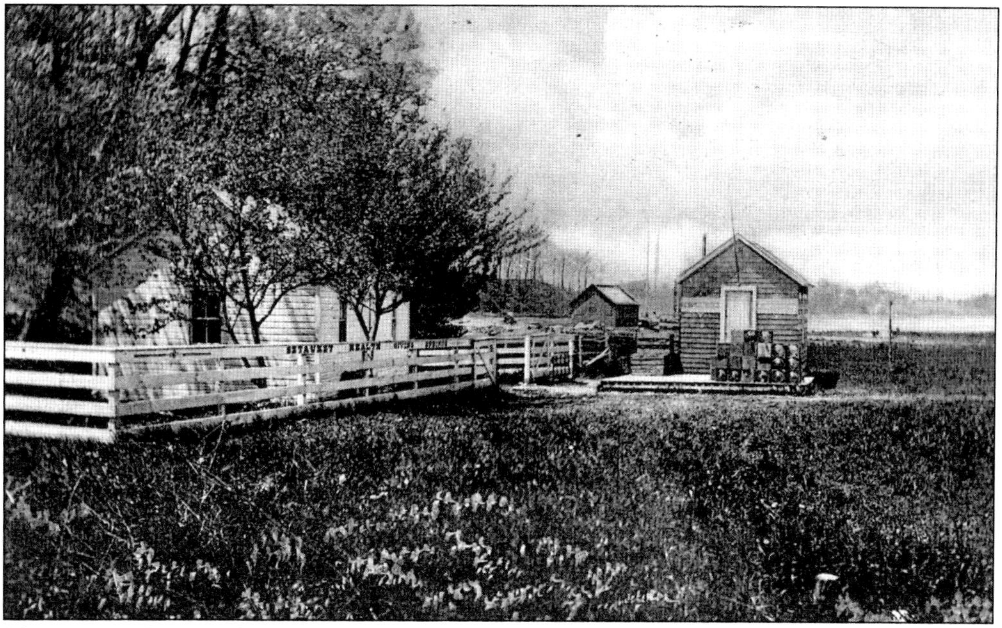

"SETAUKET HEALTH GIVING SPRINGS," C. 1910. This springwater company was located on Scott's Cove at Van Brunt Manor Road and Shore Road. William Risley, who started in the oyster business in the 1890s, built the oyster houses at the shore. After the oysters were gathered and sorted, they were stored in these sheds while awaiting shipment to market. About 1910, Risley's springwater company converted the oyster houses into a bottling operation that sold water in Brooklyn.

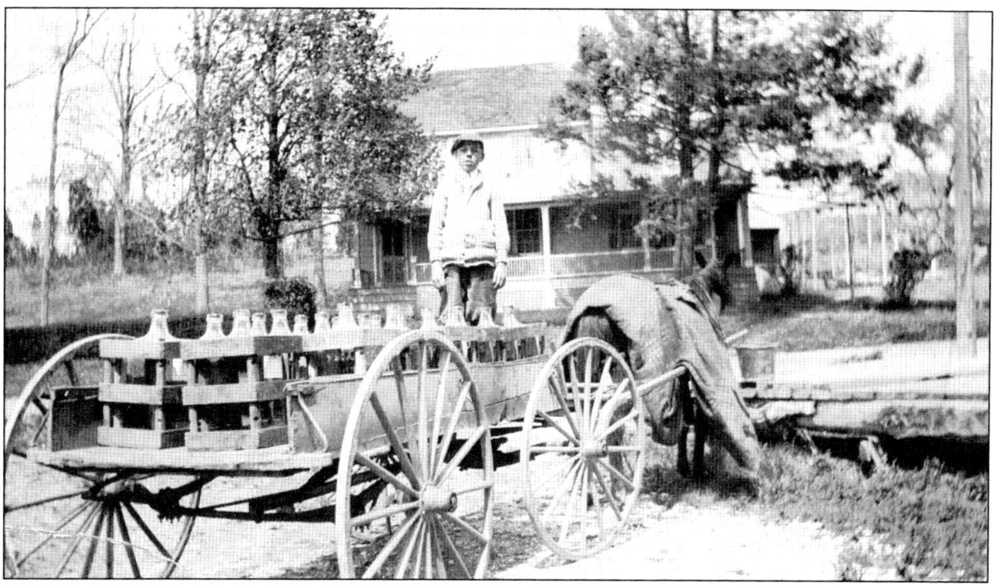

DELIVERING WATER, C. 1915. The water-delivery wagon for the "Setauket Health Giving Springs" in front of 41 Van Brunt Manor Road is depicted in this image. (Courtesy of John Lane.)

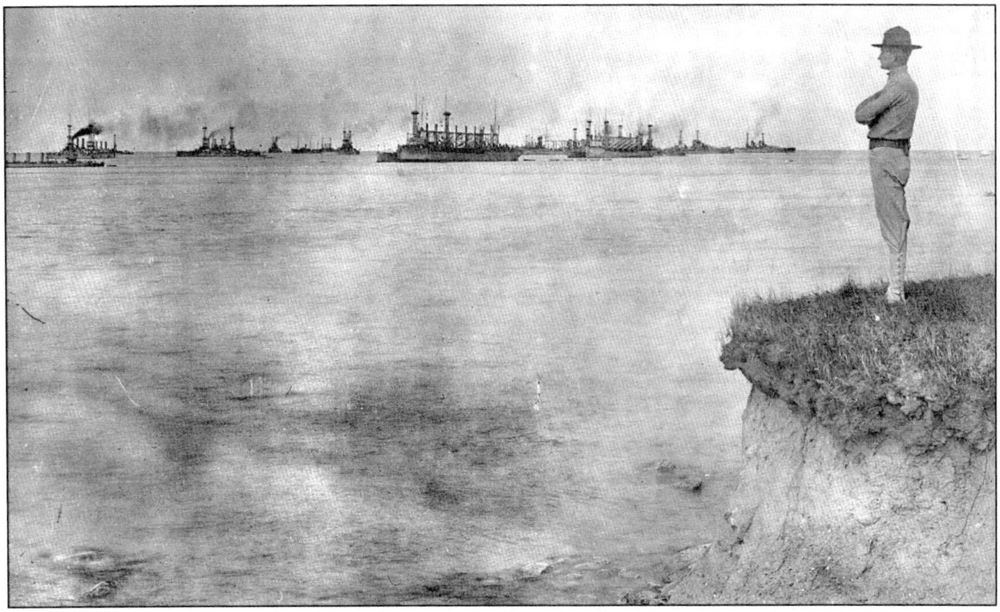

OLD FIELD POINT, SEPTEMBER 1917. The 20 vessels of the United States North Atlantic Fleet were anchored here for over a month. Among the ships in this photograph are the battleships USS *Arizona*, now resting in Pearl Harbor; USS *New York*; USS *Wisconsin*; USS *Minnesota*; USS *Virginia*; USS *Missouri (I)*; USS *Pennsylvania*; USS *Alabama*; USS *Maine (II)*; and USS *Kearsarge*. The USS *Texas* was supposed to be part of this operation but ran aground off Block Island.

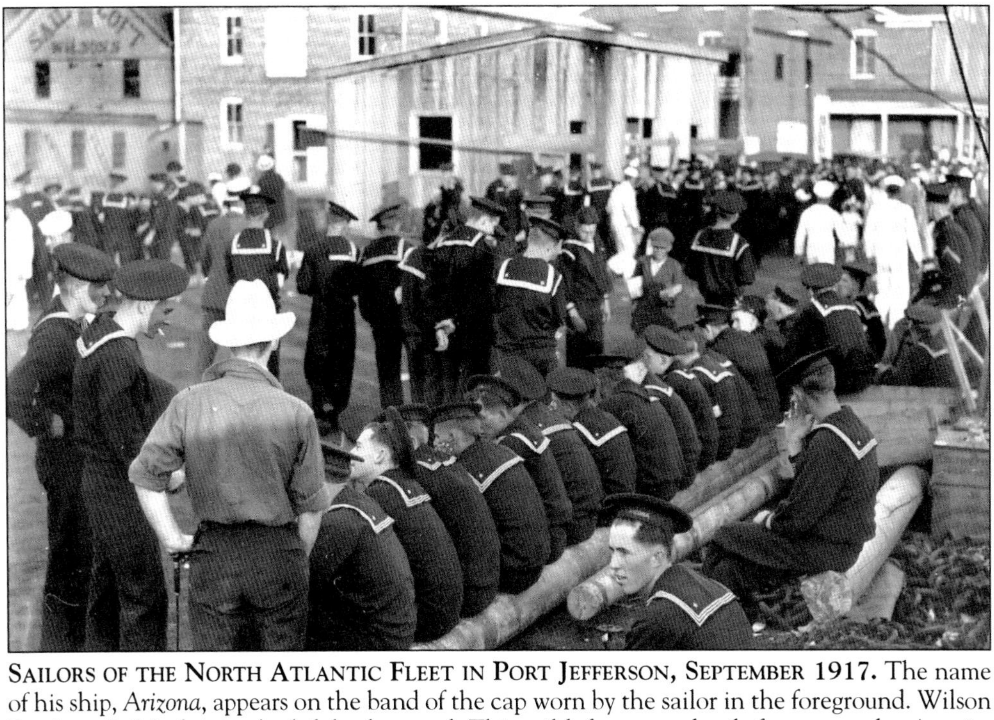

SAILORS OF THE NORTH ATLANTIC FLEET IN PORT JEFFERSON, SEPTEMBER 1917. The name of his ship, *Arizona*, appears on the band of the cap worn by the sailor in the foreground. Wilson Brothers Sail Loft is in the left background. This sail loft prepared sails for use on the *America* in its epic 1855 race.

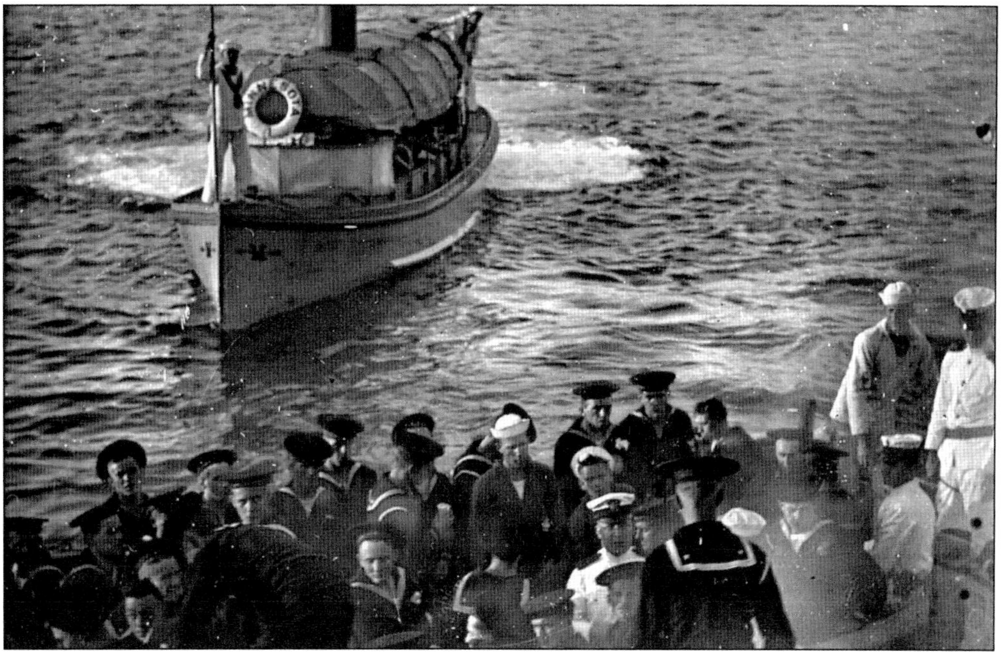

LIBERTY LAUNCH FROM THE USS *MINNESOTA*, SEPTEMBER 1917. This launch is approaching the dock in Port Jefferson; however, one of the principal landing points for the sailors of the fleet was Whitehall Beach. The sailors were then formed into units and marched from Old Field to Port Jefferson for liberty.

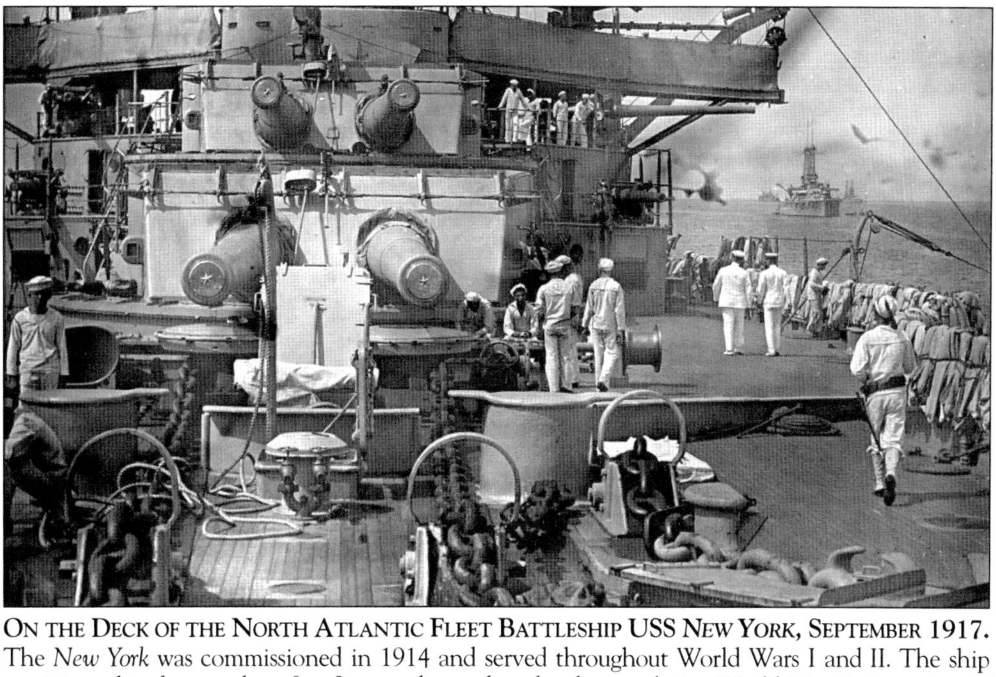

ON THE DECK OF THE NORTH ATLANTIC FLEET BATTLESHIP USS *NEW YORK*, SEPTEMBER 1917. The *New York* was commissioned in 1914 and served throughout World Wars I and II. The ship participated in the assault on Iwo Jima and won three battle stars during World War II. A survivor of the atomic blast at Bikini Atoll, the *New York* was sunk off Hawaii as a fleet exercise target on July 8, 1948. The USS *Nevada* or *Oklahoma* is at the right.

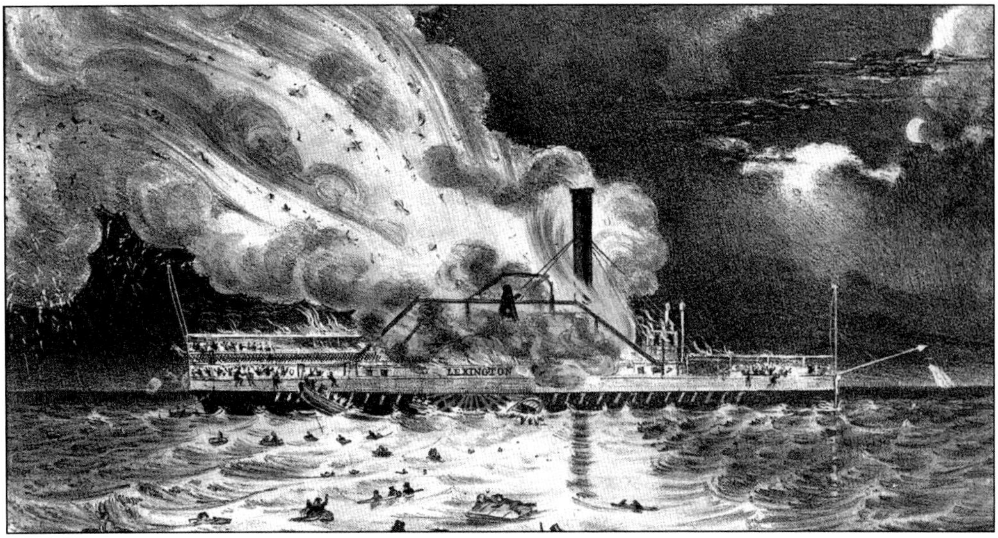

THE *LEXINGTON*. "Awful Conflagration of the Steam Boat Lexington, In Long Island Sound on Monday Eve., Jan. 13th 1840, by which melancholy occurrence, over 100 persons perished." The remains of this ship lie on the bottom of Long Island Sound off Old Field Light. This lithograph by Nathaniel Currier was a sensation and his first published image. The *Lexington* was Cornelius Vanderbilt's finest and fastest paddle wheeler, and on that fateful night, it carried a cargo of 150 cotton bales near the smokestack that started the fire. Local residents who witnessed the blaze were unable to render aid due to ice-packed harbors. Of the 150 men, women, and children on board, only 4 survived the blaze.

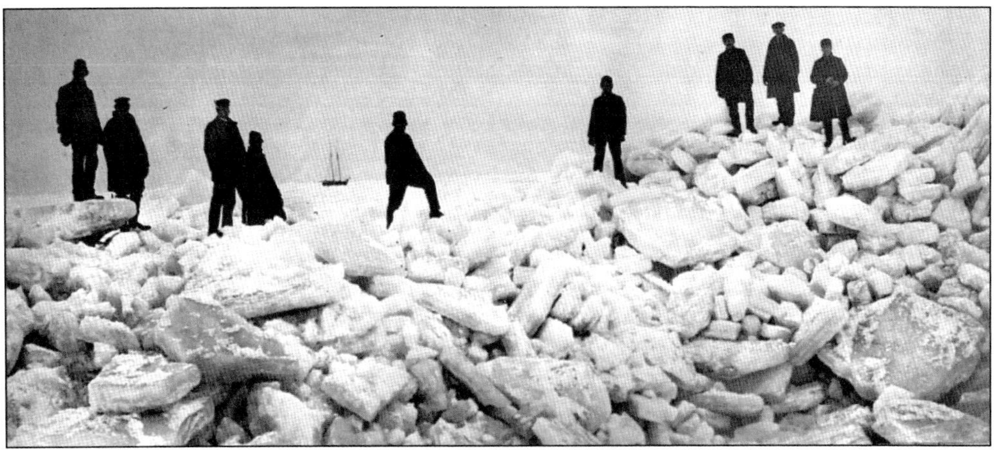

ICE AT OLD FIELD, FEBRUARY 16, 1904. Identified differently in three sources, the men pictured, from left to right, are Capt. Vincent Hallock (or Captain Edwards), Capt. Charles Harris of Port Jefferson (or Captain Hallock), Capt. John Terrell, Frank Howell (or Capt. Morse Hawkins, or Captain Hallock), Capt. Gilbert Hutchinson, Chief James Gurney, Capt. A. Morse Hawkins (or Capt. Byron Hallock), Elvin Hawkins, and Herbert Nelson. The schooner, seen one quarter-mile west of Old Field Point in the background, is either the *John Crockford* or the *Crawford*. The crew abandoned the ship for lack of food. The vessel was owned by Standard Oil Company and was loaded with oil barrels. It was salvaged by Captain Charles of East Setauket and eventually wrecked off Old Field. The dogs from the schooner came ashore at the Thatcher Estate, near the corner of Mount Grey and Old Field Roads in Old Field. (Photograph by Capt. Byron Hallock.)

Six

COMMUNITY ORGANIZATIONS

Schools, churches, synagogues, veterans' organizations, commemorative groups, fire departments, and even baseball fields provide focal points for people of similar interests. Many of these groups selflessly served the community as well as their own members. They have undergone an evolution that parallels that of society in general. What started as a series of isolated one-room schoolhouses coalesced into the Setauket School and then finally into the Three Village school district of today. Flocks of the various religious groups have waxed and waned with changes in employment and community development. In the time before television or even radio, baseball was a major community gathering point. On Sunday afternoons, teams from Setauket played teams from neighboring towns, attracting large crowds, to capture the appropriate bragging rights. The Setauket Volunteer Fire Department was organized and expanded as each new development was added to the fire district. It continues to be an important component of the community.

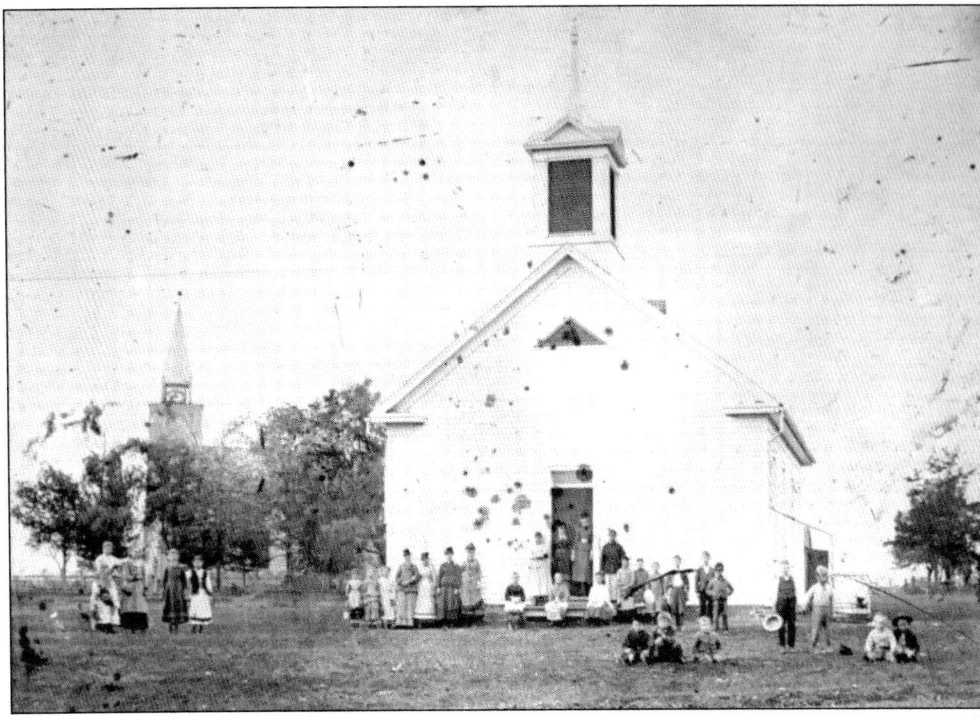

THE FIRST WEST SETAUKET SCHOOL ON THE VILLAGE GREEN, TINTYPE C. 1880. In 1893, the school board voted to expand this structure, built in 1869. The Caroline Church is seen at the left.

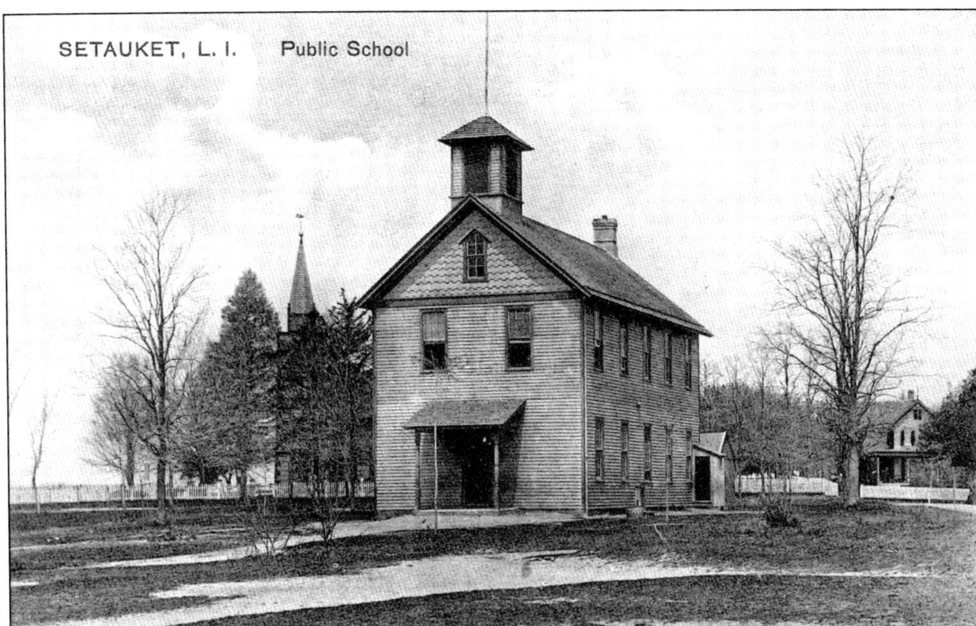

THE SECOND WEST SETAUKET SCHOOL ON THE VILLAGE GREEN, C. 1905. This view reflects the building after the addition of 1894. The second schoolhouse, with the original outhouses, remained in use until the new school on the hill was opened in 1911.

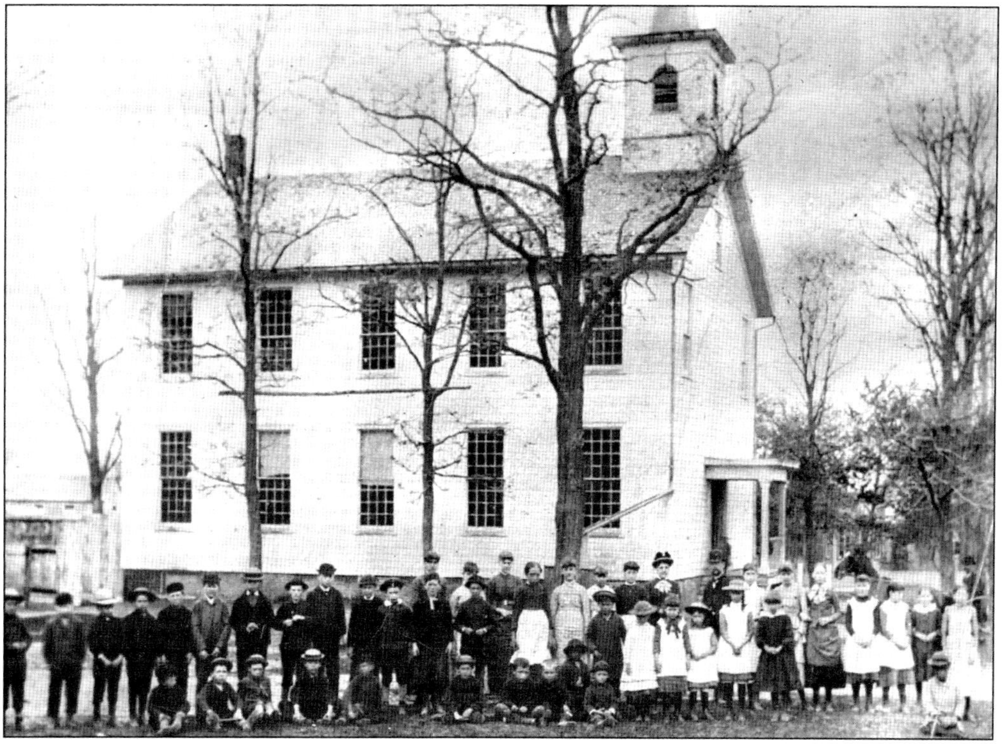

COACH ROAD SCHOOL, DISTRICT NO. 36, BUILT C. 1866. The Coach Road School, pictured here in 1898, had 44 students in grades 1 through 12, with a staff of one teacher and one principal. After the school closed in 1911, the building became an automotive repair shop. It is now an office building at Coach Road and Main Street.

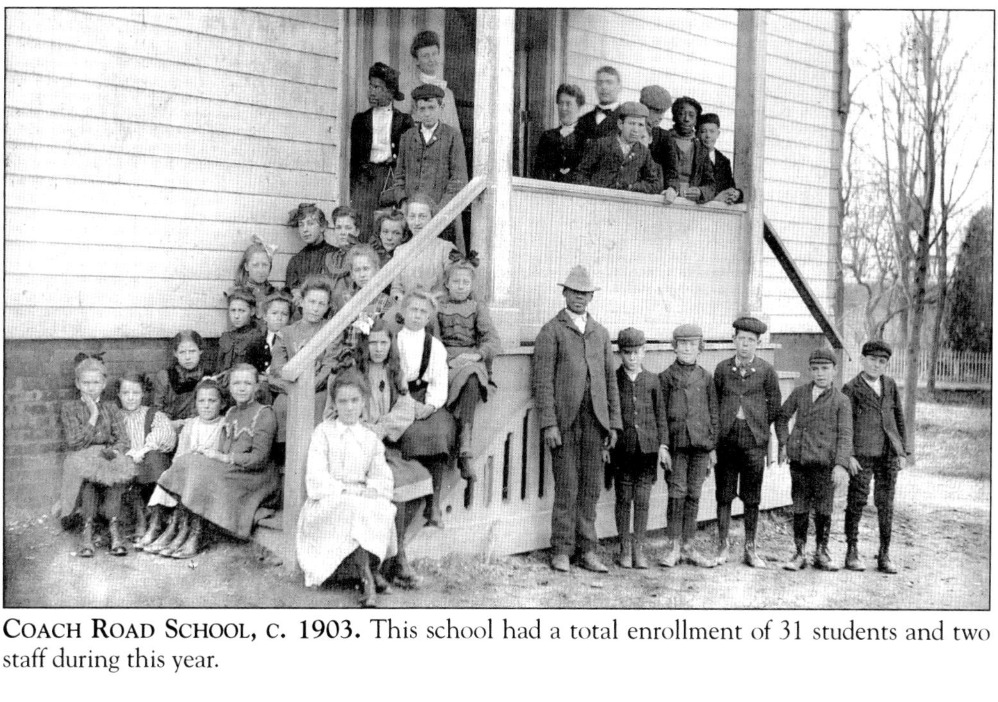

COACH ROAD SCHOOL, C. 1903. This school had a total enrollment of 31 students and two staff during this year.

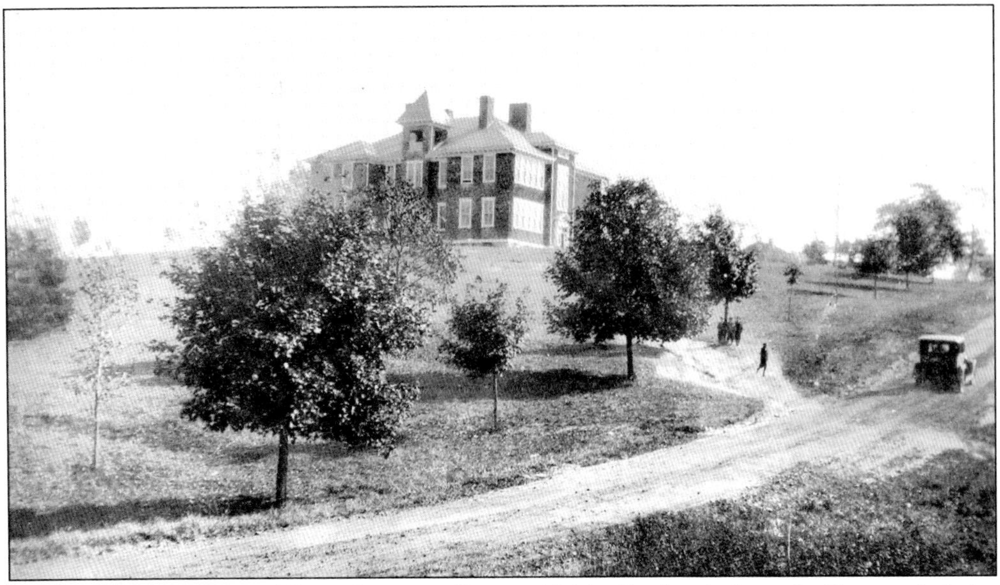

Setauket Grade and High School, Built 1911. Grades 1 through 12 attended the Setauket Union Free School, pictured here around 1925. The street in the foreground is Jones Street, with the drive to the school at the left. This school was at the top of the hill behind today's Mario's Restaurant Shopping Center. During World War II, Marge Bunn Edwards and her two young sons, Carleton (Hub) and Leroy (Beeb), were employed to clean the school after school hours. (Courtesy of Betty Voss.)

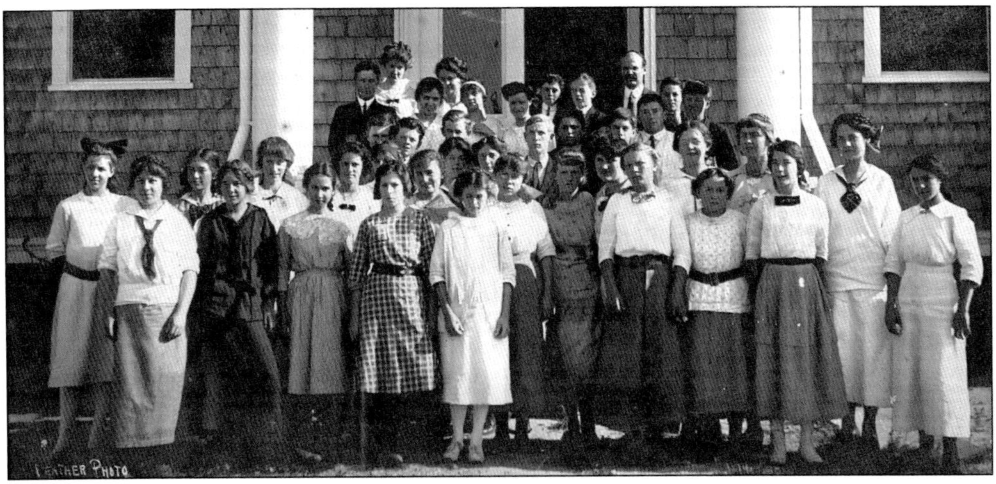

Students at Setauket Union Free School, c. 1915. As identified on the reverse of this photograph are, from left to right, the following: (first row) Ida Golden, Helen Walker, ? Fischer, Suzie Lyon, Carol Aldrich (in front, wearing white dress), Evelyn Hutchinson, Ada Jones, Grace Skidmore, Marion ?, Violet Brock, Helen Rottgers, and Lily Brock; (second row) Margaret Hutchinson, Muriel West, Lillian Hutchinson, Florence Wallace, unidentified, Libby Schlesinger, Marietta Smith, Beryl Denton, ? Schlesinger (sister of Elizabeth or Libby), Nina Davis, and Mary Jergensen; (third row) unidentified, Herb Macauley, Henry Jones, Jesse Howell, and the remainder of the row is unidentified; (fourth row) Willis Skidmore, Ruth Hawkins, Ruth Bishop, Mary West, Russel Rogers, Mark Murphy, and the remainder of the row is unidentified; (fifth row) Miss Center, Miss Quick, and Mr. Ranford. (Courtesy of Betty Voss)

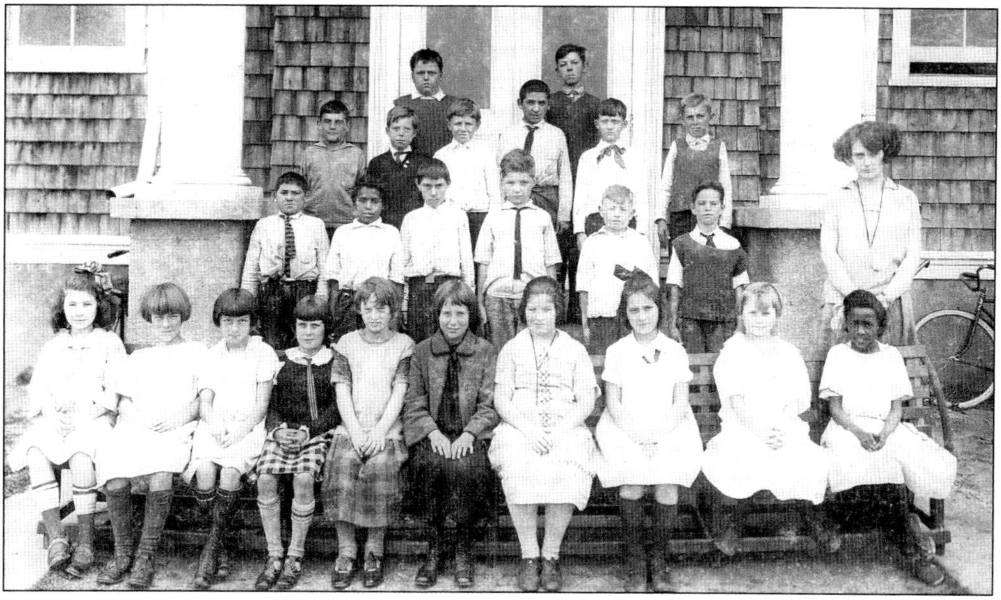

SETAUKET UNION FREE SCHOOL, C. 1929. From left to right in this photograph are the following: (first row) Sophie Stoehle, Henrietta Wells, Virginia Jayne, Kathleen Robinson, five unidentified students, and Violet Sells; (second row) Philip Laneri, Archie Stewart, Frank Gnasdowski, Andrew Lyon, Ed Pfeiffer, and William Deasy; (third row) unidentified, Beverly Tyler, two unidentified students, Thornton Hawkins, and unidentified; (fourth row) two unidentified students. The teacher is unidentified. (Courtesy of Betty Voss.)

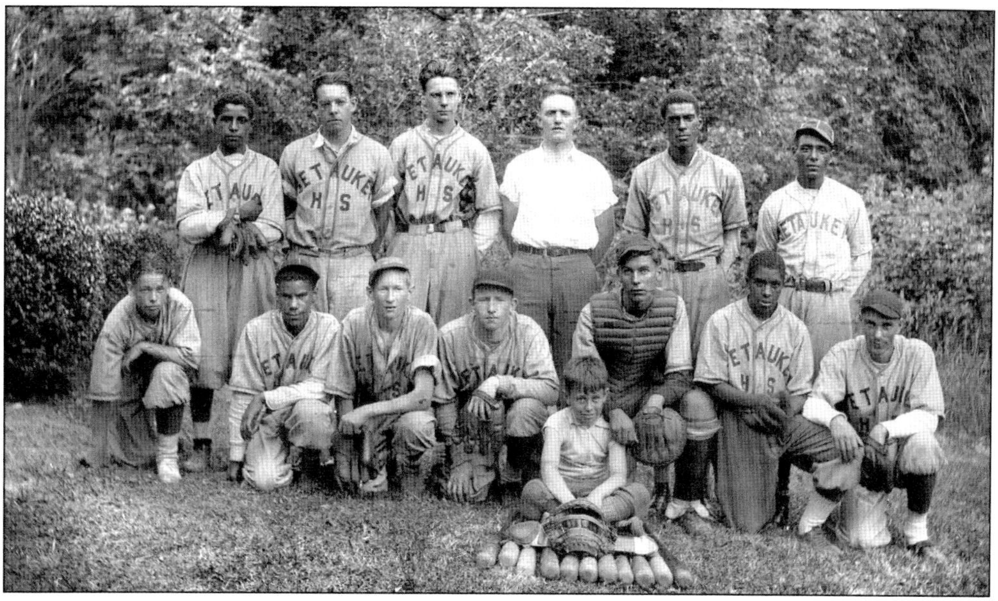

SETAUKET HIGH SCHOOL BASEBALL TEAM, 1935. Pictured in this photograph, from left to right, are the following: (first row) John Davis, William (Bo) Hart Jr., Richard (Cappy) Kapp, Edward Pfeiffer, Emmett Lyon (Bat Boy), Anthony (Ant) Matusky, Kenneth (Bones) Sells, and Frank Gnasdowski; (second row) Frederick (Douggy) Douglass, Steven Barnett, Carlyle Ritter, Dean Royce (coach), Ralph (Sam) Bunn, and Arnold (Arnie) Bunn. Edward Pfeiffer and Anthony Matusky were killed during World War II. (Courtesy of Carlton and Nellie Edwards.)

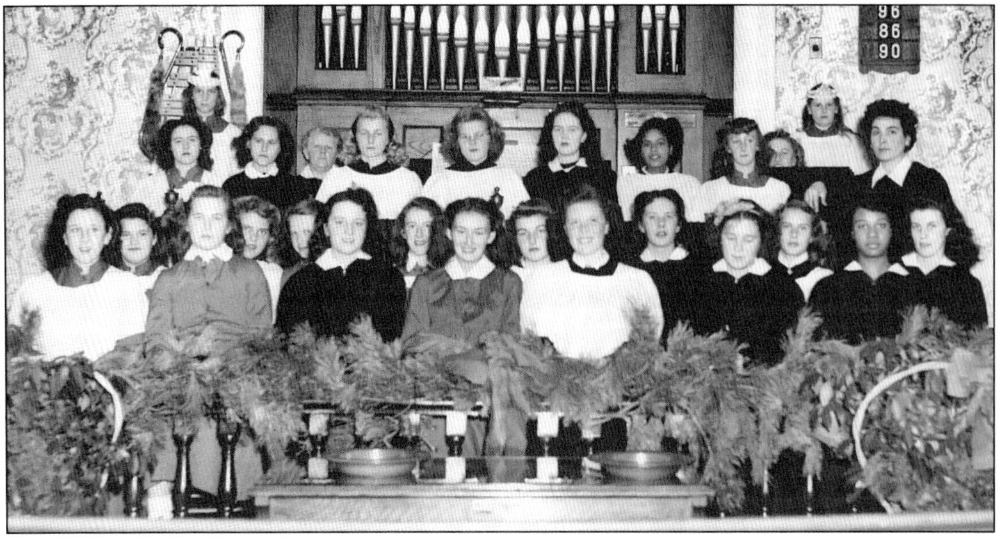

CHRISTMAS CHORAL GLEE CLUB, SETAUKET METHODIST CHURCH, C. 1945. In the this photograph, from left to right, are the following: (first row, seated) Ethelmae Emmerson, Myrna Junk, Mildred Costic, Marianne Hilliard, Pauline Costic, Betty Seiter, Barbara Meachum, Barbara Dorward, Barbara Muttit, Patricia Baker, Betty Schmeelk, Jane Stehlin, Virginia Schmeelk, Shirley Daniels, and Barbara Wolfe; (second row) Gloria Post, Marilyn Wishart, Mildred Heinz (organist), Martha Wells, Edith Hoffmoen, Florence Carpenter, Millicent Bunn, Gillian Dorward, Mary Klem, and Miss Aidala (choir director); (third row) unidentified. (Courtesy of Betty Voss.)

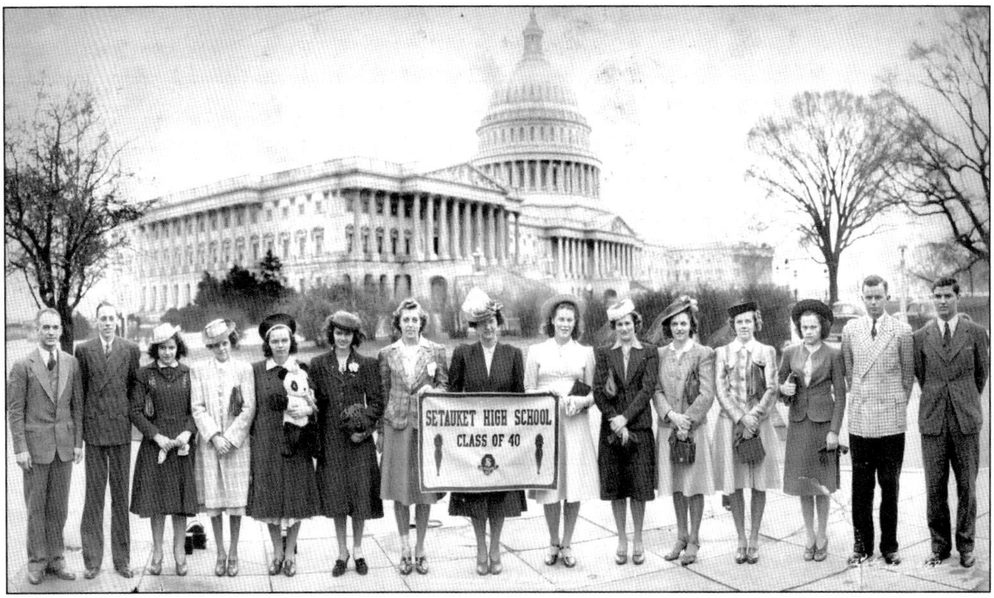

SETAUKET HIGH SCHOOL CLASS OF 1940. Class members of 1940, from left to right, are Mr. Welch (principal), Kenneth McElroy, Ethel Poulos (Contogine), Grace Osborn, Claudine Mollet (Dempsey), Freya Bruce (Szerbiak), Gertrude Kohlman (Barnett), Alice Grey (Augustitis), Norma Whiton (Glinick), Ada Shiels (Woodard), Ruth Pettit (Rothermel), Marjorie Heinz (Shawhan), Janice Washburn (Arnold), Robert Mollet, and Robert Gerard. (Courtesy of Robert and Wilma Gerard.)

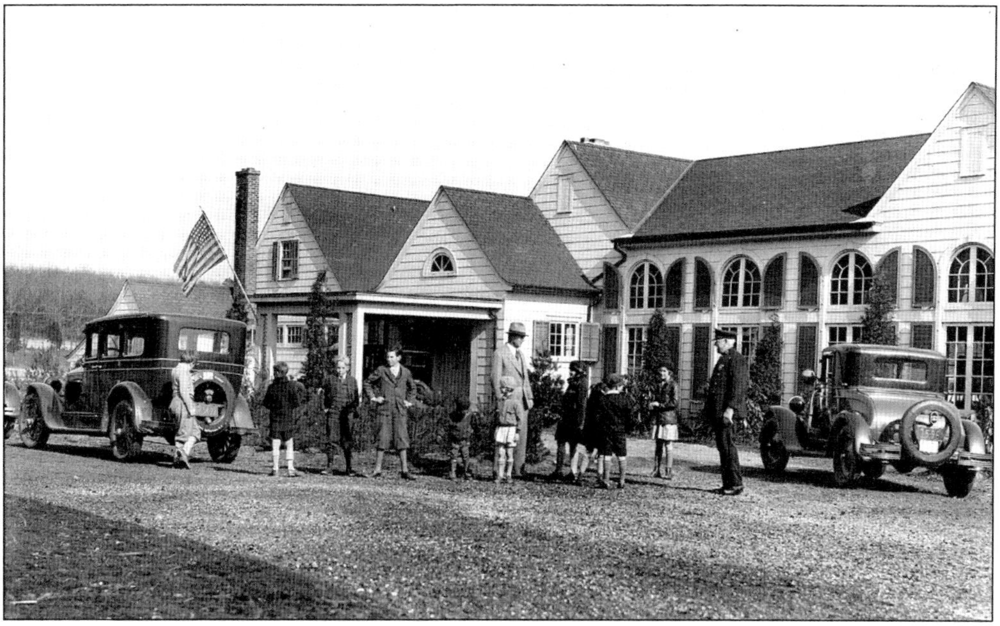

OLD FIELD COUNTRY DAY SCHOOL, 1930. Florenz Mahoney, the Old Field chief of police, is at the right next to his new Chevrolet police car.

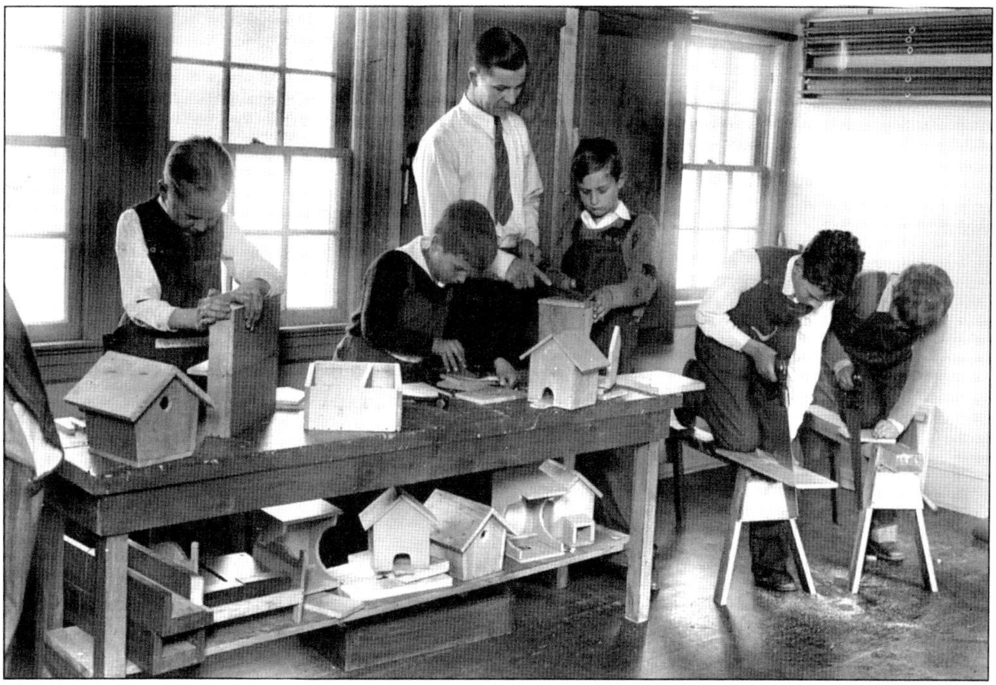

BUILDING BIRD HOUSES AT THE OLD FIELD COUNTRY DAY SCHOOL, C. 1930. From left to right are Ted Maddock, Remington Twitchell, Mr. Conklin, David Murphy, ? Haslopp, and an unidentified boy.

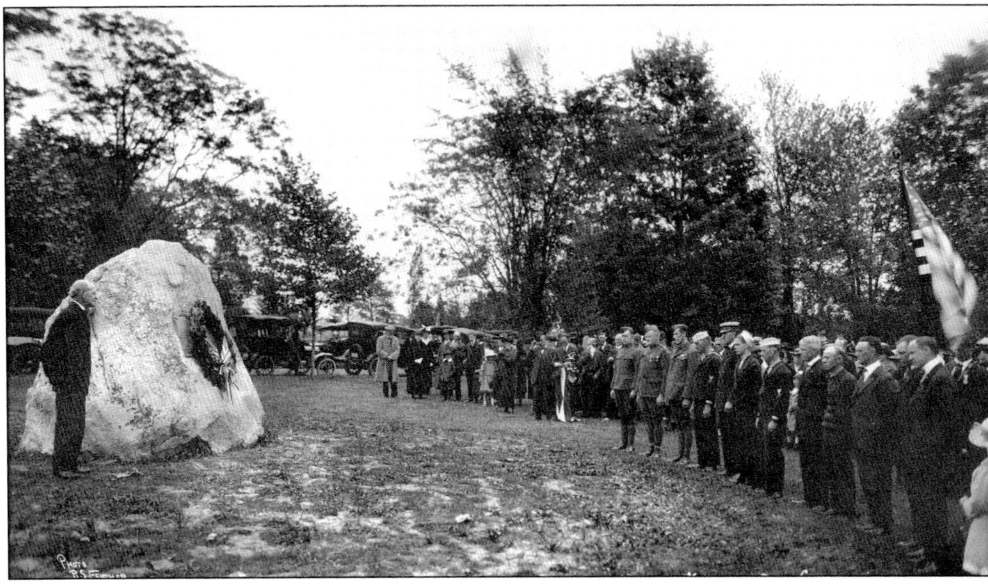

MEMORIAL DAY 1921, SETAUKET VILLAGE GREEN. This ceremony honors the World War I veterans that enlisted between 1914 and 1918. These veterans included Henry Bristol, Louis Bristol, Edwin Melville Bryant, Charles Buehrman, William Byron, Eversley Childs Jr., William Childs, Mary Elderkin, Julius Friedman, Howard Gibb, Louis Goldberg, Max Goldberg, Harry Golden (killed in action), Edward Graham, Irving Hart, William Hart, Alfred Hawkins, Daniel Hawkins, Floyd Hawkins, Raymond Hawkins, Hattie Jayne, Corneil Kiendl, Oliver Lyon, Ralph Lyon, Percy McCauley, Archibald McLaren, J. Ward Melville, George Mohlman, David O'Leary, Edward Pfeiffer, William Pfeiffer, Samuel Pinnes, Lawrence Rossiter, Silas Seaman, Albert Sells, Joseph Sells, Frank Shields, Marco Smith, Ray Terrell, Leon Tyler, Hanford M. Twitchell, Pierrepont E. Twitchell, Ernest West, George West, Harvey West, Percy West, David Wishart, and Raymond Wishart (killed in action).

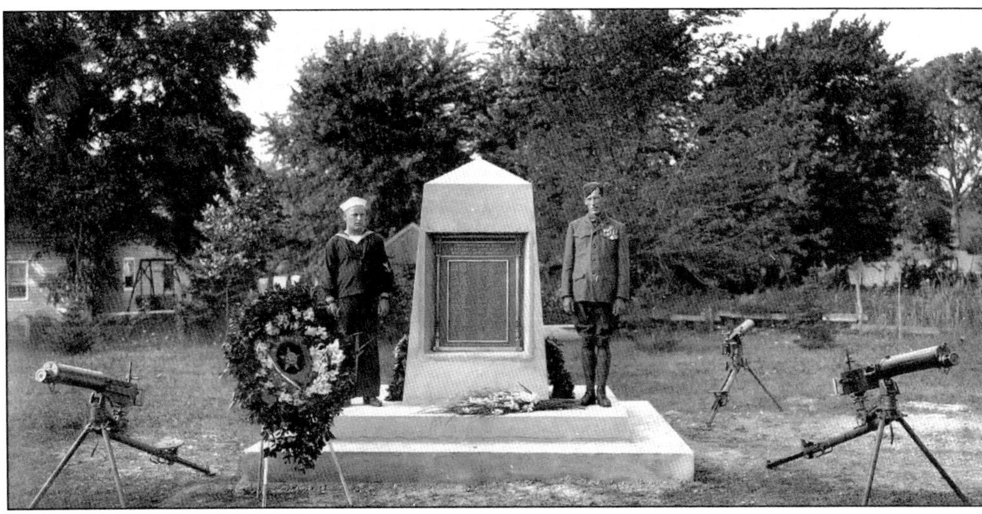

WORLD WAR I MEMORIAL ON THE EAST SETAUKET GREEN, 1925. Located at Shore Road and Main Street (Route 25A), the World War I memorial was dedicated on Labor Day, September 3, 1923. Ralph Lyon is at the left, and William Byron is at the right. The plaques from this monument are now in the lobby of the Setauket School. (Courtesy of Betty Voss)

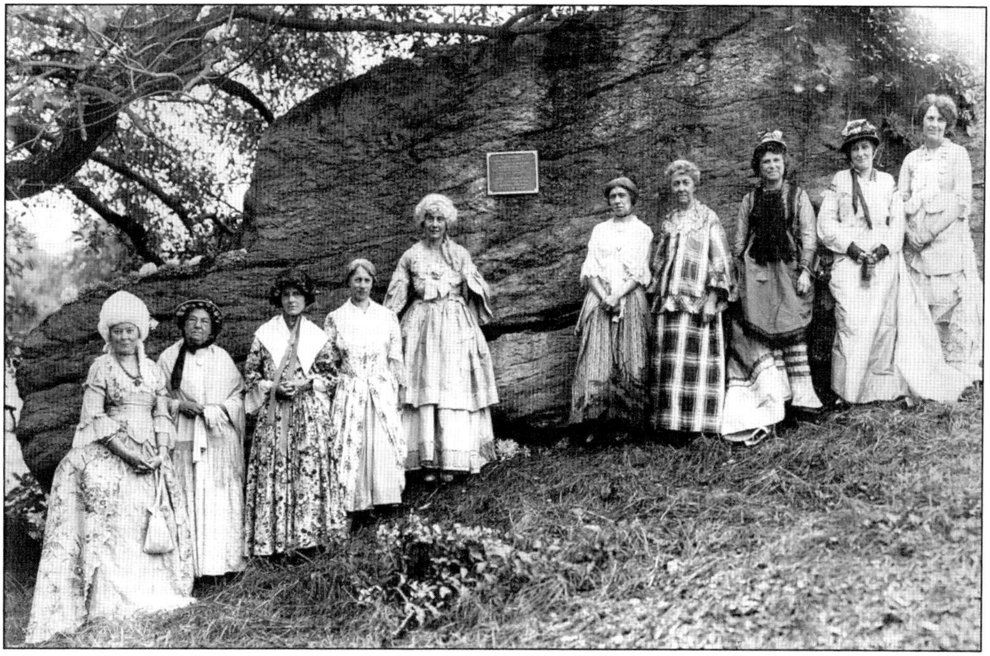

PATRIOT'S ROCK DEDICATION, DAUGHTERS OF THE REVOLUTION, AUGUST 24, 1927. From left to right are Mrs. Liftchild, Susie Williamson, Bessie Haydon, Glacie Payne, Florence Wells, Mildred Hawkins, Corrine Tyler, Buelah Smith, Abie Adams, and Amelia Clay. On August 22, 1777, patriot raiders used this rock for cover while firing on the British, who were quartered in the Presbyterian church.

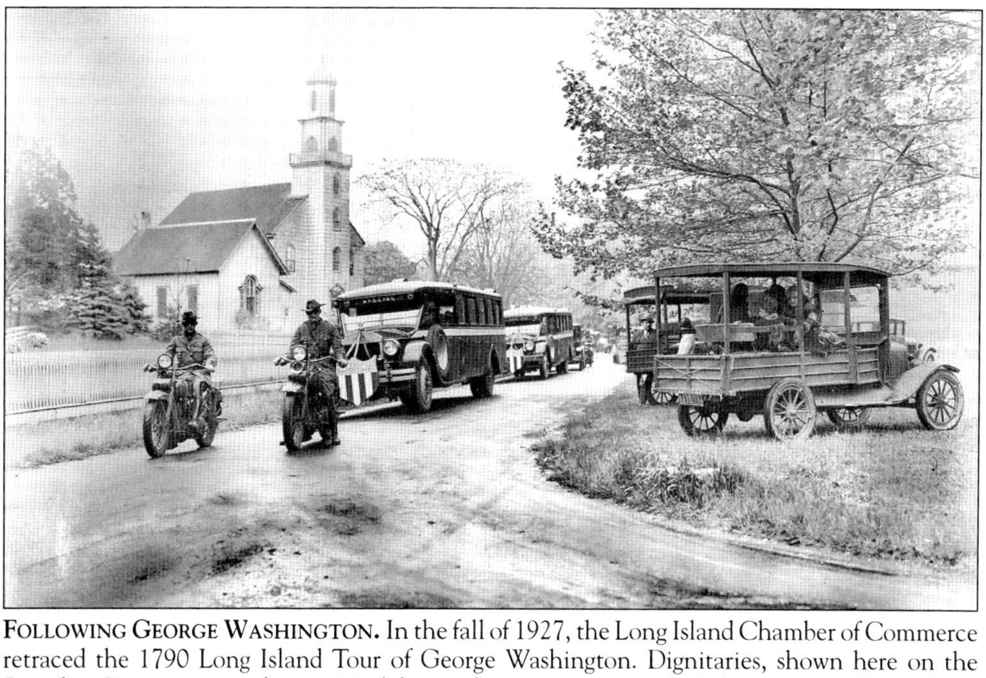

FOLLOWING GEORGE WASHINGTON. In the fall of 1927, the Long Island Chamber of Commerce retraced the 1790 Long Island Tour of George Washington. Dignitaries, shown here on the Setauket Green, are traveling in Mack buses, the state troopers ride Indian motorcycles, and the spectators are in Model T Ford Hucksters.

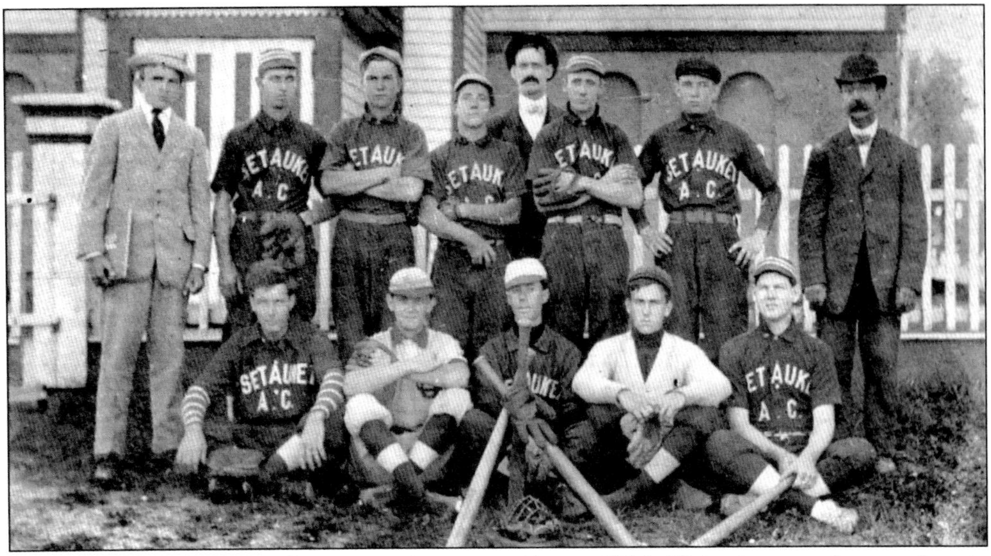

BASEBALL TEAM OF THE SETAUKET ATHLETIC CLUB, 1909. This photograph was taken in front of the Setauket Methodist Church. Pictured are, from left to right, the following: (first row) Raymond Hawes (first base), Alvin Jacobsen (pitcher), Preston (Pret) Lyons (second base), Havens Bishop (fielder), and Welcome D. Carnes (utility and Methodist minister); (second row) Lester Hand Jayne (club secretary), Ralph (Black Duck) Hawkins (third base), Roy Gildersleeve (fielder), Ray Hawkins (short stop), Al Fowler (manager), Cleveland Davis (fielder), Robert Jayne (catcher), and George Kraus (social manager).

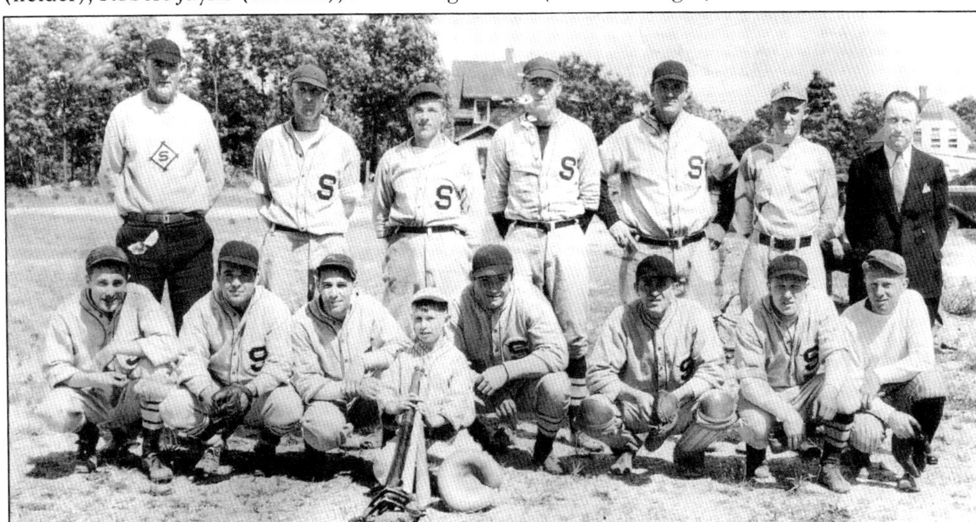

SETAUKET BASEBALL TEAM, JULY 3, 1932. Seen here are, from left to right, the following: (first row) George Smith (catcher), Harry Bedell (third base), Joseph (Jess) Eikov (first base), Bobby Emmett Lyons (batboy), Steve Buchanan (pitcher), unidentified, Ben Smith (outfield), and Arthur Chadwick (outfield); (second row) George Bruce (manager), Jeffrey (Jet) Howell, unidentified, Ed Danowski (shortstop who later played football for the New York Giants), Charles Danowski (fielder and pitcher), Pete Danowski (pitcher), and Ken McCambridge (spectator). Missing from the photograph is Bob Eikov (second base). The field in this photograph was at the corner of Route 25A and Van Brunt Manor Road, Cardwell's Corner. (Courtesy of Sherman Mills.)

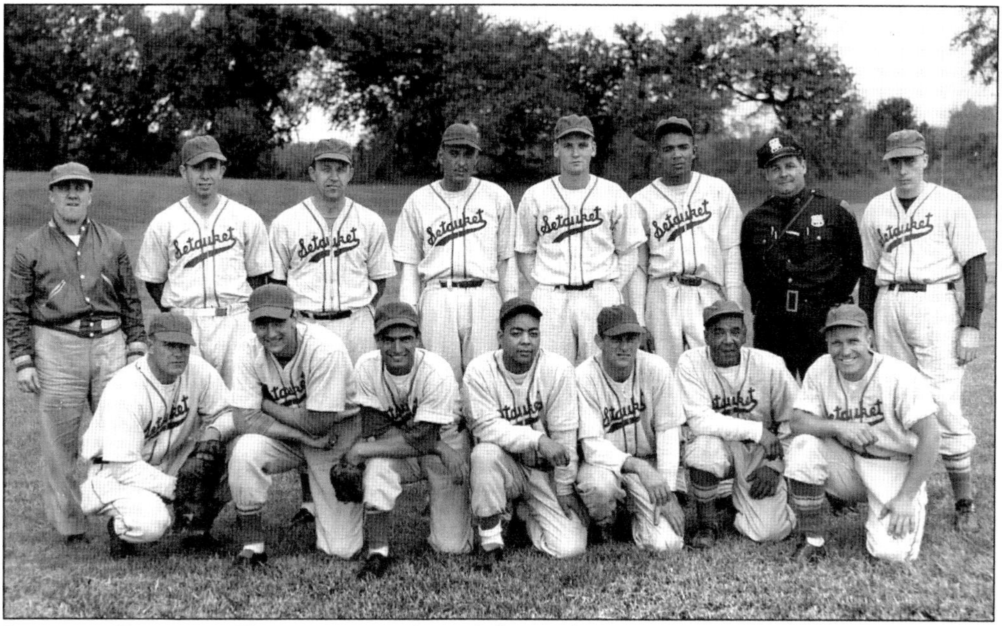

SETAUKET BASEBALL TEAM, C. 1951. From left to right in this picture are the following: (first row) Tony Mastauskas, Joe Carrabus, Rudy Carrabus, Carlton (Hubble) Edwards, Donald Jayne, William Bunn, and Wilfred Johnson; (second row) Bill Owen, Emmet Lyon, Henry Duchnowski, Ralph Bunn, Edward Lacagnin, Leroy (Beeb) Edwards, Bill Brown, and Roy Still. (Courtesy of Betty Voss.)

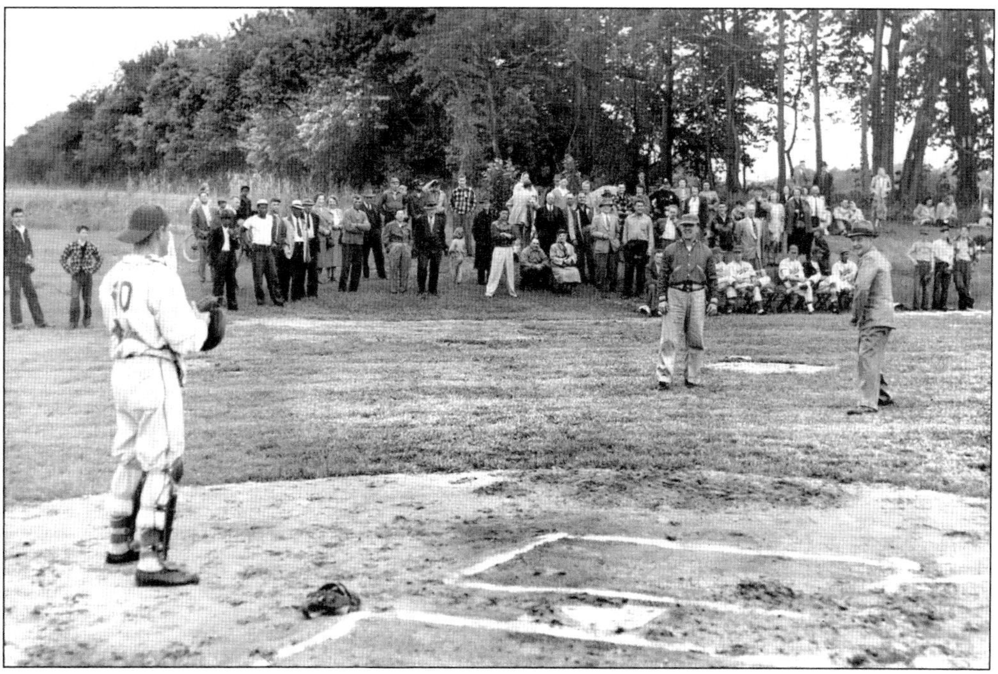

SETAUKET BASEBALL TEAM OPENING DAY, C. 1948. At Cardwell's Corner Field, Donald (Donnie) Jayne, awaits the first pitch, while coach Bill Owen watches with Sam (Mookie) Eikov at the right. (Courtesy of Betty Voss.)

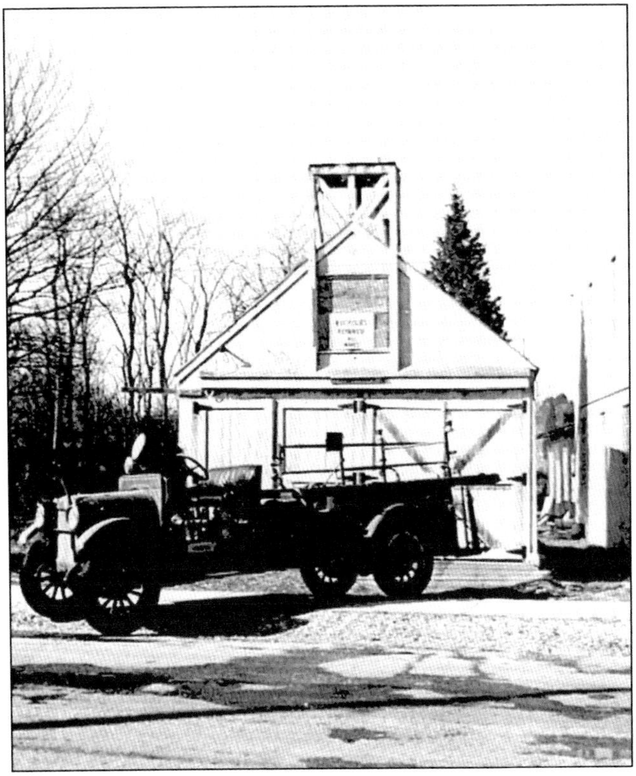

THE FIRST SETAUKET FIREHOUSE, C. 1929. The firehouse, located at approximately 28 Shore Road, is pictured here with a c. 1923 Ahrens-Fox fire truck out front. This building was moved to the Sherwood-Jayne House on Old Coach Road by the Society for the Preservation of Long Island Antiquities.

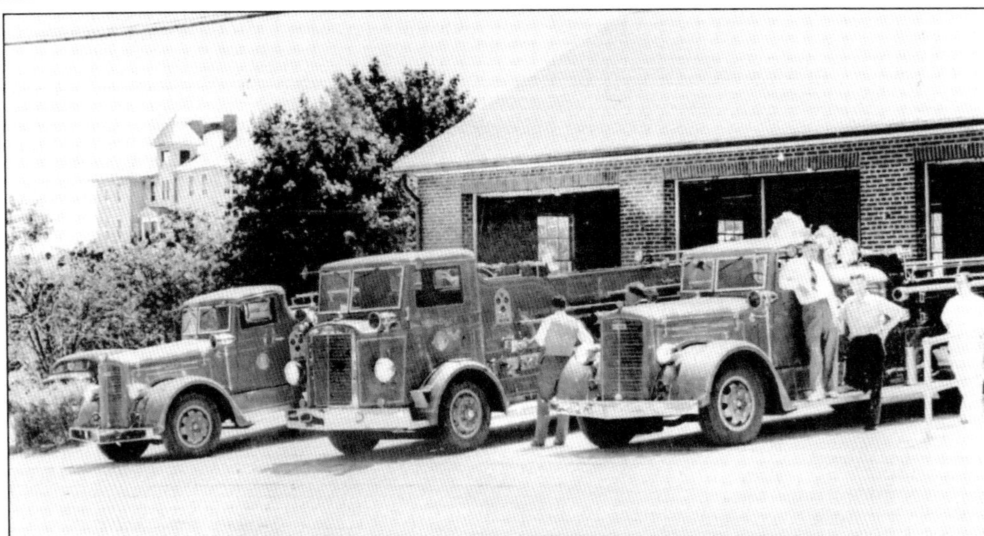

SETAUKET FIRE DEPARTMENT, C. 1940. Robert S. Gerard was contracted to build this firehouse in 1939. The 1939 Ward LaFrance trucks, from left to right, are the pumper, the hook and ladder, and the "Six Lighter" searchlight truck. The Six Lighter was sold to the Stony Brook fire department, who restored it. It was then resold back to Setauket. Royal Hawkins is in the middle of the three men at the right. The three trucks were all purchased at once with the help of J. Ward Melville. The Ward LaFrance Company was so happy for the order that they donated a fourth, a Diamond T truck.

Seven

PEOPLE OF SETAUKET

In the middle of the 19th century, the people of Setauket represented a cross section of the Long Island population. Most were farmers, selling to local and distant markets. Many cut cordwood to bring cash into the community. Skilled craftsmen worked in the shipyards or were in the employ of other community members. Some worked in the piano or rubber factories. All of these were supported by shopkeepers who provided the goods not produced locally. The descendents of the local Native Americans were present, active, and part of the community fabric. Some farmed but most provided a labor force for the community. Families of upper-middle class or greater means were present and conspicuous, but their source of income generally came from outside Setauket. They had the ability to shape portions of the community to their liking and have left the present residents with a legacy that provides a good deal of the ambience of the area. It was the "common folk," however, with their devotion to churches, synagogues, schools, service organizations, and, above all, their concern for each other, that made Setauket a community.

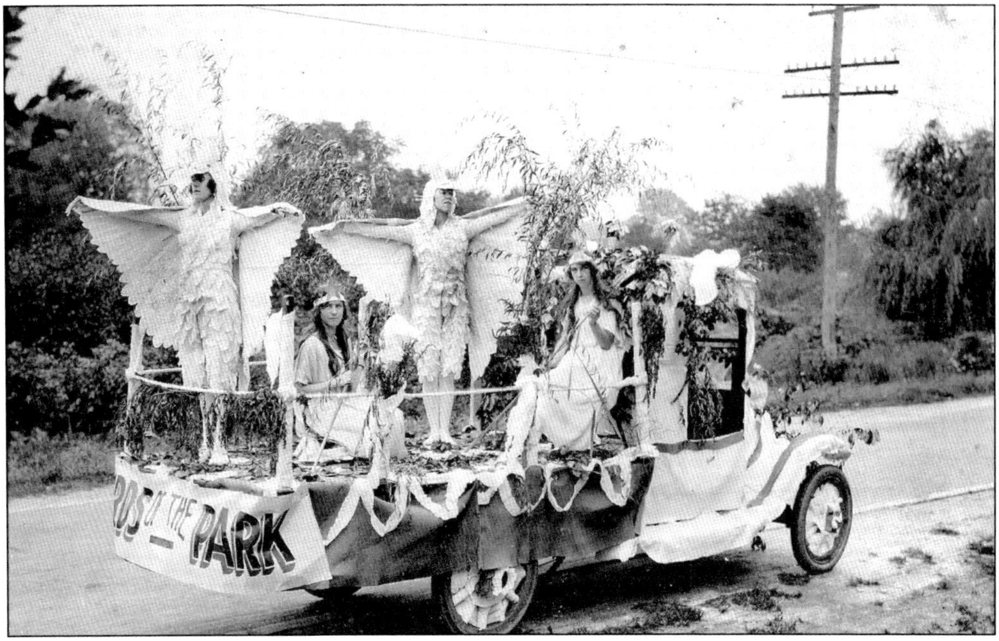

OUR HERO PARADE, LABOR DAY, SEPTEMBER 1, 1919. The celebration welcomed the boys home from World War I. "Birds of the Park" are, from left to right, Ada R. Jones (Young), Verna Baldwin (Eikov), Vivian Edwards, and Laura Hawkins.

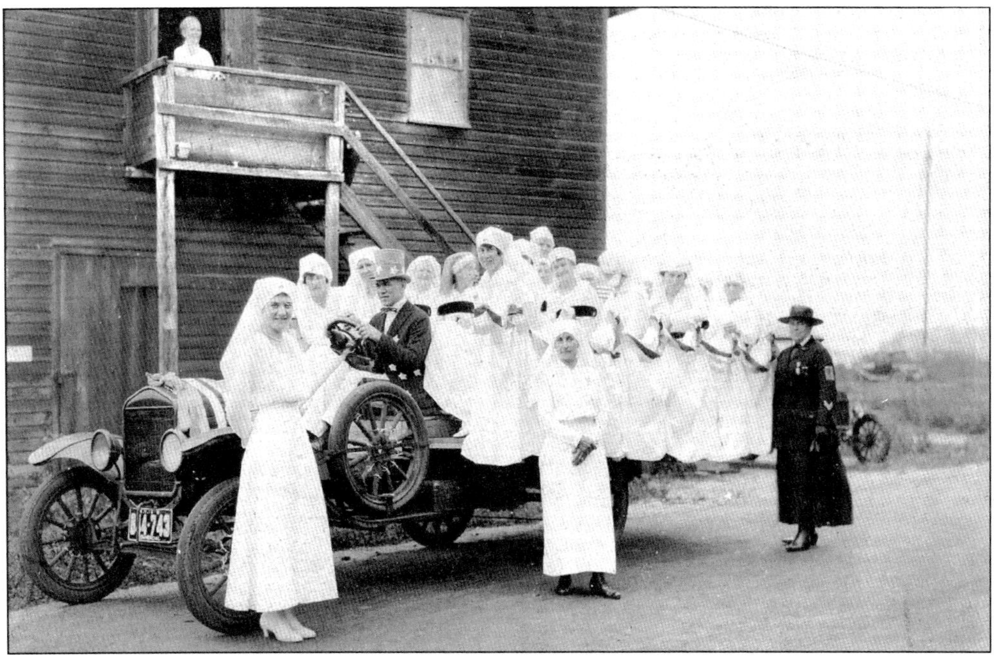

SETAUKET RED CROSS, OUR HERO PARADE, 1919. This photograph was taken in front of a woodworking shop with a residence above, originally owned by George Hand. It is east of the present town dock. Among those pictured here are Frank (Basin) Terrell, Robert Pfeiffer (driver), Mildred Heinz, Catherine Jayne, M. Wells, Bridget Deasey, Elizabeth Davis, and Helen Bennett (an Army registered nurse in uniform).

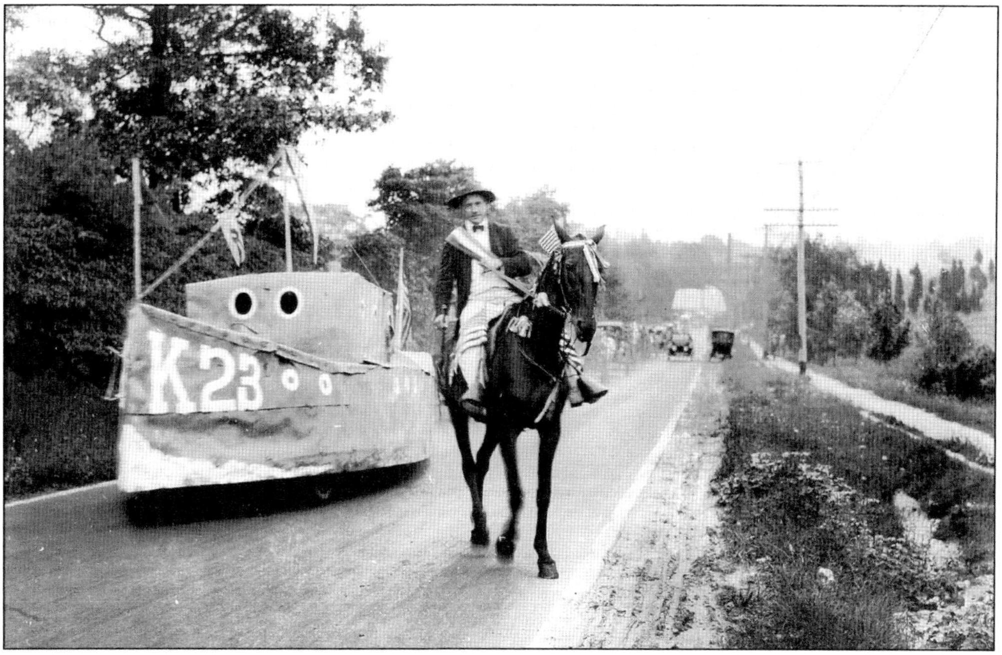

THE "K23," OUR HERO PARADE, 1919. This float represents the submarine *Haddock*, originally numbered K-1; after the war, it became K-32. This vessel was only one of four K-class vessels. Several local men served in the United States Navy, but it is unclear who served on this vessel. This view is on Main Street (Route 25A), looking east from Old Town Road.

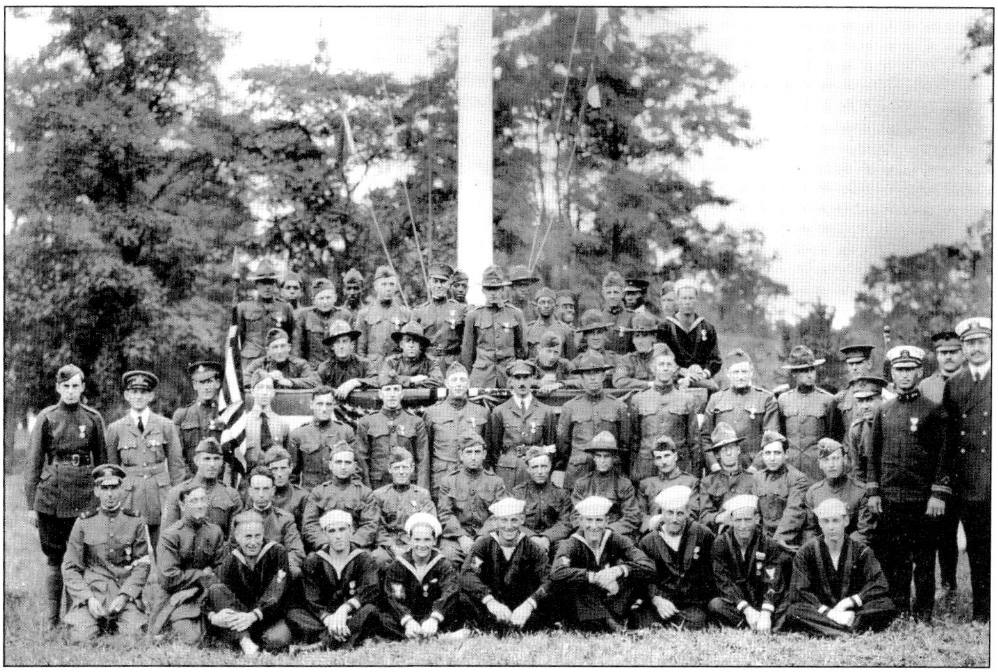

THE HEROES OF WORLD WAR I, 1919. World War I honorees are pictured at the Our Hero Parade in the Setauket Memorial Park at the corner of Shore Road and Main Street (Route 25A).

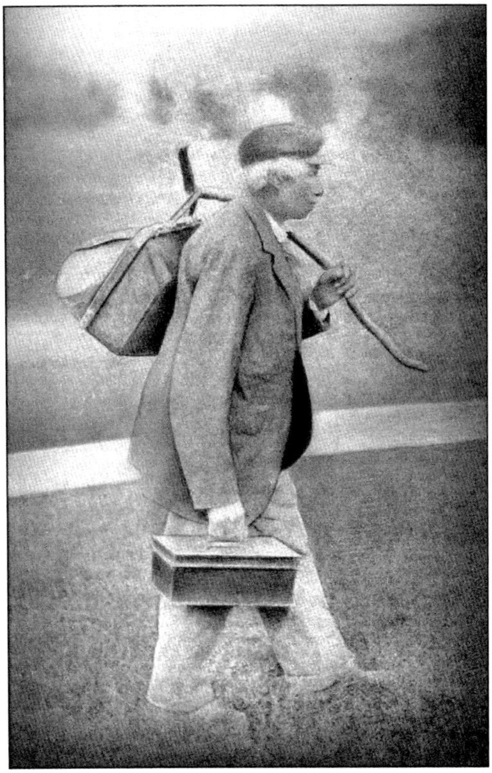

Dr. Levi Phillips Sr. (1809–1911). Widely respected as an herbal doctor, Dr. Phillips regularly walked from Brooklyn to Montauk, even as an old man, and became a local legend. Shown here about 1870, he is believed to be a direct descendent of King Phillip, chief of the Wampanoag Indians. Between 1675 and 1676, King Phillip led a coalition of local tribes against the English in an attempt to drive them out of New England. This war was a portent of future conflicts in the western United States. (Courtesy of Carlton and Nellie Edwards.)

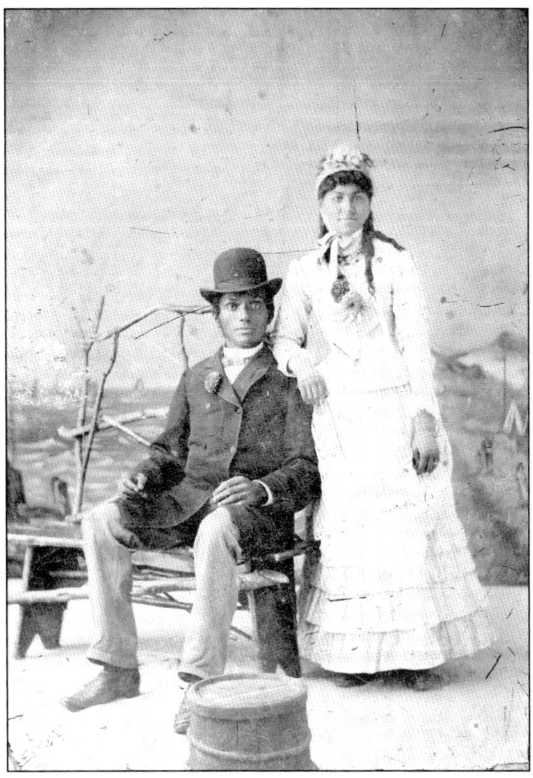

William Cuffee and Abigail (Phillips) Cuffee, Tintype c. 1900. Abigail was the daughter of Dr. Levi Phillips. The name Cuffee is common among the Shinnecock and Montauk Indians. (Courtesy of Carlton and Nellie Edwards.)

SARA ANN SELLS (1864–1964) IN A PAINTING BY RAYMOND TYLER, 1944. Known around the community as "Aunt Sara" or "Sarry Ann," this woman was often seen smoking her trademark corncob pipe.

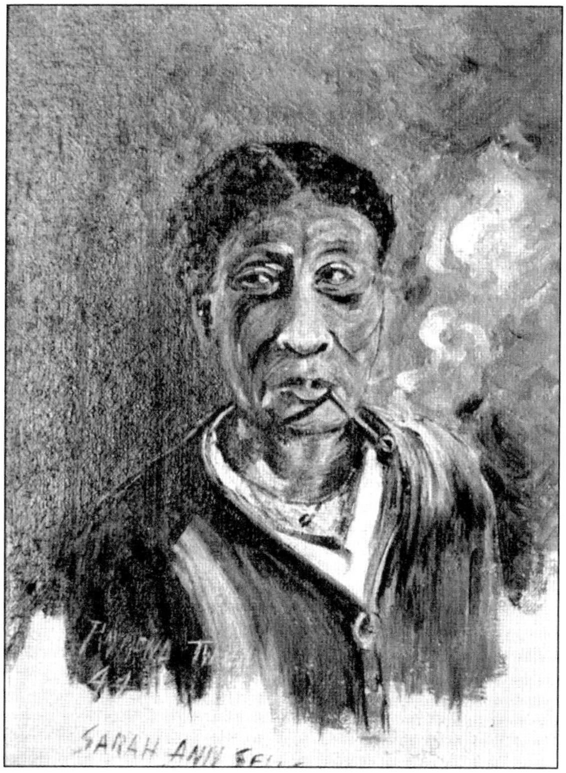

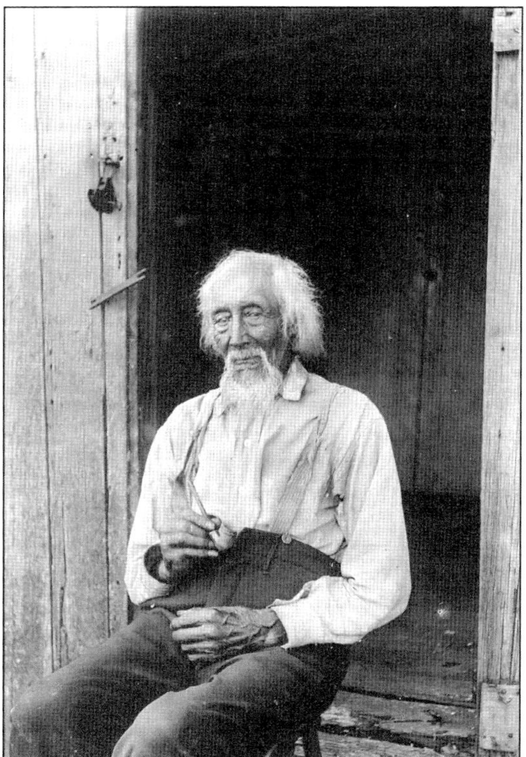

JERRY CUFFY, "LAST OF THE NISSEQUOGUE INDIANS" IN SETAUKET, C. 1905. Cuffy lived on the Woodhull farm at the end of Caroline Avenue. He was "bound" to the Woodhulls from the age of 3 until he was 21. He then remained with the family until his death at age 82 in 1910. Cuffy was a noted carver of shorebird and duck decoys.

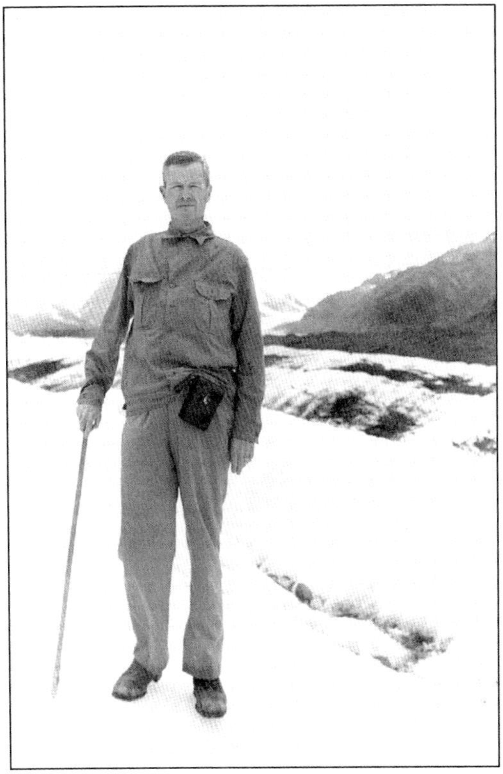

Dr. Robert Cushman Murphy on the Tasman Glacier, Mount Cook, New Zealand, 1949. Dr. Murphy was born in Setauket in 1887. As a new ornithologist and newlywed, he sailed on the brig *Daisy* from June 1912 to May 1913. He was a pelagic ornithologist at the American Museum of Natural History in New York from 1912 until his death in 1973.

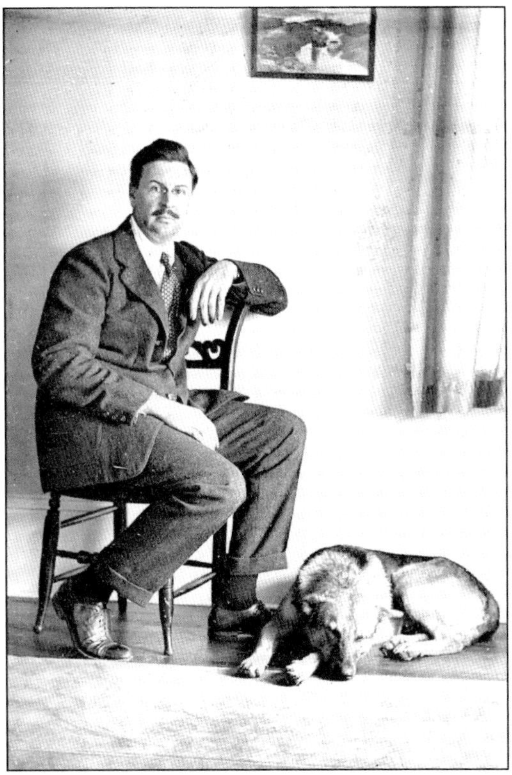

Edward Larocque Tinker (1881–1968). Edward Tinker was the founder of Tinker National Bank, which was purchased by Marine Midland Bank. His father, Henry, purchased a summer home sometime before 1891 at Tinker's Point. The point, originally the Van Brunt property, is at the north end of George's Neck. The Incorporated Village of Poquott includes the entire neck. Note that this book's cover photograph, taken by Edward, hangs on the wall behind him.

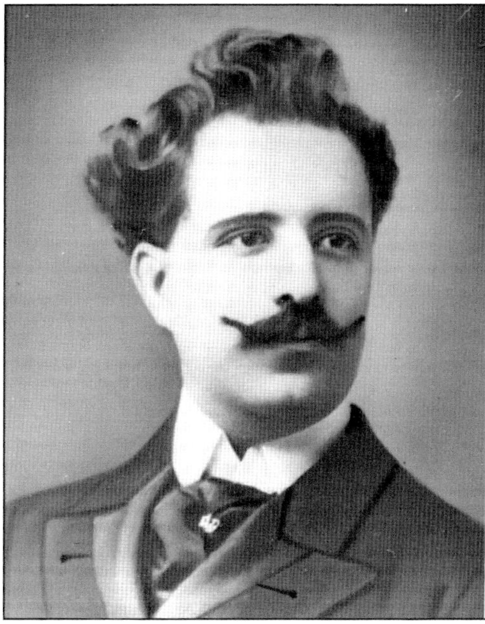

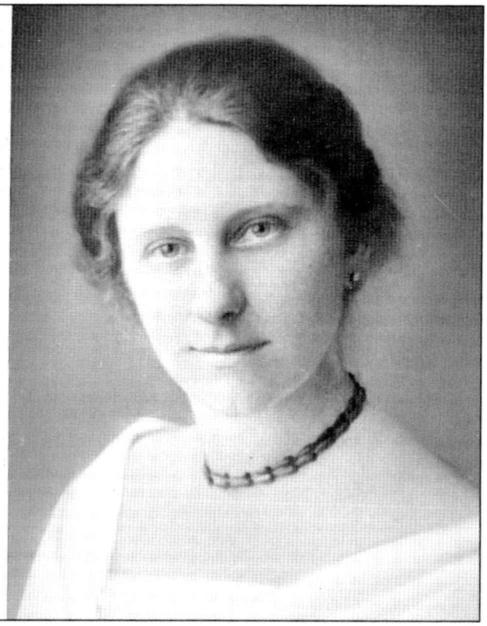

COUNT EUGENIO AND LEONA DE TEIXEIRA. Don (Count) Eugenio de Teixeira (1864–1950) was a Brazilian nobleman, doctor of law, writer, sculptor, metallurgist, civil engineer, and chemist. In 1891, he took 18-year-old Leona Hand (1873–1946) of Setauket as his second wife. She was the daughter of John Hand. The count rescued his ex-cook, Henry Smith, from the Bowery and hired him as a caretaker. Smith was locally known as "Henry No-account."

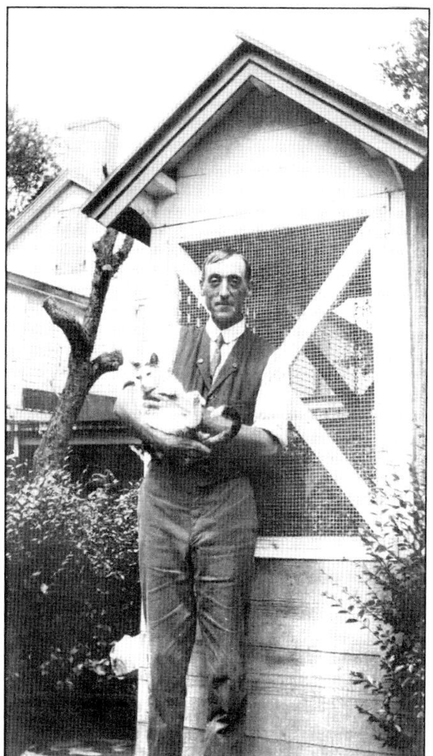

ELLSWORTH BUCKINGHAM, AUGUST 29, 1919. Born in 1885, Ellsworth (Ellie) Buckingham lived at 25 Bayview Avenue all 90 years of his bachelor life. When speaking of his school days, he said, "I went to school in the schoolhouse on Main Street and Coach Road, East Setauket. When 10 years old, I secured a job of coming early and starting the woodstove and staying late to clean the classroom. I hope [*sic*] with the money earned to buy a bicycle but Mr. Pierce, the principal, refused to pay me. I finally had to get the school board to force him and then he fired me."

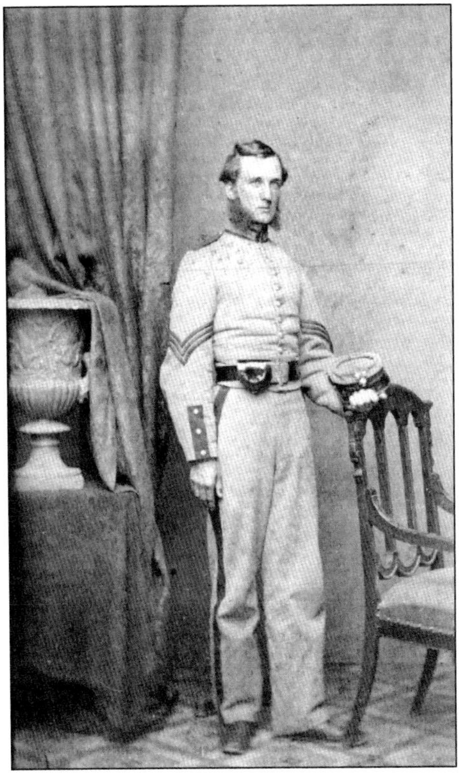

SGT. WILLIAM WHEELER, MATTHEW BRADY, MAY 1861. By October 1861, Sergeant Wheeler was a lieutenant and later achieved the rank of captain. His sister, Julia Davenport (Wheeler) Strong, was Miss Kate Wheeler Strong's mother. He served at Bull Run, Chancellorsville, and Gettysburg. He was killed by a sharpshooter on Sherman's march to the sea.

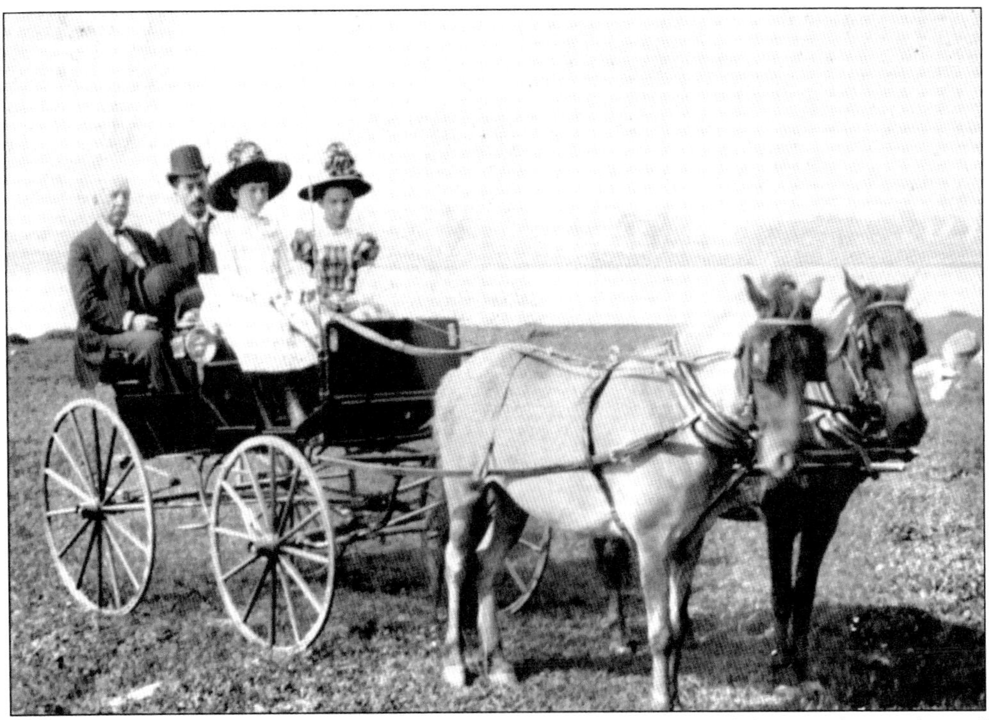

STRONG FAMILY OUTING, C. 1895. From left to right are Thomas, Selah B., and Cornelia and Elizabeth (Bessie) Strong (Selah's daughters).

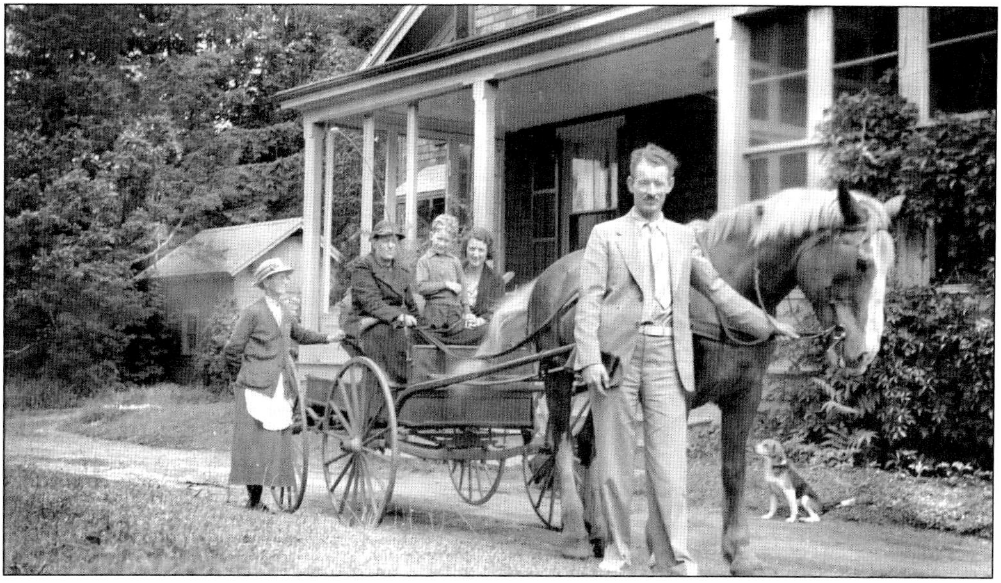

Strong Family at the Cedars, Strong's Neck, 1938. In this image, Miss Kate Wheeler Strong is seated to the left in the buckboard and her sister Elizabeth (Bessie) Strong is seen standing beside her.

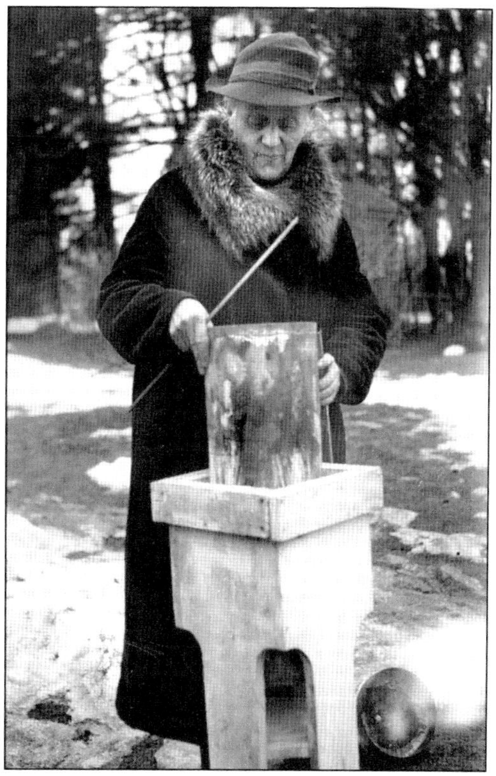

The Setauket Weather Station, c. 1940. Miss Kate Wheeler Strong (1879–1977) is shown checking her rain gauge at the Cedars on Strong's Neck. The Setauket weather station, maintained by the Strong family, operated until 1997 and was the oldest continuously operated private weather station in the United States Weather Service. After Miss Kate could no longer gather data, Bill Strong, her nephew, recorded data until 1983. Bill's wife, Sylvia, finally kept the station until 1997.

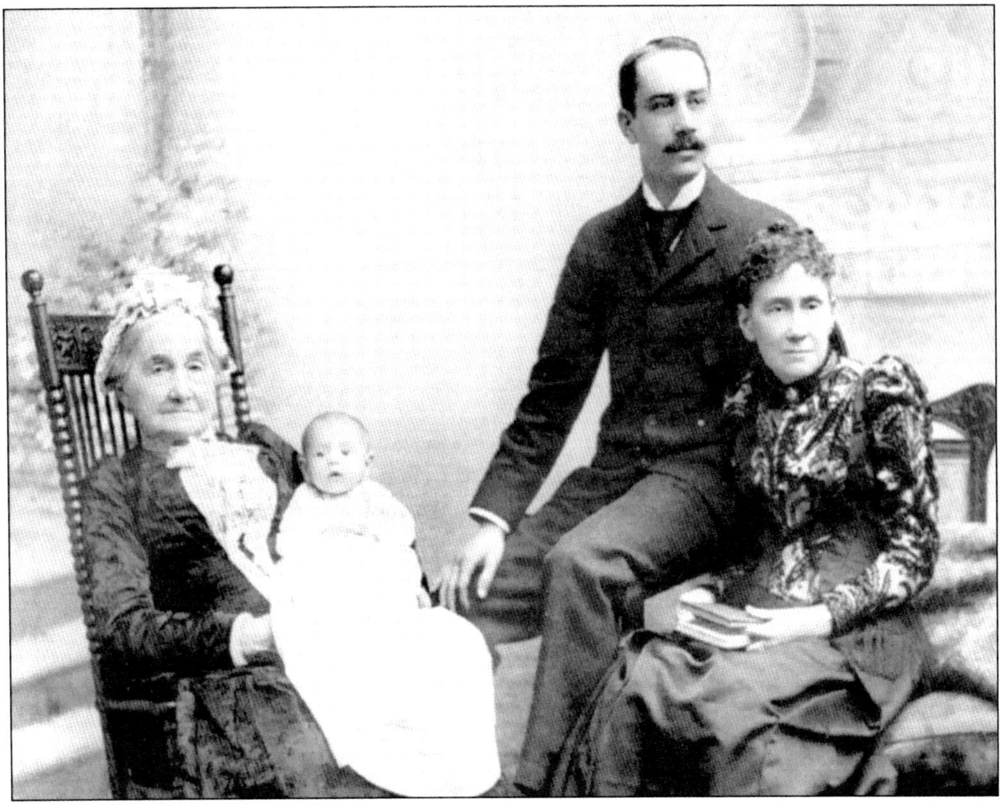

FOUR GENERATIONS OF THE CHILDS FAMILY, 1892. From left to right are Jane Ketchum Childs, c. 1807–c. 1895; Dorothy Shubrick Childs (McLaren), 1891–1935; Eversley Childs, 1867–1953; and Maria Eversley Childs, 1838–1892. (Courtesy of Margherita Abbey Childs Fidao.)

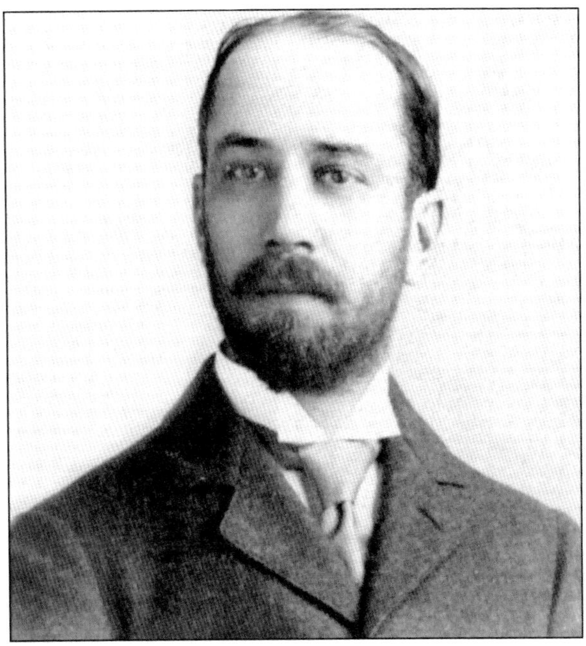

EVERSLEY CHILDS SR. (1867–1953), C. 1890. Childs was a successful industrialist and head of several corporations, including Bon Ami and Technicolor Corporation. His strong sense of civic responsibility and philanthropy led to the donation of West Meadow Beach, the Neighborhood House, and Old Field Park at the lighthouse to the community. He is best known as the founder and benefactor of the leprosarium in Cebu, Philippine Islands. (Courtesy of Margherita Abbey Childs Fidao.)

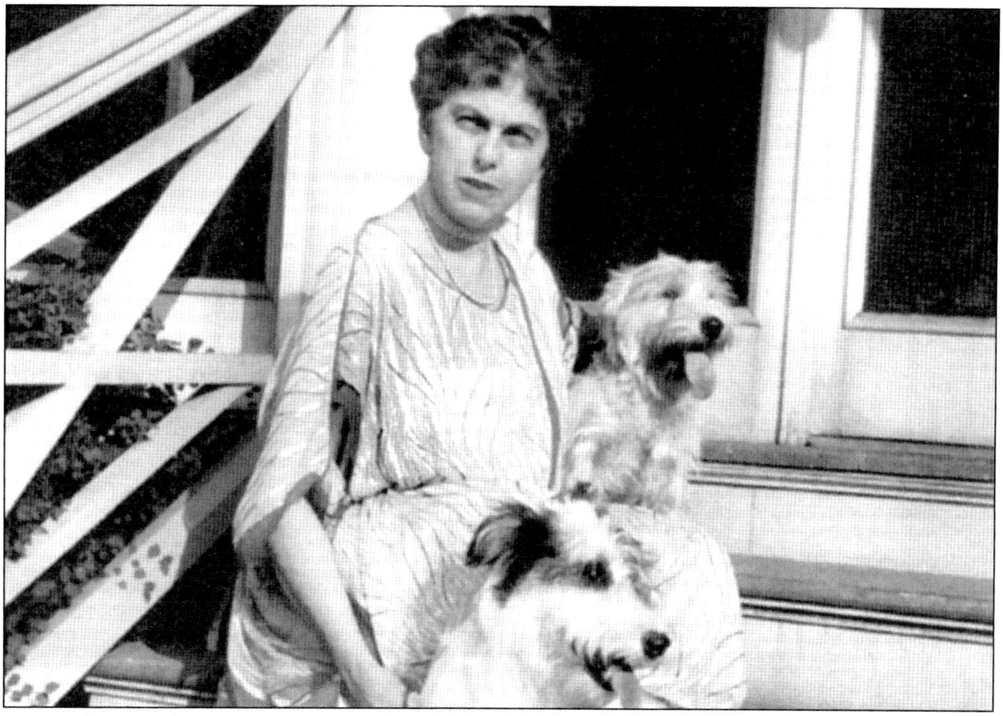

MARY (MINNIE) SHUBRICK LOCKWOOD CHILDS (1867–1944) AND HER DOGS, C. 1925. Eversley Sr. and Mary were married in 1889.(Courtesy of Margherita Abbey Childs Fidao.)

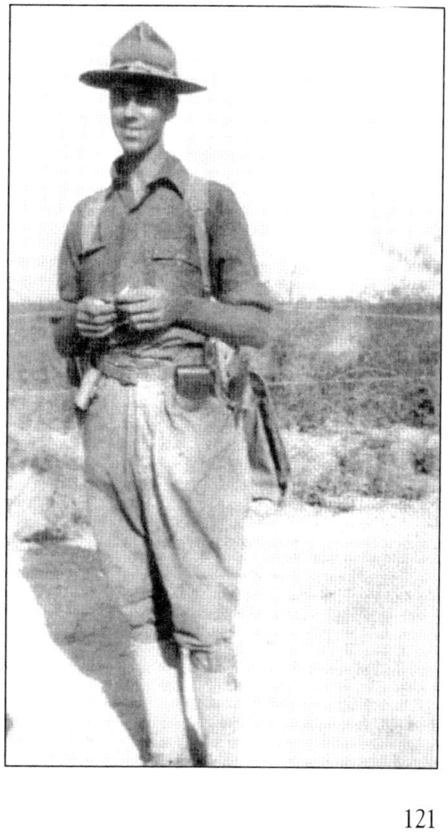

EVERSLEY CHILDS JR. (1893–1952), 1916. This man served in the 7th Regiment New York National Guard, United States 28th Infantry, on the Mexican boarder. (Courtesy of Margherita Abbey Childs Fidao.)

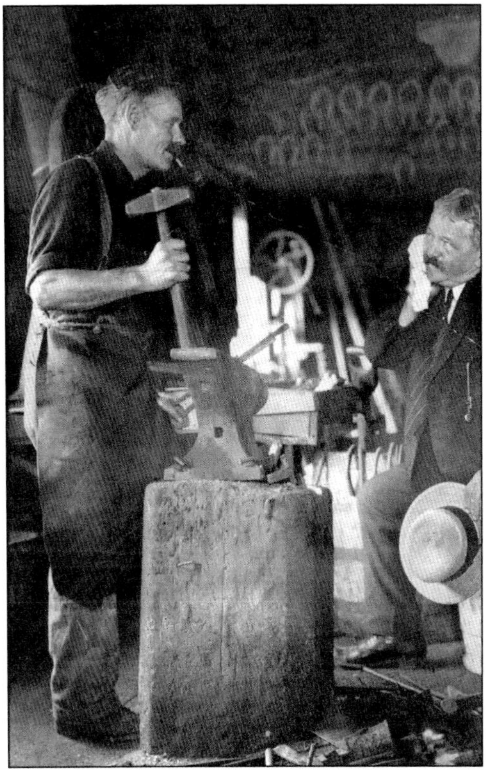

RAKOW'S BLACKSMITH SHOP, SETAUKET, C. 1910. Henry M. Rakow is at the left and customer Mr. Dunn is at the right. The shop was located at approximately 26 Shore Road. (Courtesy of Betty Voss.)

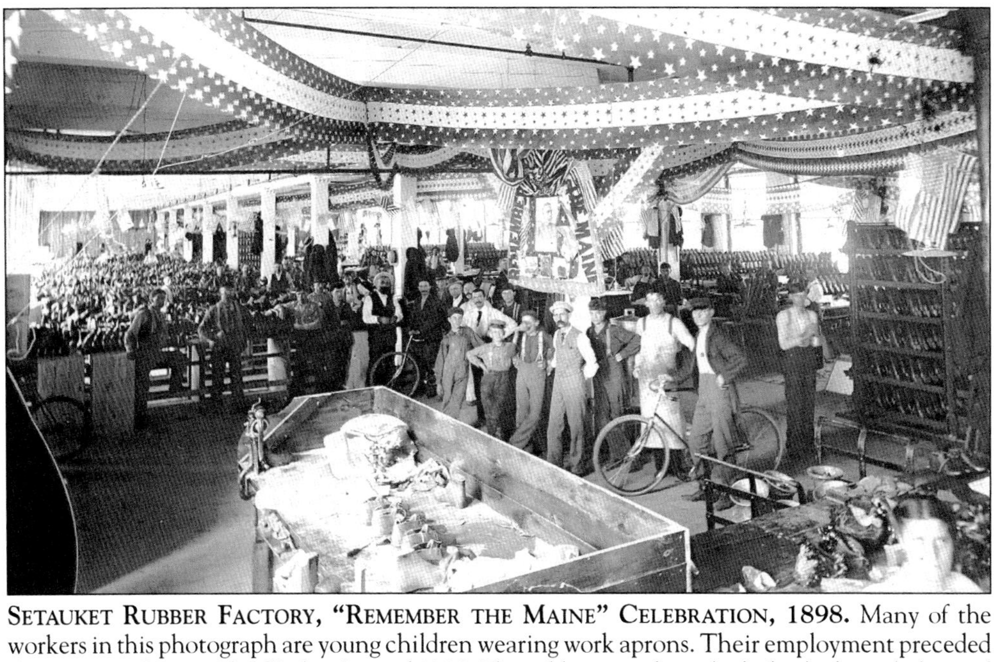

SETAUKET RUBBER FACTORY, "REMEMBER THE MAINE" CELEBRATION, 1898. Many of the workers in this photograph are young children wearing work aprons. Their employment preceded the Keating-Owens Child Labor Law of 1916. The rubber overshoes (galoshes), shoes, belts, and hose are displayed at the right.

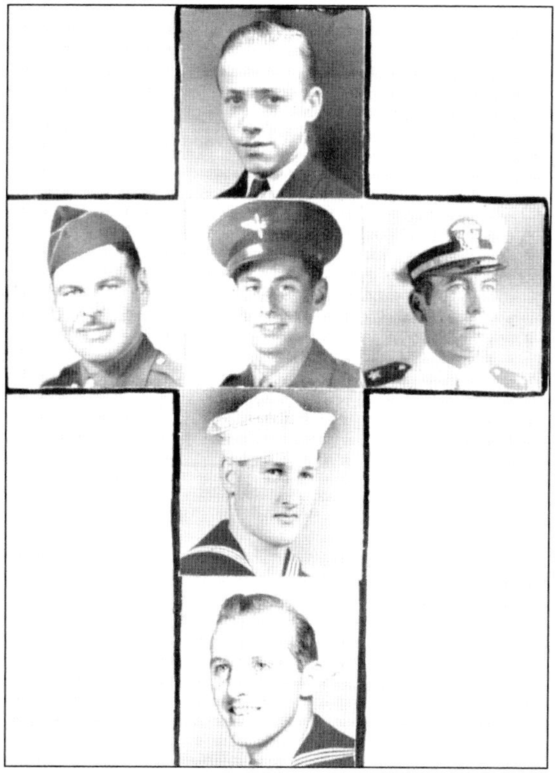

SETAUKET CASUALTIES OF WORLD WAR II. In 1946, the Setauket High School yearbook was dedicated to the alumni that gave their lives in World War II. They are, from top to bottom, Cpl. Douglas Hunter, (from left to right) Sgt. Francis Hawkins, Cpl. William Weston, Lt. Anthony Matusky, fireman 1st class Clifford Darling, and aviation machinist mate Orlando Lyons. Pictures were not available for Henry Eichacker and Edward Pfeiffer.

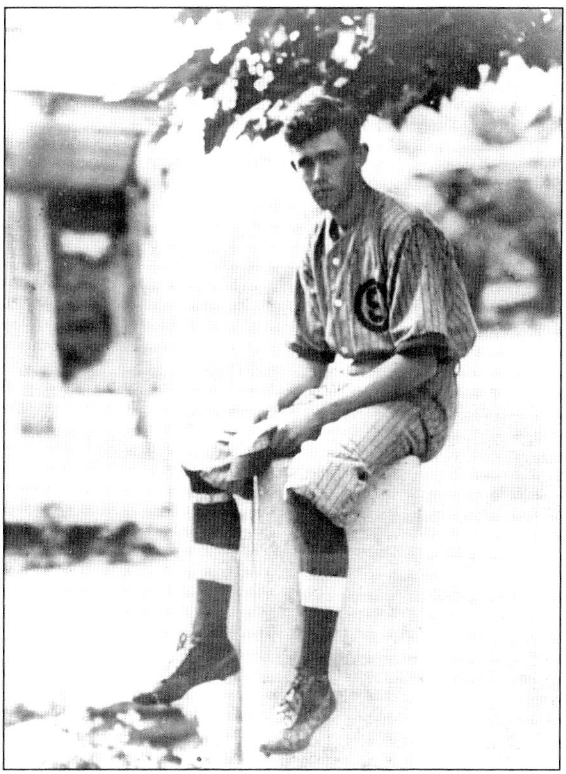

HENRY F. JONES, 1921. As a member of the Setauket Athletic Club, Jones was struck in the throat by a baseball while catching and was killed. (Courtesy of Dr. Sherman Mills.)

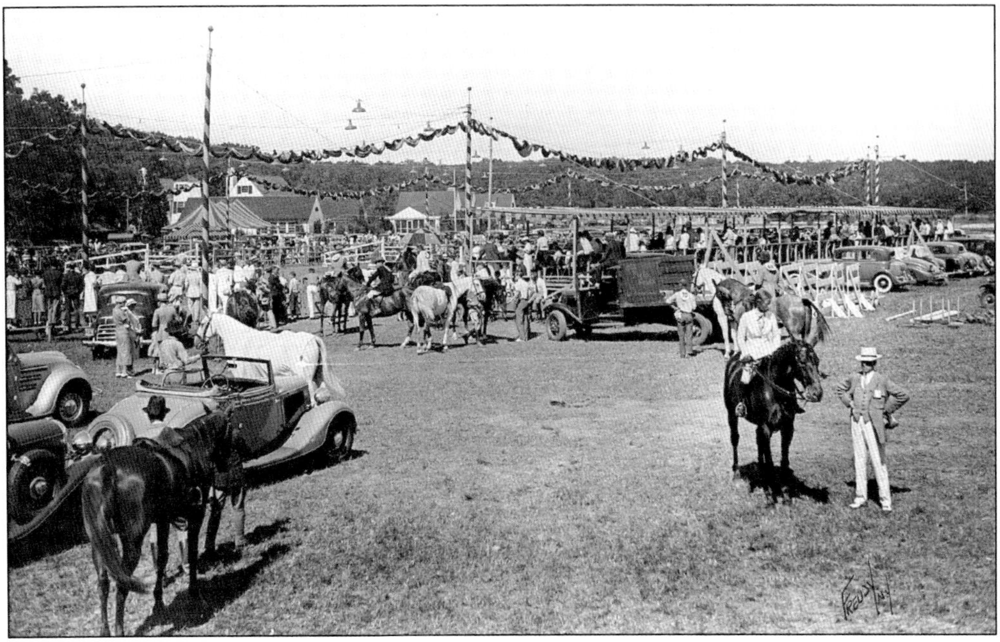

NORTH SHORE HORSE SHOW HELD AT OLD FIELD CLUB, C. 1935. Built in 1931 by J. Ward Melville, the club hosted equestrian competitions here for over 50 years. The sign on the truck at the center says "Old Field South, On Long Island Sound, Suffolk Management." This corporation was owned by J. Ward Melville.

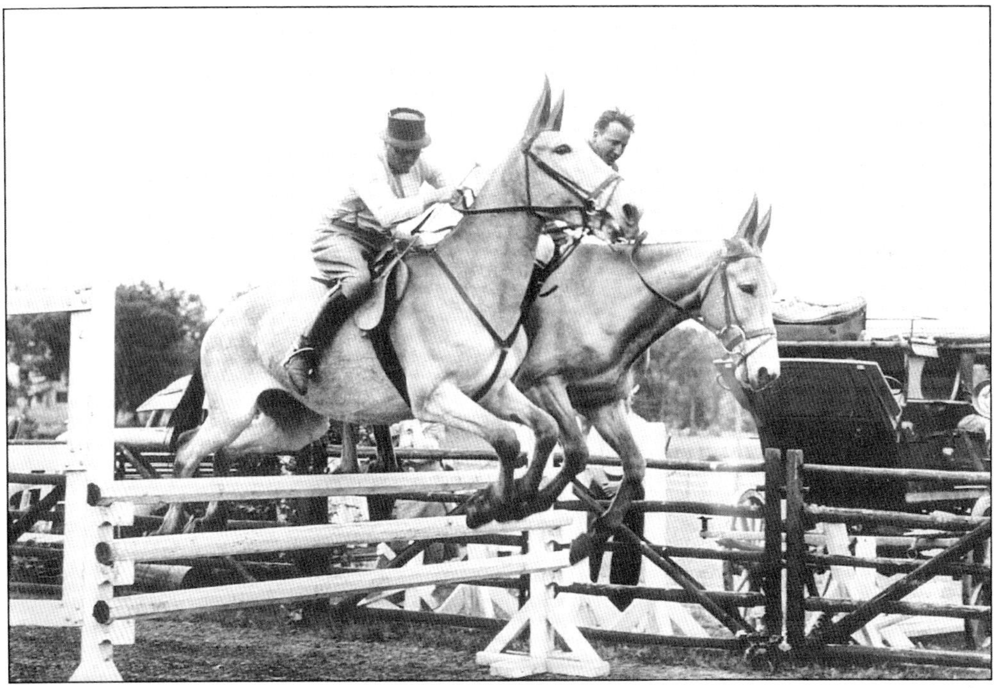

TANDEM JUMPING MULES AT NORTH SHORE HORSE SHOW, OLD FIELD CLUB, C. 1935. The horse show complex was designed by Richard Haviland Smythe, architect to J. Ward Melville. The property is now owned by Suffolk County and is undergoing restoration.

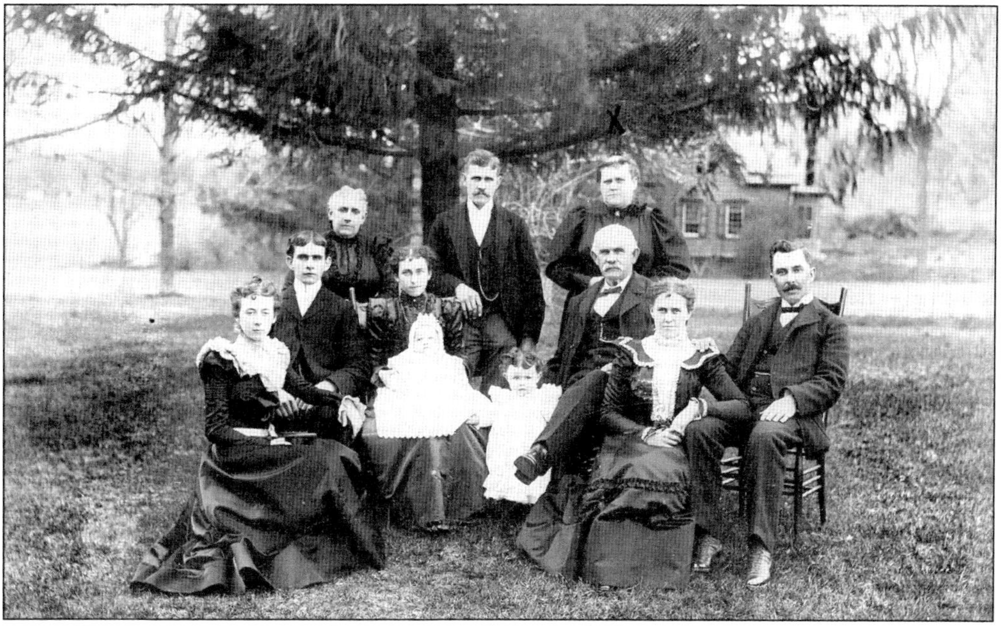

JONES FAMILY, LATE 1899 OR EARLY 1900. Photographed on the lawn of the Benjamin Jones House at 322 Main Street (Route 25A) are, from left to right, the following: (first row) Bertha Jones, Walter Jones, Lizzie Jones, Henry Jones (baby on lap), baby Gendys Jones, Walter Jones Sr., Ada Jones Williamson, and Charles Williamson (of Stony Brook); (second row) Lottie Hulse (housekeeper), Henry Jones, and Rebecca Jones. The Roe Tavern is in the background across Main Street (Route 25A).

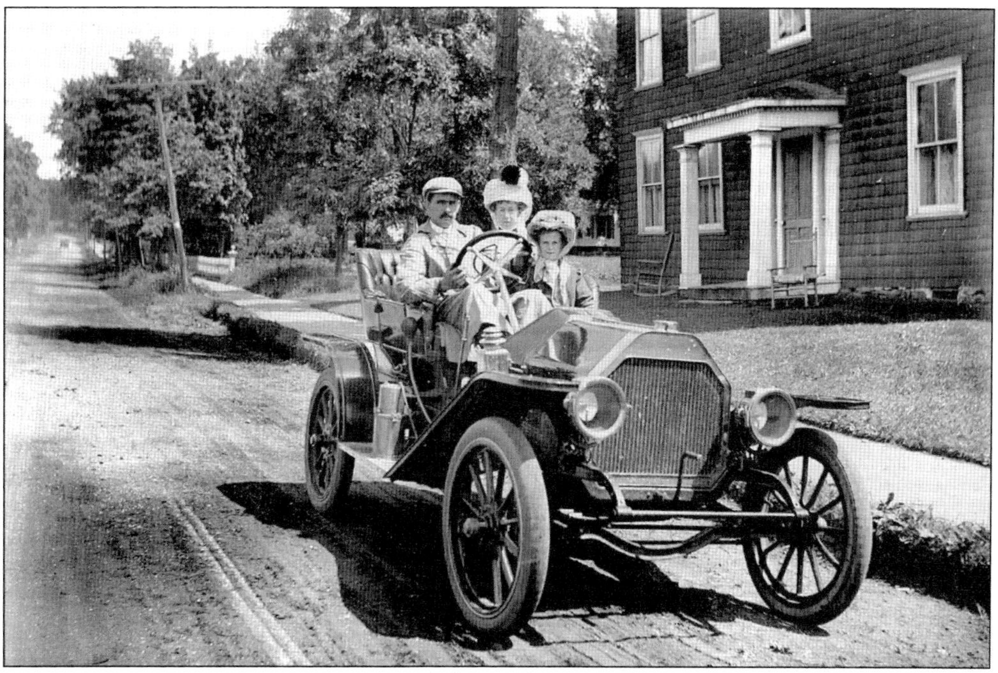

WALTER D. JONES FAMILY, 1910. From left to right are Walter, Bertha M., and their daughter, Ada Jones, in their 1910 Overland in front of their home, Old Shinglesides.

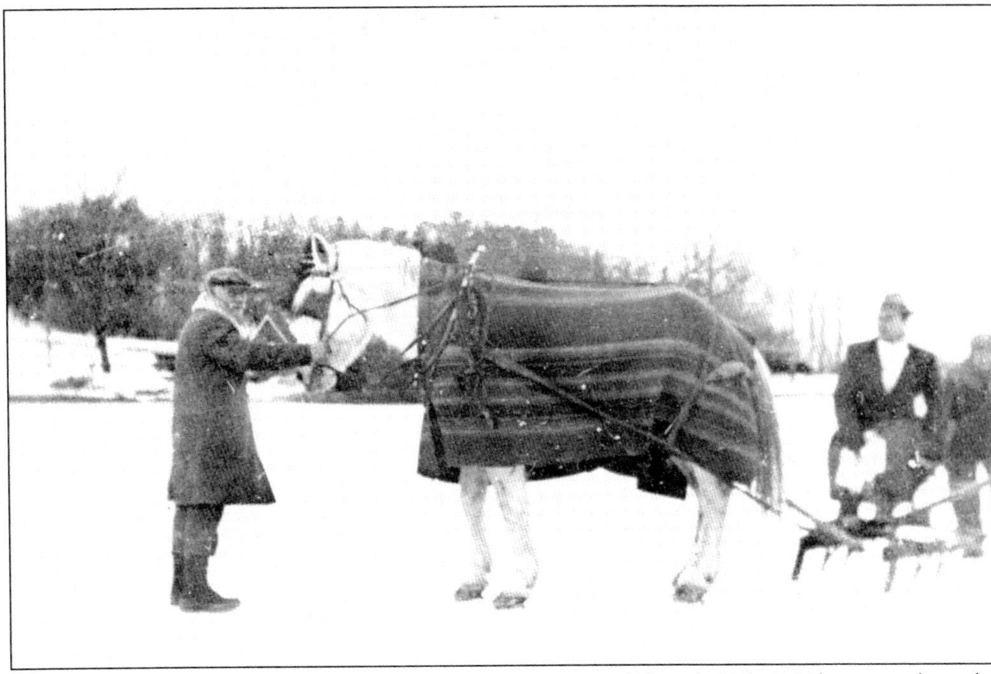

CUTTING ICE ON SETAUKET MILLPOND, C. 1935. Morris Eikov (1905–1988) is seated on the ice cutter. The horse was sharp-shodded to provide traction.

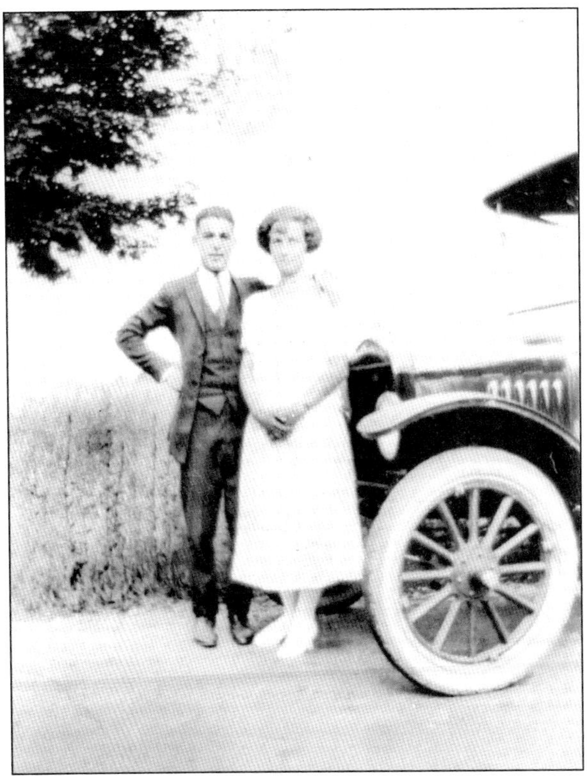

JOSEPH (JES) AND VERNA (BALDWIN) EIKOV, C. 1928. Jes drove the meat wagon for Pinnes' Meat Market and later owned the bus company with a fleet of two buses, which provided transportation for the Setauket Union Free School. His brothers Robert (Bobby) and Sam Eikov owned butcher shops on opposite sides of Main Street.

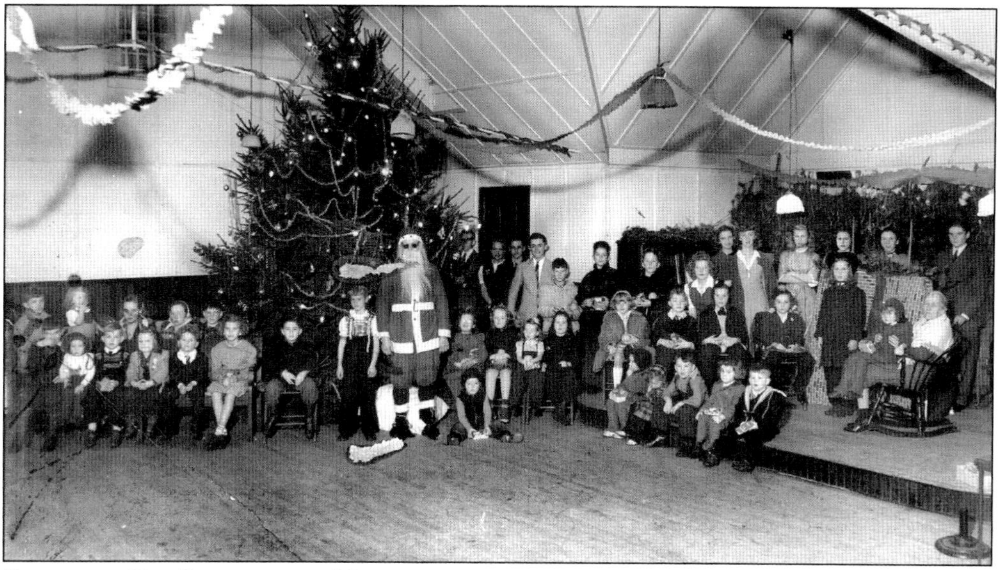

CHRISTMAS EVE PARTY AT THE NEIGHBORHOOD HOUSE, 1946. This party, open to all children, was sponsored by Miss Kate Wheeler Strong, seated in the rocking chair. Each youngster that attended was given a small bag of hard candy and an orange. To the right of the tree, in the back row, from left to right, are James Wilson, Irene Aartola, Bernard Gerard, James (Wings) Macauley, Alfonse Chervinski, Richard Meachum, Homer (Red, Eddie) Meachum, Edith Hoffmoen, Shirley Bennett, Gillian (Jill) Dorward, Martha Wells, Marilyn Wishart, Ethelmae Emerson, and Raymond Price. The rest of the children are unidentified.

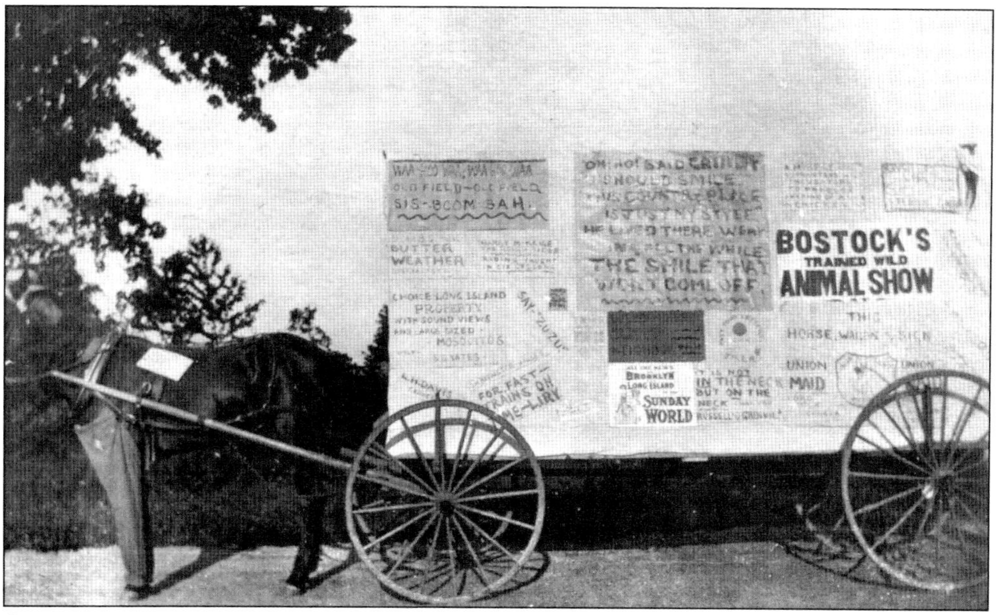

OPENING OF QUAKER PATH 1903. "Dr. James Melville" is pulling the wagon prepared by J. Ward Melville. The sign above the front wheel reads, "Choice Long Island Property with Sound Views and Large Mosquitos, apply S. S. Yates, proprietor." Quaker Path was built by Frank Melville as a more direct route from Old Field to the Stony Brook Station. Notice that the horse is wearing pants.

THE THREE VILLAGE HISTORICAL SOCIETY

The Three Village Historical Society is a tax-exempt, nonprofit, non-stock corporation chartered by the Regents of the University of the State of New York in 1966 and incorporated under the New York State Education Law. Located on the north shore of Long Island, the Three Villages—Old Field, the Setaukets (including the village of Poquott), and Stony Brook—comprise a rapidly expanding, ethnically and culturally diverse community of 35,000 people who are descendents of the original settlers of the town of Brookhaven, African Americans, and Native Americans. With the State University of New York at Stony Brook, one of New York State's four major university centers, came many of the staff of nearby Brookhaven National Laboratory and other high-technology organizations. Recognizing the diversity of the population it serves, the society is dedicated to fostering appreciation of the community's heritage through educational programs, research, and the collection and preservation of local historical structures, artifacts, and documents.

Founded in 1964 as an all-volunteer organization of old friends devoted to discovering, preserving, and disseminating Three Village history, the society has grown steadily. It has more than doubled its membership from 300 to 700, added substantially to its collections, increased the number and range of educational programs, employed professional staff, and acquired a historic house for its headquarters. Services to the community include preserving the material heritage of the Three Villages, conducting research to interpret the collections and place them in a larger context, developing interpretive exhibits and educational programs to increase awareness of the community's history, and providing assistance to the public with resources for genealogical research, historic preservation, local history, and the use of historical documents. The goal of the society is to add continually to its collections by acquiring local historical materials as they become available, thereby enhancing their value as the collective memory of the community.